[11—0]

Climbing Roses

NEW *ILLUSTRATED*
ENCYCLOPEDIA
OF GARDENING

UNABRIDGED

EDITED BY T. H. Everett

Assistant Director (Horticulture) and Curator of Education
The New York Botanical Garden

WITH CONTRIBUTIONS FROM

TWENTY HORTICULTURISTS AND AUTHORITIES IN THE UNITED STATES AND CANADA

Growers, Breeders, Exhibitors, Plantsmen, Writers, Lecturers, Professors, Editors and Superintendents of Famous Estates, who are Experts in all Fields of Horticulture, including Pests and Their Control.

VOLUME ELEVEN—Root-Sen

GREYSTONE PRESS/NEW YORK · TORONTO · LONDON

When root-pruning, bring the deep lateral roots a little nearer the surface than before. It is a mistake to add manure in any form when filling in the soil over the roots, but if crushed limestone rubble and wood ashes can be mixed in with the soil, they will prove beneficial.

It is important that the tree shall be firmly established in the ground after root pruning. As it is robbed of its main anchor roots, the stability of the tree may be considerably weakened, and, at least for one season afterwards, it will be advisable to provide support in the shape of a stout stake to which the stem is secured or to support the trunk with guy wires (see Staking).

Root-Pruning Large Trees. With trees of mature age, older than, say, 12 years, it is safest to adopt a modified form of root pruning. If all large roots are cut back at once the check might be much too severe. With big trees the usual practice is to prune the roots on one side of the tree only in one year, leaving the other half for treatment during the next autumn. In that case a semicircular trench is dug out and the exposed roots are pruned back as before.

Should a dry, cold spring follow the autumn root pruning, it is possible that the tree may suffer a greater handicap than is intended. To avoid this danger a thick mulch of rotted manure, compost, peat moss or some other suitable material should be placed on the ground all around the tree, in spring, and left on the surface to decay.

In Preparation for Transplanting. Trees which have been established in their location for several years, especially kinds such as Sweet Gum (Liquidambar), Sour Gum (Nyssa) and Flowering Dogwood (Cornus florida), which do not naturally make compact masses of fibrous roots, often suffer severely following transplanting; this may occur even though the operation is carried out with care and skill. To minimize possible damage it is a good plan to root-prune such specimens a year before they are moved. This may be done by digging a deep trench around the tree at such a distance from the trunk that the outer wall of the trench coincides with the line that will form the outer circumference of the root ball when the tree is dug. After the pruning, the trench is filled with fertile soil to encourage the development of new fibrous roots and these form part of the root ball when the tree is balled and burlaped for lifting.

ROOT ROT. See Pests and Diseases.

ROOTSTOCK. As used by gardeners, this term has two distinct meanings. The understocks to which scions and buds are united by grafting and budding are frequently called rootstocks, and the term is also used to describe the more or less elongated and usually thickened rhizomes of certain perennial herbaceous plants such as Iris, Solomon's Seal and Aspidistra.

ROQUETTE OR ROCKET SALAD. The plant known by this name is Eruca sativa, a native plant of southern Europe. It is grown in Europe as a salad plant but is rarely grown in North America.

For the best results the seeds should be sown outdoors in early spring in drills, 1 ft. apart, the seeds being sprinkled thinly and covered to about twice their own diameter with fine soil. Successional sowings at ten-day intervals should be made.

It is important that the soil be fertile and that the plants not be permitted to suffer from lack of water, otherwise growth is slow and the crop becomes tough and hot-flavored.

Late summer sowings provide a fall crop. The young tender leaves are the parts used. This plant is not satisfactory during hot summer months.

ROSA: SHRUB ROSES OF MANY KINDS

Beautiful in Flower, Foliage and Fruit

Rosa (Ro'sa). The genus from which the Rosaceae family takes its name. It consists of a large number of species or wild types from many parts of the world. From them have been developed the Roses of all kinds that beautify our gardens today. (See Rose.) Many of the wild kinds are in themselves of definite horticultural value, more especially in a fairly large garden, as they often require considerable space. Their full beauty is usually only apparent when they are allowed to develop naturally with little or no pruning. Some, such as Rosa Moyesii, are beautiful when in flower in early summer and again in autumn, when their large fruits are brilliantly colored. Rosa is an ancient Latin name.

. The term Shrub Rose is now generally applied to the Rosa species, and their hybrids, such as the hybrid Moschatas (Hybrid Musks). For a fuller discussion of the hybrid kinds than is given here, see Rose.

The species are single-flowered and bloom in clusters. The majority yield one crop only, but Rosa borboniana and Rosa chinensis may be included among the few exceptions to this rule. They are suitable for planting in isolated positions on the lawn, in a shrub border or any situation where the plant can be treated as an individual specimen.

These Roses appeal to gardeners who prefer an informal type of beauty to the more stylized appeal of the modern Hybrid Teas, and Floribundas but, as already emphasized, many need ample space, and flowering is usually confined to one crop only.

Pruning the Shrub Roses. In the management of the Shrub Roses pruning takes the form of thinning out useless or overcrowded branches rather than cutting them back. Such work is best done in winter or early spring, when the beauty of the hips (fruits) is past.

Thinning consists of cutting out old, worn-out branches, either down to the ground or back to healthy shoots on the main stems. Pruning shears or a sharp knife should be used to shorten very long shoots which may spoil the symmetry of the bushes; the thin and unripened ends of the shoots should also be cut off. The thinning and shaping of the Rose bushes is an important detail; it not only improves their appearance, but their health, by allowing sunshine and air to reach the main branches and ripen the wood.

They Like Open, Sunny Positions. The shrubs will thrive in ordinary soil which has been spaded deeply; well-decayed manure, compost and wood ash should be added. Good topsoil should be mixed in if the natural soil is poor; if it is peaty, a dressing of lime may be given. When dealing with wet or heavy clay soils, brick rubble from a builder's yard or fine coal cinders (but not fine ashes) are excellent materials to add.

Planting may be done in early fall or early spring. Mulching with decayed farmyard manure or garden compost is beneficial.

Special Uses. Of the Roses to be described, the following are specially suitable for lawn beds and shrub borders: R. Moyesii, R. Hugonis, R. Webbiana and R. Willmottiae.

These are worth growing for their attractive foliage: R. Hugonis, R. virginiana, R. Willmottiae, R. Webbiana, and R. rubrifolia.

Among those which bear the most handsome fruits are: R. Moyesii, R. Davidii, R. rugosa, R. pomifera, R. pendulina and R. Sweginzowii.

R. Eglanteria, R. spinosissima and R. Hugonis make good informal hedges.

The following species are especially suitable for small gardens: R. gallica varieties, R. centifolia varieties and R. spinosissima varieties, notably Stanwell Perpetual.

For purposes of reference the best kinds are here described in alphabetical order.

Rosa Banksiae, the Banksia Rose, a native of China, is too tender for cultivation in the North but is excellent for mild-climate gardens. It is naturalized in the southern states. The most useful varieties are the double yellow and the double white, the former scentless, the latter with a fragrance strongly reminiscent of violets. They need little pruning. Though the younger growths are killed back to the main branches or even to the ground, young shoots may develop from the live wood in spring.

R. blanda is a native of dry woods, hills, prairies and dunes from Quebec to Manitoba and southward to New York, Pennsylvania, Indiana and Missouri. This Rose has few or sometimes no prickles. It grows 3-5 ft. tall, has leaves each with 5-7 leaflets, and pink flowers, usually several together, that measure 2-2½ in. across.

R. borboniana, the Bourbon Rose, is of hybrid origin, the result of crossing R. chinensis with R. gallica. It has red or purple-red flowers, double or semidouble, that measure about 3 in. in diameter, and leaves usually having 7 leaflets. It blooms late and is hardy as far north as New England.

The Bourbon Rose, crossed with R. gallica, R. centifolia and R. damascena, gave rise to a group of Roses called Hybrid Bourbons, and these in turn, crossed with R. chinensis, produced the hardy Roses of the group called Hybrid Perpetuals.

R. bracteata, the Macartney Rose (so named because it was first introduced from China by Lord Macartney), is a beautiful evergreen trailing or climbing shrub for growing in mild climates. It is not hardy in the North. The large white flowers, 3-4 in. across, are borne singly in succession from June to September. This is one of the parents of the beautiful climbing Rose Mermaid.

R. canina, the Dog Rose, is probably the most variable of all the wild Roses; it is widely spread over northern and central Europe and western Asia, and is naturalized to some extent in North America.

The Dog Rose is worth planting in shrubberies as an informal hedge and in the open woodland. The average height is 6-9 or even 10 ft., though it is sometimes much taller in damp ground. It is the stock chiefly used by nurserymen in Europe for budding.

R. carolina, the Pasture Rose, grows wild in North America from Maine to Minnesota, Florida and Texas. It is one of the best of our native Roses and is suitable for planting in shrub borders and for other decorative plantings. The Pasture Rose forms a bush 3-6 ft. tall and spreads by means of suckers. Its leaves are ordinarily composed of 5 leaflets, and the flowers, each about 2 in. wide, are rose-pink. They are borne in June or July.

The variety grandiflora of R. carolina has distinctly larger flowers. R. carolina is closely related to R. virginiana. Unlike R. virginiana, which rarely flowers except on short branches from old stems, R. carolina produces blooms on current season's stems.

R. centifolia, the Cabbage Rose, thought to be a native of the Orient, is one of the parents of some of the old garden Roses. The soft pink

Rosa omeiensis pteracantha has only four petals. The bright red spines along its branches are attractive and so is its feathery green foliage.

blooms are very fragrant. It is 3-5 ft. in height. The variety muscosa, the Moss Rose, is even better known because it has given rise to a number of named varieties of Moss Roses, notable among which are Blanche Moreau, white, and Crested Moss, deep pink.

R. chinensis, the China Rose or Bengal Rose, is an erect-growing shrub, 3 ft. or less tall, that is semievergreen. It has few or sometimes no thorns. The leaflets number 3-5. The long-stemmed flowers are solitary or several together, each about 2 in. in diameter, and are red, pink or almost white. They have little or no fragrance. The wild variety of this plant is distinguished by the name R. chinensis variety spontanea. It was not introduced from central China into Western gardens until 1917, although varieties of it received from the Orient had been in cultivation in America and Europe long before this.

The China Rose is not hardy in the North but some of its varieties are. Among these is R. chinensis variety viridiflora, the Green Rose, a kind in which leaf-green, petal-like bracts take the place of petals. It is grown more as a curiosity than for its beauty. This kind is hardy at least as far north as southern New York.

R. chinensis variety minima, the Fairy or Pygmy Rose, is sometimes offered as R.

Lawranciana. The Rose grown as R. Rouletti is also a form of R. chinensis variety minima. Both of these kinds are hardy at least as far north as southern New York. R. chinensis minima forms vary in height from 4-15 in. Its flowers are pink, red or white.

R. chinensis variety mutabilis has flowers that open yellow and change to orange, red, and crimson. Flowers of these different colors may be seen on the same plant at the same time. R. chinensis variety semperflorens has flowers that are deep red in color and are usually borne singly.

The China Rose is of special importance because it is a parent stock of many garden Roses. Hybridized with R. moschata, the Musk Rose, it produced the Noisette Roses, R. Noisettiana. This group includes the Rose known as R. Manettii, the Manetti Rose, which is used as an understock upon which other garden Roses are grafted and budded. The China Rose, hybridized with other kinds, also gave rise to the group of Roses called Baby Ramblers.

R. cinnamomea, the Cinnamon Rose, is a native of Europe and Asia that occurs as an escape from gardens in the eastern United States. It forms an erect shrub, 4-6 ft. tall, with red or purplish red fragrant flowers each 2 in. across. The leaflets number 5-7 usually, but occasionally only 3 to each leaf. They appear in May and June.

The variety plena of R. cinnamomea has double flowers.

R. damascena. The Damask Rose is another very old garden Rose of obscure origin; one or more of its varieties supplies the attar of Rose perfume. This Rose is one of the parents of the Hybrid Perpetual type. The variety versicolor is the York and Lancaster Rose; its white petals are striped with pink or red. Omar Khayyam, blush-pink, is a very old variety, the original plant of which grew on the poet's grave at Nashipur.

R. Davidii. This is one of the newer Chinese Roses. It forms an upright bush, 6-8 ft. or more high, and bears large corymbs of rose-pink blossoms in July, followed by orange-red fruits. It is a good shrub for a lawn bed and may be planted as an informal hedge.

Rosa multiflora, sometimes called Living Hedge, should be planted only where there is ample room to allow for the wide spread of its branches.

R. Dupontii, a useful and distinct Rose, of semiwild appearance, was raised in France early in the nineteenth century by a Rosarian named Dupont. It is said to be a hybrid between R. moschata and R. gallica. It forms a vigorous bush, 6-8 ft. high, and has large white flowers tinged with pink, which open in late June. It is a useful bush for the shrub border, open woodland or wild garden.

R. Ecae. A distinct, rare and uncommon Rose from Afghanistan, R. Ecae forms a bush 3-4 ft. high, having thin, very thorny branches with small leaves composed of 5-9 leaflets. The buttercup-yellow flowers are an inch across. This Rose is most easily increased by layering. The Rose usually cultivated under the name R. Ecae is R. Primula, which see.

R. Eglanteria (rubiginosa). The Sweetbrier or Eglantine is one of the most useful Roses to plant as a closely clipped hedge, the clipping being done in early spring. In addition to the pleasing fragrance of its foliage, which is especially pronounced after rain, the pale pink blooms are followed by red fruits. This rose, which is a native of Europe, is naturalized in North America. A form with double flowers is the practical hedge R. Eglanteria variety duplex.

The Penzance Hybrid Sweetbriers resulted from crosses with Rosa foetida bicolor and the Hybrid Perpetuals.

R. foetida. The Austrian Brier, as this is called, in its typical form has deep yellow single blooms that measure about 3 in. in diameter and have a rather unpleasant odor. It grows to a height of 5-10 ft. and thrives best in localities where the atmosphere is not contaminated with impurities. It is often somewhat difficult to establish. The typical yellow-flowered R. foetida is often known as the Austrian Yellow Rose.

There is a counterpart of the Austrian Yellow known as the Austrian Copper Rose which differs in having its petals brilliant copper-red color above and buff colored on their reverses (undersides). Botanically the Austrian Copper Rose is Rosa foetida variety bicolor. Yet another variant, R. foetida variety persiana, the Persian Yellow Rose, has double yellow blooms. All of these are handsome plants but, unfortunately, are very subject to black spot disease. The brilliant yellow, orange and flame-colored modern garden Roses have R. foetida and its varieties as ancestors.

R. gallica. Possibly the oldest of all recorded Roses, this has deep-pink to crimson fragrant blooms and grows 3-4 ft. tall. The variety versicolor or Rosa Mundi has light pink flowers, splashed and striped with crimson. R. gallica is called the French Rose.

R. Helenae. This is a vigorous Chinese Rose, 12 ft. or more in height. The large leaves con-

The graceful yellow-flowered Rosa Hugonis, one of the loveliest of all shrub Roses.

sist of 5-9 leaflets, reddish beneath, dark green above. The fragrant blush-white flowers are freely produced in large terminal corymbs, in late June and July.

R. Hugonis. This Chinese Rose forms a large bush, 8 or 9 ft. in height. The gracefully arching branches are covered with leaves composed of 5-11 leaflets. The vigorous stems are often armed with large, formidable thorns; the yellow blossoms, about 2 in. across, begin to open about the middle of May. This is a useful Rose for lawn beds, for the shrub border and for the open woodland. It is readily raised from seed and by rooted sucker growths. It is called Father Hugo's Rose.

R. laevigata. This kind, known as the Cherokee Rose, is naturalized throughout the southern United States but is not hardy in the North. It is a native of China. This Rose is a vigorous grower, evergreen, and high climbing, and bears white, or rarely pale pink, flowers that are 2½-3½ in. in diameter and are fragrant. The leaves are composed of 3 or, rarely, 5 leaflets.

Hybridized with R. Banksiae, the Cherokee Rose is a presumed parent of the double white-flowered R. Fortuneana. It also gave rise to the much hardier garden variety named Silver Moon.

R. macrophylla is a vigorous shrub, 7-9 ft. high, with arching branches and large leaves, 6-8 in.

Rosa Wichuraiana, a native of Japan, is a trailing kind that has fragrant white flowers in July.

long, consisting of 7-11 pairs of leaflets. The large, warm pink flowers, 2½-3 in. across, are followed by clusters of bright red, bottle-shaped fruits. It is wild in the Himalayas and in western China. Seeds were collected during the first Mount Everest expedition.

R. moschata. The Musk Rose is one of the tallest of climbing Roses. It is found wild from southern Europe to the Himalayas. When trained to cover old buildings, high walls or arbors, or trailing through the branches of trees, it makes a delightful picture. The large clusters of cream-white flowers with yellow centers are at their best in late June and early July, pervading the air with a musky fragrance.

It is not surprising that a Rose so widely distributed and variable in appearance should have several varieties. One of the most distinct is Brunonii, the Himalayan Musk Rose, with gray-green leaves; variety plena, a tall bush, 8 or 9 ft. high, has attractive double white flowers. This kind is sometimes regarded as a distinct species and is called R. Brunonii. A valuable race of vigorous-growing Roses has been raised by crossing the Musk Rose with some of the Hybrid Teas. Neither the Musk Rose nor the Himalayan Musk Rose is hardy in the North.

R. Moyesii. This is a distinct and useful wild Rose introduced from China early in the present century. It forms an attractive bush 10 ft. or more in height. The vigorous stems are armed with large spines, and the leaves are composed of 7-13 leaflets. The rose-red or wine-colored flowers, 2-2½ in. across, are different from those of any other Rose, and are very striking.

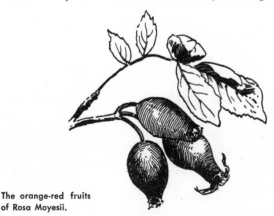

The orange-red fruits of Rosa Moyesii.

The handsome fruits are pear-shaped, and orange-red in color.

Seedlings of this Rose vary very much in the color of the flowers, and for this reason the best forms are propagated by budding, as cuttings do not root readily and layering takes a long time. The variety Geranium, raised at the Royal Horticultural Society's garden in England, is especially good.

R. multiflora. A native of eastern Asia, this Rose is commonly cultivated, and also occurs wild as a garden escape, in parts of North America. During recent years it has attained considerable popularity as a subject for forming hedges, and for this purpose has been publicized under the name "Living Fence." While it is a useful hedge plant for surrounding large areas, and soon forms an impenetrable barrier, it is ill-adapted for planting in most home gardens because it spreads widely and takes up considerable room.

The stems of this Rose are recurved, climbing or scrambling. The plants may attain a height of 6-8 ft. Its leaves consist of 7-11 leaflets. The flowers are white and fragrant and are borne in many-flowered clusters. They are followed by small, globular, bright red fruits.

Rosa multiflora shows considerable variation. Often the flowers are partly double. Its variety nana is dwarf, compact and bushy. Its variety platyphylla, which has pink or red flowers that are larger than those of typical R. multiflora, is known as the Seven Sisters Rose.

R. multiflora and its varieties have entered into the parentage of many garden varieties, the well-known Crimson Rambler being one of these. Rosa multiflora is much used as an understock on which to bud garden varieties of Roses.

R. nitida, an eastern North American Rose that grows 18-24 in. high, is suitable for the front of the shrub border. It has very prickly stems, shining green leaflets, rosy-red flowers 2 in. across, and globose red fruits. In autumn the leaves turn rich red before falling. It is found wild from Newfoundland to Connecticut.

R. Noisettiana. The Noisette or Champney Rose is a hybrid between R. chinensis and R. moschata that was raised at Charleston, South Carolina, early in the nineteenth century. It is an erect shrub, 7-10 ft. tall, and has leaves each with 5-7 leaflets. The flowers are borne in large clusters and are white, pink, red or yellow. This Rose is not hardy in the North.

The Manetti Rose, sometimes called R. Manetti, is a form of R. Noisettiana. The Manetti Rose is used as an understock upon which to bud and graft other garden Roses. It is not hardy in the North.

Well-known varieties of the Noisette Rose are Maréchal Niel, William Allen Richardson and Chromatella.

R. odorata. This is the original Tea Rose, a parent of the garden varieties of Tea Roses which, hybridized with other garden roses, gave rise to the popular Hybrid Teas. The Hybrid Teas, in turn, have been crossed with yet other Roses to produce the group called Floribunda.

R. odorata is an evergreen, or semievergreen, partially climbing kind, with tea-scented, usually double or semidouble flowers, of white, light pink or yellow coloring. It is hardy only in the South. The flowers are borne two or three together or occasionally singly. The leaflets number 5-7.

R. omeiensis pteracantha. This is a vigorous shrub Rose, very distinct in growth, foliage, flowers and fruit. Growing 10 ft. or more in height, it is an attractive Rose for large shrub borders and open woodland. It has fernlike leaves and four-petaled white flowers. The very large red, translucent thorns are extremely sharp.

R. pendulina, the Alpine Rose. This, which is often grown as Rosa alpina, is the Alpine Rose of the mountains of central and southern Europe. It is 5-7 ft. high, and is distinct because the stems have few or no thorns. The rich pink flowers are followed by large, bottle-shaped, pendulous red hips.

R. pomifera, the Apple Rose of central Europe and Asia, is so named because of its large, dark-crimson, apple-shaped fruits. It grows 5-6 ft. high and has rose-pink flowers in June and early July. It is a most useful wild Rose for the shrub border.

R. Primula is a very early-flowering species with dark-red, thorny stems and creamy yellow flowers. The foliage is aromatic and has been compared to the smell of incense. It grows 4-5

ft. high. This Rose is frequently grown under the name R. Ecae although this latter name belongs to another kind. It is a native of Asia.

R. rubrifolia, the Red-leaved Rose, is very well named, for it has distinct foliage of a pleasing reddish-gray color throughout the season. The bushes grow 5 or 6 ft. high and bear rose-red flowers, which are followed by clusters of globose, dark red fruits. It is a native of central Europe. It should be planted in gardens for its colored foliage, which is most useful to cut for indoor decoration.

R. rugosa, the Japanese Brier, is one of the best-known shrub Roses. It is a native of China, Japan and Korea, where it is among the oldest of cultivated Roses. The bushes grow 5 or 6 ft. high and bear large, purplish-red flowers which are followed by tomato-shaped red fruits.

A number of varieties are in cultivation, notable among which are Rosa rugosa alba, white, single; Blanc Double de Coubert, white, double; Agnes, apricot; Vanguard, salmon; Delicata, soft lilac, double; F. J. Grootendorst, crimson, fringed petals; Pink Grootendorst, clear pink; Conrad Ferdinand Meyer, pink; and Roseraie de l'Hay, velvety crimson-purple, very large double.

R. rugosa is a good seaside shrub, thrives in very light soils, and is used as a stock for standard Roses. It is naturalized in parts of North America, especially near the seashore.

R. setigera, the Prairie Rose, grows as a native

Rosa rugosa alba, a white-flowered variety of the Japanese Briar.

from Ontario to Iowa and southward to North Carolina, Georgia, Louisiana and Texas. Its stems are climbing and are 10-15 ft. long. Its leaves have 3-5 leaflets. The flowers are pink, fading almost to white as they age. They are scarcely scented.

The variety inermis of this Rose is a thornless kind. R. setigera is a parent of the garden variety Baltimore Belle.

R. Soulieana. This is a vigorous Rose, 10-15 ft. or more in height, with very thorny, gray-green stems. The leaves also have a gray-green tint. In July the large bushes produce cream-white flowers, which are followed by numerous rather small, orange-red fruits. It is a native of western China. It is too vigorous for the average border, but it is most effective in the open woodland or wild garden.

R. spinosissima, the Scotch or Burnet Rose, in its very numerous varieties is a most useful and attractive Rose for poor soil. It is of value for the shrub border and the wild garden, and makes an excellent low hedge.

Rosa spinosissima is wild in Europe and northern Asia. The average height is 2-4 ft., but in poor ground it may be less. The Scotch Rose spreads freely by means of creeping stems, which

The Apple Rosa, Rosa pomifera, has pink flowers which are succeeded by decorative, apple-shaped, red fruits.

provide the best method of propagation. The short, erect-growing stems are closely set with slender spines and bristles. The smallish leaves, 1½-2½ in. long, consist of 5-9 leaflets. The flowers, which open in late May and June, vary from white to pink, rose, purple, yellow and red; there are single, semi-double and double varieties, including a perpetual flowering pale-pink form known as Stanwell Perpetual. A particularly fine and vigorous variety is the one named altaica, which has large white flowers.

R. Sweginzowii. This is a vigorous Chinese Rose, 8-10 ft. or more in height. The stems are armed with large flattened spines and the leaves, 3-5 in. long, are composed of 5-9 leaflets. It has deep rose-colored blooms during June. The orange-red fruits are flask-shaped.

R. virginiana, of eastern North America, grows 3-5 or 6 ft. high, and makes a very pretty hedge, for it forms a close mass of upright stems. Propagation is thus quite easy by division or suckers in fall or early spring. It has glossy-green leaves and pink flowers 2-2½ in. across. There is also a white variety, alba. The small fruits are red.

R. Webbiana. This is a Himalayan Rose of graceful growth, forming an attractive bush 5 or 6 ft. high, with gray-green leaves. The pale pink flowers, 1½-2 in. across, are borne in June and are followed by pitcher-shaped red fruits. This is one of the most decorative of the wild Roses, both in flower and fruit.

R. Wichuraiana. The introduction of this distinct Japanese Rose of trailing growth in 1891 gave rise to an entirely new type of rambler Rose, and many present-day varieties are descended from it.

When no support is given, the long, slender shoots are of prostrate habit, attaining a length of 6-8 ft. in a season. It is evergreen in mild climates, deciduous where winters are severe, and has glossy green foliage, and bears clusters of very fragrant, white flowers in July. R. Wichuraiana is good for covering sloping banks or trailing over old tree stumps.

R. Wichuraiana is known as the Memorial Rose.

R. Willmottiae. This Chinese Rose was one of the first introductions of the famous plant collector E. H. Wilson early in the present century. It forms a densely branched shrub, 8-9 ft. high, with gray-green foliage that is very agreeable for decorative purposes. The light purplish rose flowers are 1-1½ in. across, and are followed by roundish-oval fruits, orange-red in color, which hang long on the bushes.

R. xanthina, a native of northern China and Korea, attains a height of about 10 ft. and, in the form usually cultivated, bears semidouble, yellow flowers. R. xanthina variety spontanea has single yellow flowers.

ROSA DE MONTANA. Antigonon leptopus, which see.

ROSARY PEA. See Abrus.

ROSCOEA (Rosco'ea). Dwarf perennial flowering plants which are very lovely when in flower, although they are not hardy. Only two or three kinds are in cultivation. Several plants which were formerly included in this group—R. gracilis, R. elatior and R. lutea—are now known as Cautleya.

The two principal kinds to be found in gardens are R. cautleoides and R. purpurea, both of which grow 9-12 in. in height and have tuberous roots. The leaves are lanceolate (lance-shaped), and sessile (without stalks.)

The flowers are produced singly or in small clusters, on each of the upright leaf stems. They are tubular at the base, the segments at the tips being two-lipped. The broadest lips hang downwards and the narrower upright portion enfolds the stamens. Surrounding each flower is a large calyx which is tubular and split down one side.

These plants belong to the family Zingiberaceae, and are found wild in India and China.

For a Warm Climate. Roscoeas should be planted outdoors in mild climates only. They may also be grown in pans or pots in cool green-

Floribunda Rose "Fanfare".

houses. They require light, rich soil. Sandy loam and leaf mold, to which a liberal amount of sand is added, suits them to perfection. Ordinary garden soil needs only the addition of leaf mold or humus, but heavy clay must be excavated and replaced with suitable compost.

Planting. Early spring is the best time for planting; the tuberous roots are placed 4 or 5 in. deep and 9 in. apart. During the summer months the soil is watered if necessary and kept moist, and in the autumn a mulch of ashes or of salt hay or some similar material is applied to protect them in severe weather.

Very little attention is required until the plants show signs of deteriorating in vigor. Then they are lifted and divided in spring, the soil is enriched with leaf mold or other organic matter, and the Roscoeas are replanted. This is also the principal method of propagation.

The Chief Kinds. R. alpina, 4-8 in., purple; R. purpurea, purple, autumn; R. Humeana, 8 in., violet-purple; and R. cautleoides, primrose-yellow, summer.

ROSE: QUEEN OF THE GARDEN

A Complete Guide to the Cultivation of All the Popular Types

The Rose is still the most popular garden flower, beloved by all for its fragrance, form, and infinite variety of color. During the present century, immense progress has been made in raising new varieties by crossbreeding and selection; new types have arisen; the season of blooming has been prolonged to such an extent that numerous modern varieties, including climbers, flower

This attractive border is planted
with the Floribunda Rose Circus.

intermittently or in some instances continuously throughout the summer and autumn months. In fact, only a severe frost puts an end to their season of beauty.

The species of wild Roses have already been discussed under Rosa and there, too, are described a few hybrids between species that are shrublike and generally resemble wild kinds. For garden purposes, the remaining types are classified or grouped in various ways: according to their habits of growth (for example, Shrub Roses, Trailers, Climbers); according to their ancestry (for example, Teas, Hybrid Teas, Hybrid Sweetbriers); according to the manner in which they are grafted, budded or trained (for example, Bushes, Standards or

Trees); and in a number of other ways.

These groups are not always clearly distinct. They often overlap, are not entirely logical, and sometimes lead to minor confusions; but they are generally convenient and fairly practicable, and represent the only classifications we have. They are the terms used in books, magazines and catalogues to classify Roses.

It is quite essential for the person interested in Roses to be familiar with the various types of Roses even though he may not be able, at sight, to place any given Rose in its specific category. Even experts cannot always do this with Roses with which they are not familiar. The following descriptions of Rose classes should be helpful.

Hybrid Tea type, including Pernetiana Roses,

Konrad Adenauer, a dark red-flowered Hybrid Tea Rose.

Polyanthas. They bloom intermittently all summer and fall.

Dwarf Polyanthas or Polyanthas. These are sometimes known as Baby Ramblers. Their individual flowers are small but they are borne in profusion, in great clusters after the fashion of the climbing Rambler Roses. They are low, shrubby plants that bloom over a long season.

Hybrid Perpetuals. These were the forerunners of the Hybrid Teas. They have great vigor, are hardy, and bear large, but sometimes not

which are now merged into the Hybrid Teas and can no longer be regarded as a separate group. The Hybrid Teas carry their blooms singly for the most part.

Grandiflora. A name now being given to hybrids of Floribunda and Hybrid Tea Roses in which the blooms approach the Hybrid Tea in size and form. They are borne in the clusters on long main stems but the clusters consist of fewer blooms than is usual in the Floribundas. They bloom all summer into autumn.

Floribunda Roses, comprising those varieties which bloom in clusters. These include Hybrid

Hybrid Perpetual Roses, such as this, are sturdy growers and bloom freely in June.

Many single-flowered Roses are very attractive for garden decorations.

very shapely flowers (by Hybrid Tea standards), on erect-growing bushes. Most kinds are exquisitely fragrant. They are sometimes known as June Roses.

Shrub Roses. This name is applied to a miscellaneous group of wild species, simple hybrids between wild species, and more complex garden hybrids, with little in common except their growth habit, which is that of a sizable shrub, rather than that of the dwarfer and lower Bush Roses such as the Hybrid Teas, and is distinct, of course, from the lax growth of the Ramblers and Climbers. Many of the Shrub Roses are dealt with under their species name under Rosa, which see. Others are discussed on pages 1914 to 1918 under Hybrid Sweetbriers, Moss Roses, Hybrid Musks, Cabbage Roses, French Roses, Damask Roses, Rugosa Roses, and Other Shrub Roses.

An attractive arbor covered with Climbing Roses in full bloom.

Climbing Roses are very decorative when trained on low fences.

Ramblers and Climbers. These have long canes growing from the base or from the main branches of the plant, and are especially suitable for covering walls, fences, pillars, arches and pergolas.

Miniature China Roses are tiny bushes. The blooms are less than an inch across and are borne throughout summer and autumn on plants 6 to 12 in. high. They are frequently planted in rock gardens and pots, and used as edgings for Rose beds.

Making a Rose Garden. Bush Roses look best, like most other flowering plants and shrubs, when they are grouped or massed. They should,

A formal Rose garden starting into growth in early spring after winter covering is removed and the bushes are pruned.

A garden may be formal or informal. Privacy is afforded here by a high trellised fence. The formal Rose beds in the center are balanced by the informal beds of annuals and perennials along the borders and by the Climbing Roses at the side.

The same Rose garden in full bloom in June.

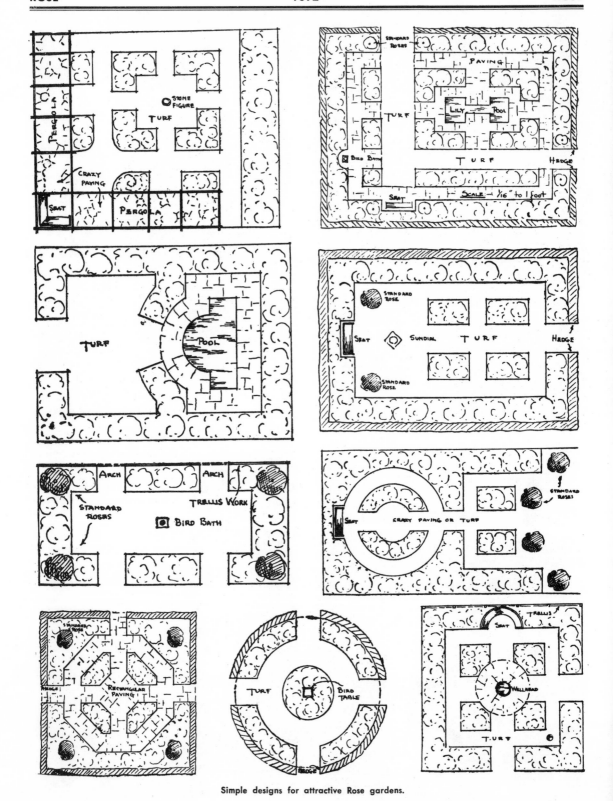

Simple designs for attractive Rose gardens.

therefore, be planted to form a Rose garden wherever possible, not scattered about in beds and borders in various parts of the garden. One possible exception is Floribunda Roses.

In a limited area a Rose garden of formal design is to be preferred; there the different varieties can be arranged to furnish delightful color schemes which not only show off the Roses to the best advantage, but afford charming color combinations. The accompanying illustrations give designs for Rose gardens of various sizes.

A Rose walk can be made a striking feature in a garden provided it is of fair length, say not less than 80 to 100 ft. The Rose beds arranged on each side of a wide grass path provide a very beautiful display in the summer and early autumn.

The effect can be heightened by using Tree and Pillar Roses as accents at intervals along the length of the Rose beds.

Roses are more attractive in beds than in long wide borders; they show to better advantage when the varieties are grouped together and are separated by grass paths, than when large unbroken masses are planted in a border.

How to Arrange Rose Bushes. Beds of mixed Roses are less effective than others in which the varieties are kept separate. If possible, each bed should be of a different variety; if the garden is not large enough to allow of this being done, two or three varieties may be grouped in each bed. That will be found far more satisfactory than mixing the Roses indiscriminately.

Another detail that must be considered when planting Roses is the height of the variety. Although they may be of the same class or type, they vary greatly in height and vigor of growth, and unless those of approximately the same height are associated the result will be unsatisfactory. Nursery catalogues often supply data on the height and character of Bush Roses such as Hybrid Teas, Floribundas and Polyanthas.

The Value of Pillar and Tree Roses. If the Rose garden is of fair size, its design is improved by the use of a few Standard or Tree Roses, Weeping Trees, and Pillar Roses. In a small garden, room cannot always be found for Weeping Trees and Pillar Roses because of their size.

A Standard or Tree Rose.

However, even a pair of Tree Roses, used at either side of a walk leading into a small garden, can lend character and charm. Flat beds of low-growing Hybrid Teas and Polyanthas improve in appearance when Tree Roses are spaced at intervals down the center. Pillar Roses may be used to frame a vista by placing them to the rear of Rose beds running down a long garden path. Pillar Roses need not, in fact, be confined to Rose gardens. They are effective at the back of broad perennial borders.

A Frame for the Rose Garden. Climbing or Rambler Roses make an admirable frame for

Tree or Standard Roses are used in this garden to give height and added interest to the beds of lower-growing Roses.

Climbing Roses trained to arches are a feature of this Rose garden.

the Rose garden. They look well if planted against posts connected by rope or chains, along which the long shoots will be trained to form festoons. Furthermore, they may be trained over picket or wooden fences, stone walls or other enclosures around the garden. Rope should not be stretched tightly between the posts, but allowed to droop slightly.

Best Width for Rose Beds. Care must be taken not to make Rose beds too wide or they will cause a good deal of inconvenience when such operations as pruning, spraying, cultivating, and

Climbing Roses are shown here trained to chains hung between wooden posts.

Rose beds should not be excessively wide. This bed measures only about 4 ft. across.

[11–2]
Japanese Brier
(Rosa rugosa)

[11–2a]
Shrub Rose, Harison's Yellow

Roses

[11—3a]
Hybrid Tea

[11—3]
Hybrid Musk

[11—3c]
Polyantha

[11—3b]
Floribunda

the removal of dead blooms and winter covering have to be carried out. Bush Roses should be planted 18 in. to 2 ft. apart and "staggered," that is, planted alternately, so that those in the second row come halfway between those in the first and third rows. A bed 6 ft. wide will take three rows of plants without undue crowding. Tree Roses are best planted not less than 4 to 6 ft. apart.

Soil Preparation. The preparation of the ground is a matter of the first importance, for Roses must be regarded as a permanent plantation, not likely to be disturbed for several, possibly many, years. Rose bushes will flourish on almost any kind of ground if it is prepared correctly.

Provided drainage is perfect, land on the heavy side gives the best results. It is, however, quite erroneous to suppose that clay is essential for first-quality Roses. Clay soils are often badly drained and require the addition of cinders, sand or gravel as well as adequate liming to open them up.

A plentiful supply of moisture in the subsoil is the first essential and the subsoil should be broken up by digging to a depth of 20 to 24 in. Where the subsoil is thin and of poor texture, moderate quantities of manure, as well as compost or other organic material that will provide humus, can be added with advantage. The manure must not be placed in separate layers, but should be well mixed with the soil, and should never come in direct contact with the roots, or it may burn them.

The upper soil should be broken up and plenty of humus-forming material, such as compost, chopped decomposed sod, leaf mold, peat moss, or very rotten manure, should be well mixed with the soil. Half a pound of bone meal to each square yard should also be added. Many rose nurseries now supply Rose food which can be used in place of bone meal.

If these instructions are carefully carried out, the plants will have a satisfactory root run, which is a very important aid to flower production.

Liming. Roses grow best in a slightly acid soil. Where a soil test indicates that the land tends to excessive acidity, a dressing of lime or ground limestone should be given in autumn. Liming will not usually be necessary for light soils, and at least a month must always elapse between liming and the application of fertilizers.

Fertilizers for Roses. It is advisable to fertilize Rose beds annually to keep them healthy and vigorous. Well-decayed manure should be put on the Rose beds as soon as pruning is finished, and forked lightly beneath the surface. If manure is not available, bone meal and dried blood or other organic fertilizer, together with rotted compost, may be substituted. A complete Rose fertilizer may also be applied as required, but not after the end of August; otherwise, soft growths unable to ripen before winter sets in are likely to be produced.

Many Rose fanciers today supplement spring feeding with liquid fertilizer applied to the soil. Some liquid fertilizers are completely soluble and can, with discretion, be sprayed on the foliage alone, or in mixture with plant sprays. This method of application is called foliar feeding.

Pest and Disease Control. There was a time when the gardener had to be able to identify not only the pests most easily seen on Roses, such as aphids, Rose slugs, Japanese beetles and Rose bugs, but also the destructive but tiny ones, including red spider mites, midges, thrips and leaf hoppers.

Not all of these pests are likely to be serious in any one garden at any one time, but one or more may cause serious damage unless controlled.

Added to the task of coping with insects is the additional menace of diseases including mildew, black spot and rust.

Rose specialists do mix separate materials used in controlling all these pests and diseases, such as DDT, malathion, miticides, ferbam, Captan, Mildex and sulphur. Not all chemicals are compatible, however, and one who lacks the proper technical knowledge may mix combinations which will seriously damage the plants.

The major manufacturers of garden chemicals now produce Rose sprays and dusts which are capable of keeping Rose plants free of all pests. A spray or dust may have the same brand name from year to year, but the ingredients will be changed to include the newest and most effective materials available.

Control of pests and diseases depends upon regular use of sprays or dusts. Both dusts and sprays are efficient. Light-weight equipment is to be had which makes the task of application easier.

In most gardens, weekly applications are advised, beginning early in the season as the new leaves unfurl. In spring, when rains and winds are prevalent, spraying often is more effective than dusting. Spraying should be done early in the day so that the foliage can dry before nightfall. All tips of new growth, as well as the undersides of the leaves, should be covered with a mist-like spray. Dusting should be done when there is no wind blowing, as in early morning or toward evening. Always work with the breeze, if there is any, so that the dust blows away from you, rather than into your face and eyes. Whereas sprays and dusts may not be seriously poisonous, you should always avoid inhaling them, and, if any material adheres to the skin, it should be washed off completely immediately after the work is done.

Mulching the Rose beds is one means of at least partially preventing the spread of diseases from the soil. Mulches, furthermore, are great labor savers. They keep down weeds, making cultivating almost entirely unnecessary in the summer. They also conserve water, and keep the roots cool, particularly in hot dry weather; they protect young roots from dying during drought. When Roses are splashed with rain, a mulch prevents disease spores, such as those of black-spot, from spreading from the soil onto the bottom leaves.

Mulches are applied to Rose beds as soon as the ground has been leveled, spring pruning done, plant food applied, and when the soil has dried enough to be workable. Many different products are used, depending upon availability. They include ground corn cobs, buckwheat hulls, peanut hulls, peat moss, shredded bark, sawdust, salt hay, cottonseed hulls, and straw. The depth of mulch will vary from 1 to 4 in., but it should cover the ground sufficiently to keep weeds from coming through.

Most mulches are left on all summer. Subsequent feeding of the plants, as at flowering time, can be done by applying liquid plant foods through or over the mulch, or by first drawing the mulch away from the plants and working the plant food into the soil.

The best time to plant dormant Rose bushes is in autumn, if you live in the North, but where zero or subzero temperatures rarely occur. In really cold climates early spring is the best time to plant. In the South any time from mid-November to mid-February is a suitable planting time, when conditions are favorable—that is to say, when the ground is neither frozen nor sodden, and when the weather is mild. Roses planted in spring do not, as a rule, start into growth so early or so vigorously as others put in the ground in autumn. Some growers consider that planting in spring is always preferable, as it is then that the sap starts to rise.

Planting dormant Roses in autumn is particularly advisable on light land, for should a hot, dry period set in during April and May, as often happens, bushes which have only recently been planted may suffer unless care is taken to keep them moist. It is worth while taking great care in planting Roses, for attention to detail may make a big difference in the result.

When Rose bushes arrive from the nursery they should be unpacked with the least possible delay and placed in the soil, care being taken that the roots are covered. If the weather is mild, the bushes should be soaked with water after being planted temporarily. This work, which is called "heeling in," is done by digging a trench 10 in. or more deep, laying the bushes in thickly and then filling in with soil. They will be perfectly safe until an opportunity can be found to plant them in their permanent locations and, of course, the sooner that is done the better. Should the land be frost-bound, leave the package untouched in any unheated place until the thaw comes.

If the branches appear to be somewhat shriveled when the bushes are unpacked, they should be buried completely in the soil for three or four days and soaked with water; when they are taken out, it will be found that the stems have freshened up considerably.

Cut Back Damaged Roots. Before a dormant Rose is planted, broken and bruised root ends should be cut back to sound portions with sharp shears or knife and any long roots which are without fibers should be shortened by about

If it is not possible to plant Roses soon after their arrival from the nursery, they should be placed in a trench and covered with soil (heeled in), as shown.

one-third or, if very long, they maybe shortened by half.

Because dormant Roses must have long canes in order to be of top grade, nurseries and local garden centers sell them this way. From the standpoint of the gardener, however, such long stems may be undesirable. For this reason, at planting time it is wise to prune back the tops somewhat, cutting off thin shoots entirely, and shortening each heavy cane so that it has only three or four dormant buds left. Cut cleanly about ½ in. above the top bud. Remove all

Cutting the tie that holds together the branches of a packaged dormant Rose plant.

Pruning the stems of a dormant Rose before planting. First, thin, weak, surplus shoots are cut out entirely.

Next, the strong shoots that remain are cut back to a length of 8-9 in.

labels attached to the canes, and fasten them to heavy wire stakes placed by the plants.

The hole should be about 15 in. across and of sufficient depth to take the roots when they are

Before dormant Roses are planted any damaged or bruised roots should be pruned back.

The roots are spread in a hole of ample size to take them without crowding.

spread out horizontally; it is a great mistake to cramp the roots in a hole which is too small for them. Never dig a hole that is narrow and deep, but make it wide and reasonably shallow. If an all-around spread of the roots is not feasible, set the bush against one side of the hole.

During planting, cover the roots of Roses awaiting their turn with a moist mat or burlap to avoid exposure to wind and sun or keep the bushes with their roots immersed in water.

Depth to Plant. One of the greatest mistakes

Good topsoil is worked among the roots.

The soil is made firm by treading it with the feet or by packing it with a stick.

The bud or graft-union, where understock and scion are united, should be just beneath the soil surface when planting is finished.

that can be made is to plant Roses too deeply. Three precautions can be taken to avoid this mistake. The uppermost roots should not be covered with more than 2 or 3 in. of soil, and the junction of stock and scion, the place at

Planting is finished by piling a temporary mound of soil to a height of 6-8 in, around the stems.

which the Rose was budded, should be covered with about an inch of soil at the final grade. Further, the soil mark on the stem, denoting the depth at which the bush was growing in the nursery, acts as a guide to the planter.

Rose bushes do not flourish in loose soil; it is necessary, therefore, to tread it very firmly around the roots of dormant Rose bushes. It is a mistake to fill in all the soil before treading it down. It should be made firm after a few spadefuls have been put in. Often some of the roots are lower than others; they should be covered with soil and made firm before the higher roots are dealt with.

Rose bushes should not be planted in soil that is freshly dug. The beds ought to be prepared a few weeks in advance of planting to give the soil a chance to settle. Too much stress can scarcely be laid on firm planting; there is little doubt that many failures can be traced to planting in loose soil. This is especially true with Tree Roses.

If the ground is rather wet when planting is done, so wet that it cannot conveniently be trodden, dry soil should be spread over the roots. When that has been made firm, the wet soil may be put on top and left as it is until dry enough to tread really firm.

If the weather is dry at the time of planting it is a wise precaution to water the bushes after planting to ensure that they are moist and that all roots are in close contact with the soil. Later, when the soil is drier, if the bushes can be moved with only slight effort, they must be refirmed immediately.

For the first two weeks after planting, dormant Rose bushes should have a mound of soil over the base of the branches to a height of 6 to 8 in. This protects the bark from sun and wind and prevents shriveling until the roots have time to become established and new shoots begin to develop. Thereafter, level the soil.

Planting Container-grown Roses. Many nurseryman offer for sale container-grown Roses. These are plants in full growth, well supplied with foliage and often with flowers at the time of planting. Container-grown Roses are produced by planting dormant plants in containers in good soil in spring. The containers are usually pots

Container-grown Roses can be set out in late spring and summer. In preparation for planting one, a large hole is dug in fertile soil.

Decayed organic matter is thrown into the bottom of the hole and is mixed thoroughly with the undersoil which is then made firm.

Some gardeners believe that container-grown Roses do not become established after they are planted as readily as dormant Roses and this, if true, is a disadvantage. Certainly, container-grown plants which are allowed to grow in their containers too long before they are planted out are inferior to good dormant plants. In no case

A container-grown Rose, in full foliage and flower, ready for planting.

The container, made of an asphalfum-paper composition, is carefully removed before the Rose is planted.

made of an asphaltum-paper composition but sometimes are of other materials. The newly potted Roses are placed in a favorable environment and are carefully tended to encourage sturdy growth. A great advantage of container-grown Roses is that they may be set out at any time during the growing season. Another possible advantage is that the purchaser may see the plant in bloom before buying.

Without breaking the ball of soil about the roots the Rose is carefully lowered into the hole.

Fertile soil is then shovelled around the root ball.

should Roses be left so long in the containers that their roots form a dense mat around the inside wall of the container.

Because container-grown Roses are pruned when the dormant plants are set in the containers they need no pruning, other than, perhaps, the removal of ill-placed branches or stems, when they are set out in the garden. Because the plants are in full growth at planting time, it is most im-

portant not to disturb, break or damage the roots or ball of soil in which they grow.

A few hours before container-grown Roses are planted they should be watered very thoroughly. At planting time a hole considerably wider than the diameter of the container should be made in ground that has been thoroughly spaded and fertilized. Rotted manure, compost or other rich decayed organic matter and a handful or two of bone meal should be placed in the bottom of the hole and be well mixed with the under soil. The soil in the bottom of the hole should then be packed firm and made level at a distance from the top which allows the Rose bush when set in position to be at the correct depth, that is with its graft or bud union just beneath the surface.

After the Rose plant has been very carefully removed from its container and set in place in the hole fertile top soil is filled in around the root ball and is packed firm with a stout stick. Great care should be taken not to break the root ball when the soil is being packed. When the hole is filled to within 3-4 in. of the top with firmly packed soil it is filled with water two or three times and this is allowed to drain away before more soil is added to bring the surface to or almost to the finish grade. A mulch of hay, straw, leaves, peat moss or other suitable material is then placed over the soil surface around the plant.

It is especially important that container-grown Roses receive adequate attention in the matter of watering during their first season in the garden. During dry weather the ground around them should be soaked to a depth of at least 8-9 in. every 5-6 days.

Winter Protection. In many parts of the United States and Canada most Roses must receive special protection against winter cold. The necessity for this varies with the type of Rose and with the degree of cold that is likely to be experienced.

Many Shrub Roses (species and simple hybrids of species that form large, shrublike plants which are generally used as shrubs rather than as subjects for ordinary flower beds) are hardy without protection even in the severest cold. Nevertheless, where temperatures are likely to drop lower than 20 below zero, at times when the

The soil is made firm by ramming it with a stick.

ground is not protected with a thick layer of snow, it is sensible to hill soil to a height of 1 to 2 ft. around the bases of the shrubs in late fall.

Rambler Roses should be given protection wherever the winter temperature is likely to go below zero. The canes should be laid along the ground and covered with a weighted board; in addition, mounds of soil should be hilled around

Before the hole is completely filled with soil it is thoroughly soaked with water.

their bases to a height of 1 ft. If the thermometer is likely to read lower than 10 degrees below zero the entire length of the canes should be covered with soil after they have been laid along the ground.

Hybrid Perpetuals, Dwarf Polyanthas, and Large-flowered Climbers should be protected, wherever the temperature is likely to go lower than 5 above zero, by hilling soil about their bases to a height of 8 to 12 in. If the temperature is likely to fall below 10 below zero the

After the water has drained away the surface soil is levelled and is covered with a mulch of hay or other suitable material.

canes of the Large-flowered Climbers should be laid along the ground and covered with a board weighted down. If the temperature may go to 20 below zero or lower, the entire canes should be laid on the ground and covered with soil.

Hybrid Teas, Floribundas, Miniatures, and Climbing Hybrid Teas need special winter protection in locations where the temperature may go to 10 above zero or lower. A mound of soil raised about the bases of the plants to a height of 8 to 9 in. (this may cover Miniature plants completely) is usually sufficient. However, if the temperature is likely to go as low as 15 degrees below zero, a heavy mulch of evergreen branches, straw, salt hay or similar material should be given in addition to the soil mound.

In cold climates, before the ground freezes, mounds of soil are heaped around the lower parts of the stems of Roses to protect them from excessive cold.

Tea Roses are unsuitable for growing where temperatures are likely to drop below zero. They should be protected by having a mound of soil 8 to 9 in. high heaped about their bases, wherever temperatures are likely to drop lower than 20 degrees above zero.

Roses grown as Standards (tree form) should receive special attention in places where the temperature is likely to go lower than 15 above zero in winter. A minimum protection consists of laying the plants down and covering them with soil. Should it be possible that the temperature will drop lower than 10 below zero, a mulch of leaves, evergreen branches, straw or salt hay should be placed over the mound of soil after it has frozen. If there is likelihood that the temperature may go below 20 below zero, tree-trained Roses should be taken up in the fall and buried in a trench over winter. In fact, many gardeners have found that this is the easiest method, regardless of how cold winters get.

How to Give Protection. A mound of soil heaped about the bases of the Rose bushes is the most effective basic protection against winter cold in all cases, where protection is needed, except with Tree Roses.

Such mounds of soil should be at least 8 in. high, and an even greater height is desirable. The soil, in intimate contact with the earth beneath, conducts warmth from the deeper layers of the soil, and even though the outside temperature is below zero and the surface of the soil mound is at the same temperature, an inch or two below that surface the temperature does not drop to the critical killing point, usually not lower than 20 above zero.

The soil mound, of course, protects only that part of the plant it covers. However, with many Roses, if the lower 6 to 8 in. are preserved, sufficient new growths will come from that portion to renew the upper part of the plant in a single season, and most kinds (not the Ramblers and Climbers, however) will flower freely on the new growth. The killing back above the soil mound simply acts in such cases as partial pruning.

Mounds of soil around the bases of the plants do not give protection to the upper parts of Ramblers and Climbers. These, if killed down to the top of the soil mound, will produce new shoots from live portions below, but flowers will not be borne on these during the first year. In climates where killing of the tops of these Roses is likely, the canes should be taken down from their supports in the fall and laid along the ground; boards should be placed on them, weighted down with stones or bricks.

In very severe climates, soil should be heaped over the canes after they have been laid down and pinned to the ground with wire "hairpins," or forked wooden pegs cut from tree or shrub twigs.

Where protection is needed for Tree Roses it is best to cut back the tops so that the branches are not more than 12 to 15 in. long, then lay the plant along the ground, peg it down, and cover it completely with soil.

To facilitate laying down, it will usually be necessary to take a few spadefuls of soil away from one side of the plant and then to carefully keel the plant over away from that side; this will permit the stem to be laid horizontally without snapping it.

In extremely cold climates Tree or Standard Roses may be dug up in the fall and completely buried in a trench outdoors.

The mounding of the soil should begin after the first really hard killing frost of fall and should be completed before the ground actually freezes up for winter.

Before the mounding begins, all shoots on Teas, Hybrid Teas, Floribundas and Dwarf Polyanthas that exceed 2½ ft. should be cut off at that height.

When Roses are planted closely together, by far the best method of mounding is to bring the soil used for mounding from another part of the garden, as this plan avoids the danger of baring the roots. The soil can be kept in place with stiff waterproof paper collars tied around each plant.

Where the Roses are widely spaced, soil may be mounded up with a hoe from between the plants themselves and from around the edges of the bed, care being taken not to expose roots. When this plan is followed it is a good practice to fill the hollows from which the soil has been drawn with the hoe with straw, leaves, salt hay or littery manure after the ground has frozen. This assures protection for roots that may be uncomfortably near the surface.

The soil mounds are broken down and the soil moved away in spring just at about the time new growth begins.

In extremely cold climates additional protection may be needed. This is supplied by covering the soil mounds, after they are well frozen, with a good layer of salt hay, coarse straw, evergreen branches or littery, loose manure. This covering acts as insulation and checks the too-rapid loss of heat from the soil beneath.

Replanting Old Rose Beds. Sooner or later Rose beds, no matter how well they were made in the first place, begin to need renovation. The soil may have become "rose-sick," which may be due to impoverishment, sourness or waterlogging, and obviously any new Roses planted in it will have little chance of success. The question arises whether to clear the whole bed and make a new one, or to replace the bushes that have deteriorated.

If the majority of the bushes are in poor condition, it will be most economical in the long run to dig them, remove the soil to a depth of 18 in., break up and enrich the subsoil, and then put in good loamy topsoil. If this is impracticable, then the best plan would be to rest the soil from Roses for two years, taking steps during this period to bring it back into condition by the good cultivation of other kinds of flowers. The old Rose plants may be replanted in rows in the cutting garden.

Replacing Individual Bushes. If comparatively few of the bushes are unhealthy, these may be replaced individually, but in each case the soil, to 18 in. deep, should be removed and replaced with fresh topsoil before putting in the new bush. If the bed is of one variety, then replacement with bushes of the same kind will be a simple matter; but if of mixed varieties, to maintain the balance of the bed careful choice must be made of new varieties equal in vigor to those left in the bed.

In many instances, Rose bushes which sprouted and began to grow in spring eventually die before flowering time. This can be the result of winter injury. Replacement of these plants can be accomplished through the use of potted plants which come in heavy paper or metal containers. Replant in the bed by removing the plant carefully from the container so as not to disturb the roots and mass of soil. Set the plant with the crown 1 in. below ground level. The growing tops should not be pruned. Keep the plant watered, especially in hot, dry weather.

Hybrid Tea Roses

When to Prune. Newly purchased bush Roses

Winter pruning. Roses are trimmed back to 16 or 18 inches high after the first killing frost. It is not advisable to cut them any shorter in the fall.

of the Hybrid Tea type, planted after the end of February, are best pruned before planting; otherwise, prune at the usual time.

Pruning during late autumn or winter, when the bushes are dormant, is advocated by some enthusiasts. It is claimed that with this method the bushes never bleed, and are not susceptible to damage by late spring frosts. It seems doubtful whether any real advantage is gained and the orthodox advice to prune when growth begins in spring is still sound.

Summer pruning is of questionable value. The growing bush needs the plant food manufactured by the foliage, and even pruning or cutting the blooms with very long stems, especially on young bushes, tends to weaken the plant.

Light Pruning Is Preferable. Generally, Hybrid Tea Roses bloom most freely when pruned lightly. The object of the pruner is to force the bushes to produce fresh, strong shoots, for the more vigorous and more numerous these are, the finer will be the display of bloom. It might reasonably be thought that, if pruned hard, the bush would produce stronger shoots than if pruned in any other way, But with Hybrid Tea Roses

which are well established in good soil, and which are well fed, that does not always prove to be the case. They are naturally free-growing, and if moderate or light pruning is practiced they will produce more shoots, quite strong enough to yield good blooms, than if they are hard-pruned. Gardeners who grow Roses for exhibition do prune harder to produce quality flowers on strong stems.

Too severe annual pruning seems to make the bushes stunted and deprive them of their natural vigor. The best advice that can be given to those who are disappointed with the display of bloom which results from hard pruning is to try either moderate or light pruning as described later.

How to Cut Back the Branches. The pruner should remember always to cut back to a dormant bud which points in the direction in which the new shoot is wanted. Except in pruning Roses of drooping or wide, spreading growth, when the branches are cut to buds which point inwards, it is wise always to make the cut just above a bud which points outwards. This precaution will prevent the center of the bush from being filled with shoots. That is a condition to

When pruning Roses first remove all unwanted canes.

Unpruned Hybrid Tea Rose after winter protection has been removed.

Canes that are shortened should be cut just above a dormant bud.

Injured wood should be cut off to the nearest live leaf bud. At same time, trim out weak branches.

be avoided; the pruner of Roses, as of fruit trees, should endeavor to preserve an "open center" so that the branches will be fully exposed to air and sunshine.

The ideal dwarf Rose bush is one which has a limited number of branches well apart from each other, and is free from small, weak shoots. Such shoots are not only worthless in themselves, but, in some measure, hinder the development of other and better ones.

Many amateur gardeners never really prune their Rose bushes at all; they merely snip off the ends of long shoots until the bushes are all more or less the same height, and do not thin out dead, diseased and weak shoots. The result is

A newly pruned Hybrid Tea Rose. Old stems have been cut about 8 in. from the ground. Some gardeners prefer to leave the stems 10-12 in. long.

A Hybrid Tea Rose making strong new growth following spring pruning.

that in the course of a few years the bushes become tall, lanky specimens which start into growth at the top only, produce weak shoots and, as a consequence, poor blooms. They become bare at the base and are unsightly.

The difficulty which most people experience is

Tree Roses are pruned in the same manner as Hybrid Teas and Floribundas. The branches are cut back to within 6-8 in. of the crown, or top of the trunk, to encourage a compact vigorous new growth. This is done in early spring.

to hit the happy mean between hard and light pruning; this end is most easily achieved by following the practice already outlined.

The Correct Way to Prune. All cuts must be made above a dormant eye or bud. A slanting and not a horizontal cut is essential because, with the former, moisture runs away more quickly, allowing the wound to heal promptly.

Pruning Newly Planted Hybrid Teas. These should be cut back to the third or fourth eye from the base of the bush. On very poor land pruning may be less drastic. The reason for hard pruning the first season is the inability of the bush to carry a heavy crop the following summer. The establishment of a sound root system is essential before a large plant can be supported.

Pruning Established Hybrid Teas. It has already been explained why drastic pruning often produces disappointing results. Moderate pruning is as follows. After removing all dead, wornout and weak wood, any crossing stems and those growing towards the center of the bush, reduce the main stems and laterals of the previous summer to about half their length. Light pruning differs only in that the cutting back is confined to the old flower stems, which are pruned back just enough to shape the plant and to eliminate thin stems.

Lightly pruned Rose bushes will not necessarily respond with stronger growth and more flowers unless they are in really good soil. This explains why light pruning is sometimes a failure. Judicious feeding is helpful under such conditions.

When pruning, look for stems showing diseased brown areas (canker) on the bark, or other signs of stem or bark injury. Prune these back to solid live wood. Remove also very old canes which last year made poor growth and no strong side branches. Frequently, these must be pruned back almost to the base of the plant to force new vigorous shoots to grow.

Hybrid Teas are still the favorite type of Rose at the present time, though Floribundas are becoming increasingly popular. The appeal of Hybrid Teas lies in the excellence of their individual bloom, the high proportion of fragrant varieties and the wide color range, which is largely absent from other classes of Roses.

Hybrid Tea Rose, Helen Traubel.

It is important to realize that Roses, in common with many cultivated varieties of plants that are propagated vegetatively (that is, by any method other than seed) invariably deteriorate in time. This may take fifteen or twenty years, or even longer, but unless the Rose is a species or only the first or second cross from one, in due course it will almost surely cease to be worth growing. Hence the need for the continual production of new varieties. Breeding is also stimulated by the American gardeners' interest in the latest horticultural developments.

Color Selections. The following list includes some of the best modern varieties of Hybrid Teas, listed by color groups. Fragrant varieties are indicated with an (F).

Red. Charlotte Armstrong, rose-red; Christopher Stone, crimson scarlet (F); Crimson Glory, velvety crimson, one of the most fragrant of all Roses; Etoile de Hollande, dark crimson (F); Mirandy, dark maroon (F); Christian Dior, crimson-red; New Yorker, bright red (F); Nocturne, cardinal-red (F); Aida, spectrum red (F);

Americana, a beautiful rich red (F); Red Radiance, light red (F); Rubaiyat, crimson red (F); Texas Centennial, brick-red (F); Konrad Adenauer, dark red (F); Detroiter, crimson.

Pink. Betty Uprichard, salmon-pink and carmine (F); Enchantment, pink (F); Peaceful, coral-rose pink; Pink Lustre; Helen Traubel, apricot-pink; Katherine T. Marshall, glowing pink; Royal Highness, pastel pink (F); South Seas, coral pink; Radiance, cameo-pink (F); The Doctor, satin-pink (F); Tiffany, clear light pink.

Yellow. Eclipse, pure yellow; Arlene Francis, golden yellow (F); Golden Masterpiece, butter-yellow (F); Golden Scepter, bright yellow; Lowell Thomas, sunflower-yellow; McGredy's Yellow, buttercup-yellow (F); Mrs. Pierre S. duPont, golden-yellow; Soeur Therese, buttercup-yellow.

White, Cream and Blush. Blanche Mallerin, crystal white; Kaiserin Auguste Viktoria, cream-white; White Queen, sparkling pure white; Virgo, pure white, good form; White Knight, pure white; Pedrables, cream-white; Rex Anderson, ivory (F); White Swan, pure white (F); White Wings, single, silvery white.

Blends, Multicolors. Arpege, pink, apricot and yellow; Condesa de Sastago, fiery copper and gold (F); Forty-niner, vermilion and gold; Kordes Perfecta, cream-white edged with pink (F); Hawaii, orange-coral (F); Gail Borden, pastel pink and apricot; Pageant, pink and yellow (F); Diamond Jubilee, buff-yellow (F); McGredy's Sunset, yellow and scarlet (F); Mrs. Sam McGredy, scarlet-copper-orange (F); Mojave, scarlet-vermilion (F); Peace, yellow edged rose-pink (F); President Herbert Hoover, yellow, copper and pink; Pageant, pink and yellow (F); Personality, golden yellow overlaid with red.

Lavenders. Lavender Girl, clear lavender; Sterling Silver, lavender-pink (F); Orchid Masterpiece, deep orchid shaded lavender.

Hybrid Perpetuals

The class of Rose known as Hybrid Perpetual is less commonly grown now than formerly, its place having been taken in popular esteem to a large extent by Hybrid Teas and more recently by Floribundas. Nevertheless, Hybrid Perpetuals have much to recommend them apart from the sentimental appeal of growing old-time Roses. They have the great advantage of being hardier than most Hybrid Teas and Floribundas and they withstand severe winters with little or no protection. They are also comparatively resistant to disease and grow with great vigor.

Hybrid Perpetual Roses resulted chiefly from hybridizing R. centifolia, R. chinensis, R. damascena, and R. gallica, and attained their greatest popularity towards the end of the nineteenth century. The first varieties are believed to have been originated in France in 1837.

The red-flowered Hybrid Perpetual Rose, Captain Hayward.

The blooms of Hybrid Perpetual Roses are usually exquisitely fragrant but lack the refined form of most of the Hybrid Tea Roses.

The flowers of these kinds are large, heavy in appearance, and flat-topped; as a rule they lack the high, pointed centers that give added grace to most Hybrid Teas. The colors are mostly white, pink, and a crimson-red which often changes to a rather disagreeable bluish tone as it fades. The flower stems are generally short, but this fault is partly compensated for by the delicious fragrance that is so characteristic of almost all Hybrid Perpetual Roses.

The flowers of these Roses are chiefly borne in June, in a glorious display, but some flower sporadically through the summer and they usually provide a second, but less profuse, con-

centrated showing in the fall. They are sometimes called June Roses.

Hybrid Perpetuals, although they lack the refinement of form and clarity of color of the Hybrid Teas and Floribundas, are splendid plants for those who want Roses with a minimum of trouble.

How to Prune. Early spring is the time to prune these Roses. The usual procedure is to begin by cutting out all dead, weak or injured shoots and any that are badly placed or are obviously crowding their neighbors. From 4 to 8 vigorous, well-placed canes are left. These are

The Hybrid Perpetual Rose, Earl of Dufferin. It has very fragrant, red flowers.

then cut back to 2 to 3 ft. above ground level, the height depending on the vigor of the plant; the thinner and weaker ones are shortened more severely than the stouter ones. If taller plants are desired, the canes may be left longer, but this means that most of the flowers will be borne above eye level unless a special form of training, such as that described below, is followed.

A Good Method of Training. In order to have Hybrid Perpetual Roses produce more blooms, below eye level and all at approximately the same height, the shoots may be trained in this manner. Allow stout, new shoots to grow naturally during the summer. In fall, after all growth has ceased, bend these shoots down so that they spread radially from the center of the bush, and tie them to a series of stakes that are driven firmly into the ground and that protrude about a foot above soil level. The object is to secure the Rose canes in a horizontal position, paralled with the surface of the ground and about a foot above it. Only sufficient canes should be tied down to fill the available space, and these should be the strongest and best that the bush has; unwanted canes should be pruned out.

Established Hybrid Perpetual Roses that are trained in this way may be pruned in either of two ways. In the first, sufficient number of new shoots may be allowed to grow erect each summer to replace those that have been tied down; in fall the tied-down ones are cut out and are replaced by tying into position the new, erect shoots. In the second method, during the summer strong vertical growths that appear from near the base of the bush are cut off 3 to 4 in. above the horizontally trained shoots and are thus encouraged to produce side shoots that will bloom later. If the second plan is followed, the horizontal canes are retained for more than one year, and each spring the vertical shoots that grow from them are pruned back to within about an inch of their bases.

Varieties of Hybrid Perpetual Roses that are still obtainable from commercial sources include the following:

American Beauty. A large, full flower, crimson-carmine shaded with rose. Of vigorous growth and a profuse bloomer. Richly fragrant. The true, original favorite of the "Gay Nineties."

Baroness Rothschild. A large, full flower, light-pink with suffusions of white and pale-rose. An erect grower of considerable vigor.

Captain Hayward. One of the best red Hybrid Perpetual Roses. Flowers are large, semidouble, and scarlet-crimson. Of vigorous habit.

Duchess of Sutherland. Flowers large, rosy-pink. Plant of vigorous habit. Not to be confused with the Hybrid Tea variety of the same name, which has long, pointed buds and high-centered flowers that are rose-pink with lemon yellow at the bases of the petals.

Ferdinand Pichard. A strong-growing, free-flowering variety that bears semidouble flowers streaked pink and scarlet.

Frau Karl Druschki. One of the very finest Roses. Flowers very large, snow-white, double. Very vigorous. Not fragrant.

General Jacqueminot. A very fine Hybrid Perpetual Rose with long, strong stems and clear red flowers. Sometimes known affectionately as "General Jack."

George Arends. A vigorous plant with large, full flowers of an exquisite shade of delicate pink.

Gloire de Chedane-Guinoisseau. This variety has large, well-formed flowers of a bright crimson color. A vigorous grower.

Henry Nevard. Characterized by having large, crimson-scarlet flowers of pleasing form. A vigorous grower; bushy.

Louise Crette. In this variety the flowers are very double and high-centered. They are well formed, white with creamy white centers. The canes have few thorns.

Mrs. John Laing. A rather low grower that produces long-stemmed, very large, fully double flowers of a soft pink color.

Mrs. R. G. Sharman-Crawford. A vigorous Rose that has large, cupped flowers that are rosy-pink, with the outer petals lighter.

Oskar Cordel. A variety of compact growth that bears bright carmine flowers that are large, double and abundant.

Paul Neyron. A very vigorous variety with flowers of immense size that are lilac-pink to rose-pink. The flowers are double. Richly fragrant.

Prince Camille de Rohan. A vigorous-growing

variety that has very double, dark-crimson flowers that are shaded with black-maroon. Its flower stems are rather weak.

Roger Lambelin. A vigorous grower of distinctive appearance. The flowers are irregular and semidouble, the petals crimson, margined or streaked with white, and fringed.

Ulrich Brunner. A long-time favorite among Hybrid Perpetuals. The flowers are large and bright carmine red. A vigorous grower and a free bloomer.

Tea Roses

Tea Roses are characterized by rather spreading growth and delicately scented blooms of pale coloring that are produced freely in summer and in autumn. In the South and in California, many varieties grow at least 5 ft. high. The Tea Rose is descended from Rosa odorata, a Chinese Rose which was introduced early in the nineteenth century.

Throughout several generations of crossbreeding and selection, numerous varieties have been raised. Comparatively few are now in cultivation; they have been superseded by the Hybrid Teas, which are hardier and better suited to planting in the open garden, and produce flowers of richer and more varied coloring. There is, however, a revival of interest in Tea Roses in mild-climate areas, the South and on the West Coast, to the climates of which they are best adapted. There they grow much more vigorously and yield a long succession of bloom. They are not very subject to black-spot disease.

Tea Roses thrive best on warm, well-drained soil; they are scarcely suitable for planting in clay ground unless it has been prepared by replacing some of the clay with loam and sand. Most are not reliably hardy in the North, and even in parts of the South in cold gardens they generally need some protection during the winter months. This is best provided, if the Roses are dwarfs or bushes, by placing mounds of soil or old ashes over the base of the branches. If they are grown as Tree Roses, the branches should be tied loosely together and sacking wrapped around them when severe weather is expected. But in mild climates they come safely through the winter months without protection of this sort.

In well-drained, loamy soil some varieties of Tea Rose will grow into fair-sized bushes and their flowers usually can be gathered until quite late in the year. One would scarcely recommend them for general planting in the open garden except in mild climates and in sheltered gardens.

The Best Tea Roses. These are the chief varieties now in cultivation:

Anna Olivier. Light rose with buff shading. One of the best of the older Teas. Fragrant, moderately vigorous.

Bon Silene. Produces abundantly over a long period its charming, large, double, rose-pink blooms.

Bridesmaid. A vigorous kind with soft pink flowers.

Comtesse Riza du Parc. A free-flowering kind with large salmon-rose flowers that are tinted with copper.

Duchesse de Brabant. This, the favorite Rose of President "Teddy" Roosevelt, is free-blooming. Its flowers are pink.

Earl of Dufferin. A very large, full-petalled Rose of vigorous growth. Its flowers are red and very fragrant.

Isabella Sprunt. A Tea Rose of vigorous growth that bears an abundance of sulphur-yellow flowers.

Lady Hillingdon. Orange-yellow; the flowers are weak stemmed; the climbing form is recommended for walls.

Madame Antoine Mari. A delightful little Rose of perfect form; the blooms are of lilac-rose shade and white, very dainty; it does as well in the garden as any of the Teas.

Mme. Lombard. A fine Tea Rose. Flowers salmon-pink shaded with yellow.

Maman Cochet. A very beautiful flower of light-rose shade. White Maman Cochet is one of the best garden Roses of the South.

Marie Van Houtte. One of the best Tea Roses. Flowers are white, slightly tinted with pink and yellow.

Molly Sharman-Crawford. An attractive Rose with white flowers which have greenish shading. It is of fairly vigorous growth.

Mrs. Dudley Cross. A thornless Rose that has large, well-formed flowers of light yellow with a pleasingly attractive light pink shading.

Mrs. Foley-Hobbs. A beautiful Rose. The large full blooms are white, flushed with pink, and fragrant.

Mrs. Herbert Stevens. Without doubt the best of the white Tea Roses; the flowers are sweet-scented. It does quite well in the open garden, but, like all other Tea Roses, does not flourish in exposed, windy places.

Rosette Delizy. A good variety that blooms over an extended season. Yellow with dark carmine outer petals.

Souvenir de G. Nabonnand. Of light-rose color, fragrant, moderately vigorous.

Floribunda Roses

The Floribunda Roses, which are also known as Hybrid Polyanthas, have achieved great popularity during recent years. They were originally crosses between Dwarf Polyanthas and Hybrid Teas, but the parentage is now somewhat wider, hence the renaming as Floribundas.

The plants are as tall as the average Hybrid Tea, but the height varies greatly among varieties and some recent introductions are even taller. They bear single, semidouble, or fully double blooms, larger than those of the Dwarf Polyanthas and occasionally of Hybrid Tea quality, though somewhat smaller.

Floribunda Roses perform exceptionally well in the average garden because of their hardiness, resistance to disease, and capacity to supply more color all season long than Hybrid Teas. This class of Rose is very effective when planted in solid beds of one color, but home gardeners have found that its use can be extended to foundation plantings, shrub borders, flower borders, low hedges and large tubs and planter boxes.

The Pick of the Best. There are many

This hedge of Floribunda Roses borders a driveway to a garage. The tall specimen against the garage is a Climber.

Floribunda Rose, Masquerade.

cherry-red; Cocorico, orange-red; Frensham, deep crimson red (F); Garnette, dark red; Red Wings, deep red; Red Pinocchio, deep red; Fusilier, orange-scarlet (F); Jiminy Cricket, coral-orange (F); Siren, fiery scarlet; Chatter, bright crimson; Geranium Red, red.

Pink. Betty Prior, carmine to shell-pink; Pink Bountiful, blend of pink (F); Ma Perkins, coral shell pink (F); Pinocchio, salmon and pale pink (F); Betsy McCall, soft coral pink; Rosenelfe, clear pink; The Fairy, pale pink.

A favorite Floribunda Rose is the coral-pink Fashion, here planted around a bird bath.

excellent varieties, especially among the reds and pinks. Recent introductions include good yellows, richly toned multicolors, good whites, and now lavender and brown tinted kinds. Some varieties, notably Fashion, Masquerade and Vogue, have a distinct wild Rose fragrance. In the following selection, fragrant varieties are marked with an (F).

Red. Lilli Marlene, cherry red; Baby Blaze,

Rose Summer Snow is a white-flowered Floribunda.

Yellow. Goldilocks, bright yellow; Gold Cup, deep yellow (F); Golden Fleece, light yellow (F).

White. Irene of Denmark, clear white; Summer Snow, white (F); White Bouquet (F); Glacier, white.

Blends. Circus, orange-buff-pink; Fashion, coral pink (F); Spartan, orange-red (F); Vogue, cherry-coral (F); Masquerade, multicolor; Rochester, pink and yellow (F).

Lavender. Amy Vanderbilt (F).

Pruning the Floribundas. Pruning varieties in this group often causes needless headaches. The best method is to cut back last year's growth to the second eye below the flowered head. Two-year-old wood is pruned down to a few eyes from the base. As with all types of Roses, weak and spent wood is removed, and any criss-cross shoots cut out. Very light pruning produces a mass of thin, weak growths, which is not desirable.

Grandiflora Roses

Nurserymen and leading rosarians have given this name to Roses having the general characteristics of Floribunda Roses, but with the habit of bearing fewer flowers in a cluster and carrying them on long stems suitable for cutting for flower arrangements. The plants tend to grow tall and upright. Otherwise, Grandifloras, which are hybrids between Hybrid Teas and Floribundas, resemble Floribundas in hardiness, disease resistance, ever-blooming habit, and fine form of the buds and blooms.

Varieties which are now classed as Grandifloras include Buccaneer, clear golden yellow; Carrousel, rich dark red; Montezuma, burnt orange; and Queen Elizabeth, clear light pink.

Grandiflora Roses are pruned, cared for and used the same as Floribunda Roses.

Polyanthas

Polyanthas are very free-flowering Bush Roses. Some varieties, having originated as "sports," are likely to revert to the parent unless care is taken to remove shoots bearing off-color flowers. Polyanthas are very long-lasting as cut flowers, but have declined in popularity since the advent of Floribundas or Hybrid Polyanthas, which have larger blooms, produced with even greater freedom on taller plants. The most popular varieties include Cameo, flesh-pink; Carol Ann, salmon-orange; Cecile Brunner, the Sweetheart Rose, pink; Crimson Rosette, crimson; Margo Koster, orange-pink; Orange Triumph, scarlet-orange; Pink Rosette, soft pink.

Very little pruning is required for these Roses. Any wood which failed to bloom the previous year should be cut down to the base. Do not remove thin growths unless this is desirable to keep the center open, as the stems are naturally thinner than those of the Hybrid Teas.

Hybrid Sweetbriers

These strong growing Roses make attractive flowering shrubs and are also excellent for tall hedges, provided care is taken to combat blackspot disease, to which they are very subject. The height ranges from 6 to 8 ft., or even higher. The foliage has the typical Sweetbrier aroma. Frequent heading back of extra long canes is necessary to make the plants bushy.

Good varieties include Lady Penzance, coppery salmon; Lord Penzance, fawn-tinted lemon; Eglantine, bright pink. All bear their single flowers in late spring only.

Miniature Roses

Grandiflora Rose, Queen Elizabeth.

These fascinating little Roses, which form

A miniature Rose trained as a tree or standard.

Pruning. This and the other China Roses need little pruning. They should be looked over in spring for the purpose of cutting out dead or very weak shoots that may interfere with the development of better ones; the remaining branches may then be shortened by about one-third. China Roses are of rather thin growth, and light pruning suits them best.

The following varieties are still in cultivation: Comtesse du Cayla, red tinted orange; Cramoisi Superieur, crimson; Fabvier, crimson and white; Fellemberg, a beautiful old China Rose with sweet-scented flowers of light crimson or rose-red; Hermosa, rose-pink; Mme. Laurette Messimy, light rose. The Green Rose, Rosa chinensis viridiflora, belongs to this group.

Moss Roses

These charming old-fashioned, tall shrub-type Roses are so attractive that a corner might well be found for a few of them. They are called Moss Roses because the flower stems and the calyces are covered with a mosslike growth of glandular hairs.

The way to manage these Roses is to plant them in a sunny location in deeply dug soil enriched with decayed manure and, after the first spring, to prune them lightly. In spring, following planting, the branches of the past year's growth should be shortened to within about five buds of the base; in future years it is sufficient to cut out weak and ill-placed shoots, and to shorten the remainder by one-third. In time the plants make strong shrubs. Moss Roses bloom only in early summer.

Few varieties are available. One of the best is Blanche Moreau.

Blanche Moreau. White flowers, heavily mossed.

Capitaine John Ingram. Dark-red, double blooms, the buds well mossed.

Crested Moss, or Chapeau de Napoleon as it is sometimes called. Has large, full, deep pink flowers with calyces that are curiously and attractively fringed and frilled in a manner different from that of other Moss Roses.

Gloire des Mousseux. Rose-pink buds which are exceptionally well mossed.

compact bushes 6 to 18 in. tall bearing a profusion of perfectly formed miniature blooms, are grand subjects for the rock garden or window boxes, and they also make delightful pot plants.

Available kinds include: Rosa pumila, pink; R. Rouletti, rose-pink; Oakington Ruby, crimson; Pompon de Paris, deep pink; Pixie, white; Jackie, yellow, fragrant; Midget, rose-red, fragrant; Prince Charming, crimson; Red Imp, crimson. Miniature Rose trees are now being produced with main stems 12 in. high. Standard varieties including Bo-Peep, bright pink; Pixie, white; Red Imp and Tom Thumb, rich crimson, are being grown in tree form by nurserymen.

These Miniatures should be pruned only lightly in early spring, merely cutting out dead shoots and shortening tips of the remainder.

China Roses

Almost the only variety of this Rose which is now grown is the pink Monthly, or common China Rose, Rosa chinensis semperflorens, and that is represented chiefly by bushes which were planted many years ago. In mild climates it blooms almost throughout the year. It makes an attractive low hedge. The flowers have no pretentions to form, as judged by exhibition standards, and they have comparatively few petals. The color is a very attractive shade of rose-pink.

Jeanne de Montfort. Well-mossed buds and flat, semidouble flowers that are pink, edged with silver.

Louis Gimard. Mauve-pink flowers on long stems. It is well mossed.

Mme. Louis Leveque. Large, globular, salmon-pink flowers. Stems are well mossed.

Mousseux Ancien. Pink blooms that darken towards their centers. The calyx is well mossed.

Salet. Flowers are rosy pink with bluish margins to the petals. They are exceptionally large. This plant often blooms in the fall as well as in early summer.

Waldtraut Nielson. One of the best of the Moss Roses. Its flowers are deep pink.

Hybrid Musks

This delightful group of shrub-type Roses grows vigorously and blooms freely throughout a long period in summer and autumn. Since the Reverend J. H. Pemberton of England originated many varieties, they are sometimes catalogued as Pemberton Pillar and Pemberton Shrub Roses.

Hybrid Musks are said to have been raised by crossbreeding the Musk Rose, Rosa moschata, and various modern Roses. Some of the most vigorous ones form large bushes 5 ft. or more high, and bear a profusion of small flowers which make up for lack of size by their abundance. Tall kinds may be grown as Pillar Roses against a support.

Roses in this class are easily managed and are perfectly hardy. They should be planted in an open sunny place, 3 to 4 ft. apart, according to the vigor of the variety, and pruned lightly.

Pruning Hybrid Musk Roses. In the spring following planting it is wise to shorten the branches to within about 12 in. of the base, but in subsequent years it is necessary merely to cut out old branches or parts of them, remove dead and weak shoots, and shorten slightly the main branches of the previous year's growth. Shoots of rather weak growth may be shortened by one third or so, but only the tips of the strong ones should be cut off.

Within a few years, Hybrid Musk Roses develop into splendid bushes and are very beautiful during the greater part of the summer and early autumn. They are also delightful for indoor decoration if long shoots bearing buds and blossoms are cut.

A bed of Hybrid Musk Roses.

The Hybrid Musk Rose Clytemnestra.

The best varieties of this type are:

Clytemnestra. Copper buff-pink. Grow as a pillar.

Cornelia. This variety, of vigorous growth, has rose-colored blooms tinged with yellow. Shrub in habit.

Danae. Not so vigorous as others. Buds are yellow, the open flowers white.

Moonlight. The buds are light-yellow, the semidouble flowers are white. Vigorous, forming a fair-sized bush.

Pax. The best Hybrid Musk; the large flowers have few petals.

Penelope. This is a beautiful Rose; it is of strong growth and soon forms a bush 3 ft. or so high if pruned lightly. The flowers, produced in loose bunches, are salmon pink and sweet scented. If only one Hybrid Musk Rose is chosen, preference should be given to this variety.

Prosperity. White, tinted pink. Continuous bloomer. Grows as a shrub or pillar.

Vanity. This variety, which is less vigorous than Penelope, bears large flowers of carmine-rose coloring.

Cabbage Roses

The Cabbage Rose species, Rosa centifolia, is dealt with under Rosa, which see. This and varieties of it are shown as Cabbage Roses because of the shape of the flowers.

These Roses need pruning in the same man-

ner as Moss Roses, which procedure is described under Moss Roses, above. The following are good varieties of Cabbage Roses:

Konigin von Danemark. Very full, medium-sized flowers, flesh-pink with deeper-colored centers. Fragrant.

Rose des Peintres. A Rose of vigorous growth, the flowers of which the old Dutch painters loved to paint. Blooms are large, full, and flesh-pink, with darker centers.

Vierge de Clery. The finest white-flowered Cabbage Rose; flowers large sized, very fragrant.

French Roses

Rosa gallica, which is the original parent species of the French Roses, is described under Rosa, which see. Good varieties of the French Rose, which require pruning in the same manner as Moss Roses, are:

Duc de Guiche. Double flowers, light violet-red or orchid color.

Jeannette. Attractive double flowers are bright light-red color.

President de Seze. Flowers are a most unusual color, lilac-red shaded with violet-orchid. The large, full flowers are borne profusely.

Rosa Mundi. The rather large, semidouble flowers are white or delicate pink, boldly striped with deep pink and red. This Rose is sometimes mistakenly grown as York and Lancaster, a name which rightly belongs to R. gallica variety versicolor. See the Damask Rose, below.

Tricolor de Flandre. Flowers are double, lilac-white striped with pink, purple and crimson. Fragrant.

Damask Roses

Like the strong-growing Cabbage Roses and French Roses, the Damask Roses are very hardy. They need pruning in the same manner as the Moss Roses, which see. The type species of the Damask Rose is Rosa damascena, described under Rosa, which see. Among worth-while varieties are:

Kazanlik. A semidouble variety that is much grown in southeastern Europe for the manufacture of Attar of Roses. It grows 3 to 4 ft. tall and has clusters of bright rosy-pink flowers. Botanically this variety is Rosa damascena variety trigintapetala.

Marie Louise. This is perhaps the best Damask Rose. It forms a bushy plant and has large, double, rich pink flowers of delightful fragrance.

Mme. Hardy. This pure white Rose has large, full, fragrant flowers. One of the best white old-fashioned Roses.

Professeur Emile Perrot. This variety is grown in quantity in Europe for the perfume industry. Its very fragrant flowers are soft pink.

York and Lancaster. This Rose dates back to Tudor times and was named, it is believed, to commemorate the end of the Wars of the Roses between the House of Lancaster and the House of York in England. Botanically it is Rosa damascena variety versicolor. Semidouble flowers are fragrant. Some petals in the same flower may be entirely white, others entirely red or sometimes half-red and half-white. They are not, however, clearly striped as are those of Rosa Mundi (see under the French Rose, above).

Other Shrub Roses

In addition to the varieties called Shrub Roses (kinds that make sizable bushes and are useful for landscape groups) mentioned above under the headings Hybrid Sweetbriers, Moss Roses, Hybrid Musks and China Roses and those mentioned in the treatment of Rosa (which see), there are other Shrub-type Roses of hybrid origin that are worthy of consideration. Among the best of these are:

Autumn Bouquet. This hybrid between New Dawn and Crimson Glory grows about 4 ft. high and has large, double, very fragrant, rose-pink flowers. Remontant (blooms more than once in a season).

Hon. Lady Lindsay. A hybrid between New Dawn and Rev. F. Page-Roberts that grows about 3 ft. tall and has pink petals that are darker on the underside, flushed yellow at the base. Remontant.

Fragrant Beauty. This is a vigorous Rose that grows 4 to 5 ft. high. It has semidouble, carmine-red, fragrant flowers that have a strong, spicy fragrance. It is a continuous bloomer.

Harison's Yellow. An old Rose that forms a shapely, 6-ft. bush and carries a multitude of small, semidouble, fragrant, bright yellow flowers in early summer.

Maiden's Blush. A very old Rose that makes a shrub to about 8 ft. tall and has a profusion of soft pink, sweetly fragrant flowers.

Nevada. A vigorous shrub, about 5 ft. tall, with large, single white flowers, sometimes splashed with crimson on the outside. Remontant.

Schoener's Nutkana. This vigorous Rose has arching canes 4 to 6 ft. high. Its single fragrant flowers are clear rose-pink. It has few thorns.

Rugosa Roses

The natural forms of Rosa rugosa, both the mauve-pink and white-flowered kinds, are vigorous, extremely hardy shrubs which endure cold climates and the salt spray and sandy soils found along the seacoast.

Plant breeders both here and abroad have used the Rugosa Rose to develop a group of shrubs which are exceptionally useful in shrub border plantings and hedges, and in some cases are trained like climbers. Their rich green, heavy foliage often takes on an attractive autumn color. The plants are unusually resistant to insects and diseases.

The Hybrid Rugosa Rose, Pink Grootendorst.

Representative varieties of Hybrid Rugosa Roses follow:

Agnes. One of the few Rugosa Roses having golden yellow double flowers. Sweetly fragrant. 6 ft.

Blanc Double de Coubert. The large, semi-double flowers are pure white and delightfully scented. A shrub, 4-5 ft. tall.

Conrad Ferdinand Meyer. Tall growing, bearing large double pink blooms in early summer. Can be trained as a climber or kept pruned to shrub height.

Dr. Eckener. The large semidouble, copper-rose flowers have the quality of Hybrid Tea blooms borne on a hardy 5-ft. shrub. Remontant.

F. J. Grootendorst. Unlike most other Hybrid Rugosas, the red flowers of this variety and also those of Pink Grootendorst are small and are borne in large clusters all season long. The individual flowers are double and fringed like carnations. Grows 4 ft. or more. Useful as an informal hedge.

Sarah Van Fleet. Flowers large, semidouble, rose-pink, sweetly scented. 7 ft. high. Remontant.

Vanguard. Flowers large, double, bright orange-salmon colored. One to several flowers are clustered on long cutting stems. Foliage big, deep glossy green. A strong grower which may be trained as a Climber or pruned as a large shrub. Early summer flowering.

A Wichuraiana Rambler Rose trained to a pole.

Rambler Roses

The Wichuraiana Ramblers (familiar varieties are Dorothy Perkins and Excelsa) are distinguished by very long and comparatively lissome shoots or canes; they are very vigorous, some varieties producing shoots 12 to 15 ft. long in a year. The leaves, too, are attractive; they are rich green and often persist until well into the winter. These Ramblers were at one time planted in large numbers for covering arches, trellises and pergolas. At present they are superseded in popular appeal by the Large-flowered Climbers, yet they still have a great deal of merit in the garden.

These plants bloom profusely in June and July, and some of them bear blooms later in the year, but these are so few in number that the Ramblers must be regarded as early summer-flowering Roses only. When in full bloom they provide a magnificent display, excelling in splendor anything else in the garden at that time.

These Roses do better in the open garden,

Rambler Roses are splendid for training over arches.

The pink-flowered Rambler Rose Dorothy Perkins here shades a children's play area.

trained over a suitable support, than against a hot, sunny wall; in the latter position they are liable to be damaged by red spider mites and thrips (two pests which like hot, dry conditions) as well as aphids. If that happens, the leaves become sickly and lose their rich green coloring. They are also very susceptible to mildew when grown against walls. This is especially true of Ramblers of the Dorothy Perkins type.

Planting. The Ramblers are easy to grow if a few simple precautions are observed. They are vigorous, even rampant plants which need deeply cultivated, rich soil. When that is provided, and pruning is carried out correctly, they can scarcely fail. The way to make sure of successful results is to dig plenty of compost and moderate quantities of farmyard manure into the subsoil.

Thorough subsoil preparation is vital, as the roots extend throughout a very wide area and the bushes are likely to remain in one place for a longer period than those of Bush and Tree Roses.

In planting, the soil is taken out to such a depth that the uppermost roots will be 2 to 3 in. below the ground surface when the Rose is placed in position. The soil must be firmed before the Roses are put in, and made firm about the roots. Except when the soil is very wet, it should be

settled with water before finally hilling earth up around the stems to a height of 6 in. After two weeks the mound can be leveled.

The Rose plants should be cut back to about half their height at planting time. As new shoots grow, they must be tied to the supports, though not tightly, for the plants are certain to sink a little in the soil during the winter months.

During the first summer after planting, fresh, vigorous shoots should develop, and these will blossom the following year. Next spring, the tops of any shoots which have died off during the winter must be cut back to sound wood.

Pruning Established Ramblers. In subsequent years the pruning of Rambler Roses is a simple matter, for it consists merely in cutting out the old shoots or branches, those which have borne the flowers. The new shoots of the current year's growth are left unpruned, and are tied to the supports to provide the flowers of the following year.

Pruning is best done as soon as the flower display is over, usually in August. If that time is inconvenient the work may be done in early autumn, or even in winter, but there are advantages in finishing the pruning in late summer: the fresh shoots will have the supports to themselves and be exposed fully to the fresh air and sun-

Most Rambler Roses produce new shoots freely from their bases as soon as their blooming season is over.

Most Rambler Roses produce fresh shoots freely from the base; therefore, at the annual pruning, all the old branches can be cut out near the ground with heavy shears, and the new ones, or as many as there are room for without overcrowding, tied in to replace them. When there are too many new shoots, break off the thin ones at the base before they make much growth.

A few varieties are of somewhat different habit of growth. The fresh young shoots often develop on the old stems at some distance from the

shine. Pests and diseases are removed with the old canes, too.

The most convenient way of carrying out the pruning is to detach all the shoots, both old and new, from the supports, and lay them on the ground. It is then easy to cut out the old ones, and just as easy to tie the others to the supports. If this is attempted without first detaching all the branches and shoots, it takes longer and the work is more troublesome.

The new canes which spring from the bases of Rambler Roses are carefully tied to supports.

Pruning Ramblers consists of cutting out all the old flowering canes that can be spared immediately the flowers have faded.

The new shoots are tied somewhat loosely with soft string.

Sometimes it is necessary to retain some of the old branches of Rambler Roses. When this is done the laterals (side branches) are cut back.

A retained old branch of a Rambler Rose with its laterals cut back to within a few buds of their bases.

ground, not from the actual base of the plant. In fact, the Rose may become treelike at the base, with a thick woody stem. In pruning Roses of this type the old branches must be cut back only to these strong new shoots.

Pruning Side Shoots on the Old Branches. If, as may happen sometimes, there are not enough new shoots to take the place of all the old ones, it becomes necessary to leave a few of the latter. They are left unpruned in late summer or autumn, except that the side shoots on them may be shortened slightly if this is thought necessary. In March, the side shoots on any old branches which had to be retained should be pruned to within two or three buds of the base. They will not yield such fine flower bunches as the new shoots or stems of the past summer's growth, but they will bloom and so add to the

splendor of the display. Old shoots or stems ought not to be left if there are enough fresh ones to replace them.

The summer management of Rambler Roses begins with the development of the young shoots at the base of the plants or low down on the branches. Care must be taken that they do not get damaged or broken, for they will supply blooms the following summer. They ought to be tied loosely to the older stems, or to the supports, to keep them upright; if left unsupported, they may become bent. If the tops are broken off they will sprout several new shoots, none of which will grow so strongly as the original one would have.

If the new shoots are so numerous that it will be impossible to find room for all of them in late summer or autumn, when pruning is done, it is better to cut out a few early in summer than to allow them to reach their full height and then cut them out.

Rambler Roses are what the gardener calls gross feeders; that is to say, they benefit by rich soil and applications of manure or fertilizers. Liquid fertilizer, applied regularly, has a remarkable effect on the growth, and the stronger the growth the finer will be the flowers. Liquid fertililizer may be used every week during the time the Roses are growing freely. It should not be given when the soil is dry; if necessary, clear water should be used first.

At flowering time, shoots often develop high up on the plant among the flower bunches and detract from the beauty of the blossoms. These shoots should be cut off, for they are of no use for training later on. This does no harm to the plant.

The Best Ramblers. Some of the old Ramblers are still favorites. The following selection comprises the best of them:

Chevy Chase. A fine Rambler with rich crimson flowers. Practically mildew-proof.

Dorothy Perkins. At one time a great favorite. It was introduced early in the present century and is very subject to mildew. The showy rose-pink flowers are borne in large bunches and the plant becomes smothered in bloom in July.

Excelsa. One of the old varieties. It bears large bunches of crimson, double blooms.

Lady Gay. Very similar to Dorothy Perkins; the blooms are a slightly deeper shade of rose-pink. Makes a fine weeping standard.

Lady Godiva. An attractive Rambler which bears a profusion of double, soft pink flowers.

Minnehaha. A handsome variety having bunches of double rose-pink blooms.

Sander's White Rambler. One of the best white Ramblers; the double flowers are in large clusters.

Thelma. A beautiful free-flowering Rambler with large bunches of salmon-pink flowers.

Veilchenblau. Sometimes sold as the "Blue Rose," but by no means deserving of such a promising name. Its semidouble flowers are borne in large clusters. They open a bright crimson but quickly pass to a rather unpleasant bluish-magenta shade. A vigorous grower.

Violette. This is very much better than Veilchenblau because its early summer flowers are a good violet color and remain so without fading. It is an offspring of Veilchenblau.

Trailing Roses

Trailing Roses hardly form a distinct class. They are, rather, varieties of Ramblers and of Climbers that have very lax stems which, if unsupported, lie along the ground. Such varieties are very useful for covering steep, sunny banks and for using as a ground cover.

The Memorial Rose, Rosa Wichuraiana. An excellent Rose of this type. It is described under Rosa, which see. Other useful Trailing Roses are:

Max Graf. This is an extra hardy kind that has handsome foliage and large, single, clear pink flowers. A Rugosa Hybrid.

Carpet of Gold. This creeping kind bears a profusion of bright yellow, double, fragrant flowers.

Little Compton Creeper. A good variety with single, delicate rose-pink flowers.

Climbing Roses

In a sense Rambler Roses (discussed above) are Climbing Roses, but in addition to them there are several other types of diverse ancestry that are of climbing habit and are suitable for covering pillars, pergolas, arches, walls and fences. Among these are to be found climbing forms of well-known Bush Roses, including Hybrid Teas, Teas, Polyanthas and Floribundas. The flowers of these climbing forms resemble those of the Bush varieties from which they originated as "sports" or mutations. The only difference is in the habit of growth of the plants. In addition, there is a group of Climbing Roses known as Noisettes that are excellent for mild climates and greenhouses, and a group called Large-flowered Climbers that are hardy in the North.

Large-flowered Climbers. A very important class of Roses that has come into prominence during the present century is that known as Large-flowered Climbers. This group includes Roses of varied ancestry all of which are characterized by having larger individual flowers that

Rose Blaze, one of the most popular of large-flowered Climbers. Its blooms are bright red.

Large-flowered Climbing Roses trained along a wall and fence in a delightful setting.

are arranged in somewhat looser clusters than are those of the Ramblers.

In this group we find a much wider color range than the Ramblers possess. The earliest examples of this group were obtained by crossing R. Wichuraiana and R. setigera with Hybrid Teas and Hybrid Perpetuals, but many modern varieties are of more complicated heredity.

Typical Large-flowered Climbers bloom heavily in early summer and then do not flower again, but some have a tendency to repeat, and if weather and other environmental conditions are favorable they may have a few blooms through the summer and make a fair showing in fall. The kinds that tend to flower in summer and fall in addition to the main bloom of early summer are called Everblooming Climbers.

Pillar Roses is a name given to those Large-flowered Climbers that make only moderate growth and are better adapted for growing against posts or pillars than for covering large wall areas or extensive pergolas. Many of the more vigorous Large-flowered Climbers are not suitable for growing on pillars or posts because it is essential that their main branches be trained more or less horizontally if they are to flower well.

The planting of Large-flowered Climbers, including Pillar Roses, is the same as for Ramblers, described above.

Pruning of Large-flowered Climbers should receive attention immediately after the early summer bloom is over. A modification of the pruning plan recommended for Ramblers is followed. The modification is necessary because most Large-flowered Climbers do not produce

The large-flowered Climbing Rose Gladiator has very large and fragrant red flowers.

new shoots as freely from the base as do Ramblers, although they do produce some each year. Usually there will not be enough new shoots to replace all the old ones; some of the old ones must be retained.

Pruning, then, consists of keeping all strong, healthy new canes that push up from the base or lower part of the plant, and of cutting out, as low down as practicable, an equivalent number of the oldest canes. Naturally, dead, diseased, damaged and ill-placed canes are removed at pruning time.

The new canes are carefully tied into position, the gardener keeping in mind the fact that most of the vigorous-growing Large-flowered Climbers bloom most profusely when many of their canes are trained in a horizontal or nearly horizontal position. Some canes must be carried vertically for a certain distance, of course, so that the Rose will cover the area allotted to it. All canes, new and old, should be spaced so that they receive ample light and air circulation. They should not be crowded or tied together in bundles.

Recommended Large-flowered Climbers. Varieties of Large-flowered Climbers that are of special merit are:

American Pillar. One of the oldest varieties in the Large-flowered Climber group. A fine Rose for training up a post or pillar, or over old stone walls and fences. The stems are thick, vigorous and thorny. The flowers are 3 in. in diameter and are borne in immense clusters. They are carmine-pink with white centers.

Blaze. One of the most vigorous and free-blooming of Roses. It has large clusters of double flowers of a brilliant red color. Some strains of this Rose are classed as Everblooming.

Bobbink White Climber. Although not truly white, the flowers of this Everbloomer are nearly so. When they first open, the buds and flowers are pale lemon-yellow or creamy white.

Coral Dawn. An Everblooming variety with a clear deep coral-pink color. The flower stems are long.

Dr. Huey. The flowers of this kind are velvety maroon of a deep shade and are carried in tremendous clusters.

Dr. W. Van Fleet. An old variety with an abundance of long-stemmed, beautifully shaped flowers which bloom in a clear flesh-pink color.

Dream Girl. An Everblooming kind that is suitable for growing on posts and pillars as well as on other supports. The flower color is pink overlaid with apricot. The flowers are very fragrant.

Gladiator. The blooms of this variety are very large and fragrant and are brilliant rose-red in color.

Golden Showers. This variety bears exquisitely shaped, daffodil-yellow flowers that are delightfully fragrant.

King Midas. This is a good Pillar Rose. It produces a profusion of large, fragrant flowers of a clear yellow color, Hybrid Tea in form. It is an Everbloomer.

Mary Wallace. A very strong grower that bears pink flowers enhanced by a luminous sheen.

Mme. Gregoire Staechlin. Also known as Spanish Beauty. This Rose has huge, fragrant, delicate pink blooms that are overlaid with crimson.

Mrs. Arthur Curtis James. This Rose, which is also called Golden Climber, is of very vigorous growth. It produces a profusion of finely formed golden-yellow flowers of Hybrid Tea form that have a good fragrance.

New Dawn. This is a very vigorous Everblooming type with beautiful apple-blossom-pink blooms borne freely. Suitable for covering large areas.

Paul's Scarlet Climber. An old Rose of good character and great profusion of bloom. The flowers are brilliant red. Universally popular.

Royal Gold. A dependably recurrent bloomer which bears golden-yellow flowers.

Silver Moon. This is one of the older varieties in this class. It is a strong grower and has large, semidouble, creamy white flowers that are slightly fragrant.

Spectacular. A vigorous, hardy kind which bears a profusion of orange-red to spectrum-red flowers.

Other Climbers. The cultivation of Climbing Roses that belong neither to the Rambler group nor the class known as Large-flowered Climbers is very similar. Here belong the Noisettes, the Climbing Hybrid Teas, the Climbing Teas, the Climbing Polyanthas and the Climbing Floribundas.

Management of Large-flowered Climbers. When Roses of these kinds are planted, the usual care should be taken in preparing the soil, for otherwise they may make poor progress. A hole 2 ft. deep and 2 ft. across should be dug. If the soil is light, add compost to the excavated soil before it is filled in again. Bone meal, a pound to each bushel, should be put on the surface soil and forked in. If the soil is prepared in this way a week or two in advance of planting, the Roses will make good growth. If, however, they are planted in ill-prepared ground they will be very disappointing. The best time to plant is in autumn.

There are two principal types of Climbing Roses, those which are naturally of vigorous or climbing habit, and the climbing "sports" from Hybrid Tea and other Bush Roses. Each needs a different kind of pruning.

Pruning Vigorous and Natural Climbers. The first pruning should be done the first spring. This pruning consists of cutting out thin, weak shoots and shortening the rest to within about 6 in. of the ground. This may seem drastic treatment, but, although it sacrifices the first summer's bloom, it forces the plants to send up strong, vigorous shoots, and that is the first essential for establishing Climbing Roses.

As the new shoots make progress the two lowest should be trained as nearly horizontally as possible along the base of the wall or support; others ought to be fastened about 10 in. above them, and they also should be trained as low down as possible. If this practice is not followed and the new shoots are allowed to grow in an upright direction, the Rose will soon become bare at the base; in future years fresh shoots will develop only towards the top.

The secret of success in training Roses against walls is to spread out the shoots as much as possible, taking care that the lowest are near the base of the wall. As the years pass, Roses on walls are liable to get bare at the base and this cannot very well be prevented. It is, however, worth while occasionally to cut back one of the old branches for the purpose of forcing the growth of fresh shoots low down in the plant. When Climbing Roses are planted to cover a post, the shoots should be trained around it, instead of

[11—4]
*Coneflower
(Rudbeckia)*

[11—4a]
*Rock Soapwort
(Saponaria ocymoides)*

[11—5]
Bouncing Bet
(Saponaria officinalis)

[11—5a]
Salvia splendens,
pink-flowered variety

[11—5b]
Lavender Cotton
(Santolina Chamaecyparissus)

[11—5c]
Gloriosa Daisy
(Rudbeckia hirta variety)

A Climbing Rose trained against a wall.

being allowed to grow upright; the plant is then less likely to become bare at the base.

Corrective pruning of Climbing Roses can take place in summer. Parts of a few old branches are cut out to make room for the fresh shoots of the current summer's growth. To what extent this can be done must be decided by the gardener. It is unwise, however, to prune more severely than is required. It helps to have as many new shoots as possible on the plants, for these are naturally more vigorous than the older branches. They generally develop at some distance from the base of the plant, and the old branches can, of course, only be shortened to those places where the new shoots started to grow.

The Spring Pruning. There must always be a certain number of old branches in a Climbing Rose; it is impossible to cut them out so freely as is done with the Rambler Roses. There will be considerable pruning to be done in spring. Just as new growth begins, all side shoots on the old branches are cut back to within two or three eyes from the base. Any shoots which have died back at the tips during the winter must be shortened to sound wood.

Pruning the Climbing Sports. Particular care must be taken in the pruning of this type, for otherwise they may revert to the bush habit. It is a mistake to cut down the branches in the spring following planting, as was recommended

when dealing with the ordinary Climbing Roses. They should be pruned very lightly, or not at all, until they are established and growing freely. Thin, weak shoots may be cut out at the first spring pruning, but no further pruning is desirable.

If hard pruned before they have become established, these plants may lose their climbing habit of growth, or become stunted. If planted in ground prepared in the way previously advised, and watered occasionally with liquid fertilizer during the summer months, they will make good growth. The following year, or perhaps in two years, the plants will be vigorous enough to be pruned in the usual way, by cutting out parts of the old branches to make room for the young shoots. Never judge the Climbing Hybrid Teas until they have been established for at least three years.

Beautiful Climbing Roses. There are the best varieties of the ordinary Climbing Roses:

Allen Chandler. A Climbing Hybrid Tea with single, sweet-scented, scarlet flowers. Blooms in summer only.

Chromatella (Cloth-of-Gold). A vigorous Noisette with large, double, fragrant, dark-yellow flowers that are sulphur yellow on the reverse side of the petals. Suitable for mild climates only.

Fortune's Double Yellow. A Noisette that is also known as Beauty of Glazenwood, and San Rafael Rose. Gold of Ophir is a form of this Rose. Fortune's Double Yellow is hardy in mild climates only. It has semidouble, orange-yellow flowers that are flecked with red. It is a free bloomer.

Gloire de Dijon. A Climbing Tea Rose that has been a favorite in gardens for several generations. It is a useful wall Rose; the fragrant flowers of buff-yellow shade appear in summer and in autumn. Hardy in sheltered places in parts of the North.

Guinee. Large, blackish-red blooms. A Climbing Hybrid Tea. Very fragrant.

Lady Waterlow. A charming Climbing Hybrid Tea Rose of vigorous growth which bears semidouble blooms, salmon flushed with carmine, in summer and to some extent in autumn.

Madame Alfred Carrière. One of the old Noisette Roses which does splendidly on a sunny wall. The buds are blush, the open flowers white. It is fragrant. Not hardy in the North.

Maréchal Niel. This old golden-yellow Noisette Rose is successful on a sunny sheltered wall, but is at its best under glass. Not hardy in the North.

William Allen Richardson. A very vigorous Noisette that has been grown outdoors in a sheltered location as far north as New York City, but can generally only be recommended for southern gardens. It has small, double, fragrant flowers of a buff-yellow or apricot-yellow hue.

The Best Climbing "Sports." Of the climbing "sports," those which have developed from the bush or dwarf Roses of the same name, the following are the best. Although they bloom to some extent in autumn, as well as in summer, they are inclined to produce vigorous leafy shoots and, as a result, the autumn display is often a moderate one. Horizontal training is desirable to encourage flowering wood. Climbing sports do not bloom freely until they are well established. Plenty of water should be given during dry weather to encourage fresh growth.

The climbing forms of the following Bush Roses are especially recommended: Cecile Brunner, Charlotte Armstrong, Crimson Glory, Dainty Bess, Etoile de Hollande, Lowell Thomas, Mme. Butterfly, Mrs. Sam McGredy, Nocturne, Peace, Pinocchio, Ophelia, Show Girl, Sutter's Gold, Talisman, Texas Centennial.

Tree or Standard Roses

A Tree or Standard Rose is one which is budded on a Brier, Rugosa or other strong stem 3 ft. 6 in. or more high. Trees are not a distinct class of Rose, as amateurs sometimes believe; they are the same varieties which are grown as dwarf or bush plants. The only difference is that, instead of being placed low down on the stock, the bud is inserted on the lateral shoots near the top of a tall Brier stem. For Rugosa trees, the buds are inserted in either side of the main stem just below the top growths. Some varieties of Roses thrive better as trees than others, but they are not exclusively Tree Roses, for all of them are suitable for cultivation as Bush Roses.

A Rose grown in the form of a tree needs much the same treatment in respect to pruning,

Standard or Tree Rose showing formation of the head. Trunk is carefully tied to a stake.

fertilizing, and other care as if it were grown as a bush. In really cold climates special precautions must be taken to preserve these plants over winter.

A common mistake made in growing Tree Roses is to plant them too deeply. This is done apparently for the purpose of making them firm and safe from damage in rough weather. As a result the roots are buried far too deeply and the plants suffer. Generally, it is true that Tree Roses are more difficult to establish than Bush or dwarf Roses. It is, therefore, desirable that everything possible be done for their welfare. Trees which make poor, weak growth will never bear good blooms and, moreover, they are unsightly. A flourishing tree, on the other hand, is very attractive.

One may plant a dozen Tree Roses of which nine may flourish and the remaining three fail unaccountably. They may be planted in the same kind of soil, under exactly similar conditions, and even be of the same varieties. It is difficult to understand why some should thrive and others do badly in such circumstances.

Why Tree Roses Sometimes Fail. The explanation seems to be that, owing to the long stems, Tree Roses receive a more serious check than dwarf Roses on being transplanted, and if the check to growth is prolonged only the best will succeed. This explanation seems to be supported by the fact that Tree Roses, as received from the nursery, leave little or nothing to be desired; they appear to be, and doubtless are, perfectly healthy, with satisfactory and promising shoots. Yet, when transplanted, some of them may fail.

How to Plant Tree Roses. It goes almost without saying that the ground must be prepared by digging deeply. Before the roots are covered, the supporting stakes should be driven into the ground. When planting is finished, the Rose stem is tied to the stake, care being taken that it is securely fastened near the top, for if that part is unsupported the tree may break off just beneath the head of branches. A second tie should be made partway down the steam. Tree

A Tree or Standard Rose in full bloom. It is planted as an accent among ordinary bush Roses.

Roses should be planted in autumn where severe winters are not the rule; they are less likely to suffer a severe check then than if planting is deferred until spring. In cold climates where the trees must be protected over winter, planting is done only in spring.

The tree should be unpacked at the earliest possible moment after arrival, placed in a shallow trench, and the roots and stems covered with soil. If necessary, they should be soaked with water. Before they are planted it is a good plan to soak the roots in a thick puddle of soil and water.

Pruning should be done in spring and is the same as for Bush Roses, except that less severe cutting back is best.

If Tree Roses do not start strongly into growth it is worth while trying the following plan; its purpose is to keep the Brier stems thoroughly moist until the trees are able to look after themselves.

Keeping the Stems Moist. Strips of flannel, burlap, heavy paper or cloth are wrapped around the stems so that the latter are fully covered from top to base, and the material is kept moist by sprinkling it daily, or even twice a day, in warm, dry weather. This practice has been found to be beneficial and has helped Tree Roses over a difficult period during the first spring and early summer.

Suckers. This term is used to describe shoots which spring from the stock on which the named Rose was budded. If suckers are allowed to grow they weaken the true Rose, and unless they are removed they may cause its death. Suckers can generally be distinguished from the shoots of the named Rose without difficulty; they usually have numerous spines and smaller, light-green leaves. If any doubt arises, the matter can be decided by tracing the shoot to its source of origin. If it arose below the place where the bud of the true Rose was inserted, there can be no doubt that it is a sucker from the understock.

Suckers on Tree Roses are easily seen when they develop on the main stem, but sometimes they may grow right at the top of the stem and be more or less hidden among the branches. There, especially on weeping Tree Roses, they may escape notice unless looked for carefully.

Suckers should be cut away to their base on the roots or stem of the stock. It is useless to break them off, as they invariably grow again.

Only a limited number of varieties of Roses are grown as trees by nurserymen, but the selection includes all of the chief colors. Varieties with a stiff upright habit seldom make the best Tree Roses.

These Make Good Trees: Charlotte Armstrong, cerise red; Circus, blended tones of red, yellow, orange, pink, a Floribunda type; Crimson Glory, deep red; Diamond Jubilee, buff-orange; Fashion, coral-pink tinted gold, a Floribunda type; Golden Masterpiece, big, clear yellow flowers; Goldilocks, true golden yellow, a Floribunda type; Helen Traubel, pink and apricot; Kaiserin Auguste Viktoria, ivory-white; Mrs. Pierre S. duPont, deep yellow; Pageant, yellow and red; Peace, huge yellow flowers flushed pink; President Herbert Hoover, flame; Spartan, orange-red, Floribunda type; Tiffany, phlox-pink; Vogue, cherry-coral, Floribunda type; Blaze, bright scarlet-red; Chrysler Imperial, crimson-red; Golden Fleece, bright yellow, a Floribunda type; Jiminy Cricket, coral-orange, a Floribunda type; Mme. Jules Bouche, white; New Yorker, red; Red Pinocchio, scarlet-red, a Floribunda type; Twilight, lavender-lilac; White Swan, pure white. Other kinds are equally as good and are offered in the catalogues of Rose specialists.

Weeping Trees. These are obtained by budding a Climbing or Rambler Rose on a Brier or Rugosa stem 5 to 6 ft. high. Well-developed specimens provide a splendid show of bloom in summer; they are seen to the best advantage when set apart from other plantings, or in a Rose garden.

The management of Weeping Trees is perfectly simple. They must be staked securely, for when the head of branches is well developed it is heavy, and the stem may break unless it is adequately supported. At planting time, before the roots are covered, a strong stake should be driven into the soil. It is wise to place a piece of old rubber hose around the stake before tying the stem of the Rose to it, to prevent the latter from being chafed and bruised. There must be one tie near the top of the stem, and one or two others lower down.

Weeping Trees are best pruned by shortening the growths to about half their length at the time of planting.

In future years, pruning should be done in late summer, as soon as the flowers have faded, or in early autumn. This consists of cutting out the branches which have flowered, or parts of them. Sometimes they can be cut out altogether; generally they can be shortened only to where fresh shoots have started to grow. The object is to preserve the new shoots of the past summer's growth, and to cut out older ones to make room for them. The pruning, in fact, is similar to that of Rambler and Climbing Roses grown on arches, pillars and arbors.

Training the shoots requires some attention. Wire frames of the shape of an umbrella can be made and fixed to the supporting stake; they simplify the training of the shoots and ensure shapely trees. Or the ends of the long shoots may be tied to the Brier stem to make them droop. But if suitable varieties, those with slender branches, are chosen, the training will not be a troublesome matter, for they are naturally of drooping growth when budded on a tall stem.

Rose Hedges

Few features of a garden are more delightful than a hedge of Roses. There are many suitable kinds, some of them vigorous shrubs, which provide tall hedges, others for moderately high and for low hedges. The latter make a most appropriate frame for a Rose garden.

Rose bushes to be grown as a hedge must be planted in deeply cultivated and well-fertilized ground, for it is essential that they make strong growth. It should be dug deeply, rich compost or manure being mixed with the lower layer of soil and bone meal with the upper layer. Planting is done in autumn or early spring.

Vigorous kinds of Roses, the Penzance Briers for example, should be planted 4 ft. apart; others rather less vigorous, the Hybrid Musk Roses for instance, 2½ ft. apart; and the low-growing kinds about 15 in. from each other.

For the first two years no pruning other than removing dead wood will be needed. Subsequently, prune according to the height required

A fine hedge of the Floribunda Rose Fanfare.

and shorten the lateral growths as is necessary.

There are numerous varieties of Floribunda Roses that, if planted 18-24 in. apart, form dense hedges and bloom freely throughout the summer. They require trimming once a year in spring to assure shapeliness and the production of strong young shoots. Vigorous growers suitable for this purpose include Betty Prior, Spartan, Fashion, Vogue and Baby Blaze. Less strong growers, suitable for lower hedges, include Chatter, White Bouquet, Fusilier and Golden Fleece.

In recent years, Rosa multiflora has been advocated as a hedge plant. In farm areas, this Rose has been planted in place of stock fences to enclose pastures and to serve as a windbreak. In small gardens, however, this Rose usually is out of place because it will make too heavy growth. A hedge of this Rose must be severely pruned several times a season after it is established, to keep it down to the desired height and width. If allowed to grow naturally, a single plant will have a 15-foot spread when mature.

Roses suitable for forming a tall hedge include the Penzance Briers, Conrad F. Meyer, and Zepherine Drouhin. Frensham, Betty Prior and Salmon Spray are suitable for low hedges. The Hybrid Rugosas such as Agnes, F. J. Grootendorst and Schneezwerg form hardy hedges and are suitable for planting near the sea.

Rose Propagation

Most Bush Roses of the Hybrid Tea type are budded on Rosa multiflora understock, which is raised for the purpose from seeds or cuttings. The understocks are planted in autumn or spring, and budding (which see) is carried out in summer. Other understocks used for budding Bush Roses include Ragged Robin, Dr. Huey, Shafter and Odorata.

Rose cuttings in various stages. A. Prepared cutting. B. Calloused cutting with first root starting. C. Roots starting after callousing. D. Well-rooted cutting in early April.

Tree Roses are budded on Rosa rugosa. This stock is now widely used by nurserymen, and has proved very successful; Roses budded on it seem to bear transplanting well. During the first few years Tree Roses on Rugosa have rather thin stems, and these must be staked very carefully to prevent damage from being done in windy weather. Other understocks used include IXL and Rosa Wichuraiana.

Taking Cuttings. Rose bushes are easily propagated by cuttings. The simplest way is to set them outdoors in autumn; they may, however, be placed in pots under glass during the summer months. The great advantage possessed by Roses grown from cuttings—"own-root Roses" they are called—is that all the shoots which develop are the true Rose variety; there are no suckers. A disadvantage is that they develop rather slowly at first. Propagation by cuttings is popular in the South.

Summer cuttings should be made from shoots which have flowered and are moderately firm, or what the gardener calls "half-ripe." They may vary from 4 to 8 in. in length. The leaves should be removed, except two at the top, and these may be reduced in size if necessary; none of the dormant buds is cut out. Treating the ends with a rooting hormone will hasten root development. The cuttings are inserted in very sandy soil in a place shaded from direct sunlight. If the soil is kept moderately moist and the cuttings are set under a frame or in a greenhouse and covered with a hand light or fruit jar, they will form roots in a few weeks. July–August is the best time to take summer cuttings.

Autumn cuttings are inserted outdoors or in a cold frame in October or early November. They may be from 6 to 10 in. long, made from well-ripened flower shoots. A narrow, straight-backed trench is dug in the garden, sand is scattered along the bottom, and the cuttings are set at such a depth that they are half-covered with soil. They should be set about 5 in. apart, and trodden in firmly. They will be well rooted in a year's time. These are called hardwood cuttings.

Roses propagated from cuttings do not usually bloom until two years have elapsed, because they have to establish a sound root system. Budded plants produce a good crop the following summer as they have a root system already provided by the understock.

Rambler Roses and other vigorous kinds may also be propagated by layering.

Exhibition Roses

To grow fine Roses for exhibition requires careful attention to many details of cultivation, and constant vigilance in the spring and early summer to combat the attacks of pests. The first thing of importance is deep and rich soil. By deep digging, manuring, and adding good loamy soil to poor ground, Roses of exhibition standard can be grown in any sunny garden.

Preparing the Ground. Whether the soil is light or heavy, deep digging is essential. This consists of breaking up the subsoil or underlayer and replacing the top layer in its original position. Light sandy soil needs the addition of fibrous rotted turf that has been stacked for a year or two, with layers of farmyard manure between. Compost is good, too.

The liberal addition of rotted cow or horse manure is recommended. The manure must be well decayed if planting is to follow at an early date. The manure is well mixed with the soil, and bone meal, 2 to 3 oz. to the square yard, should be spread on the surface and forked in.

This is all the bushes will need for the first year, as the application of quick-acting fertilizers before they are well established can be harmful. In succeeding years one or two feedings with a commercial Rose fertilizer, applied at pruning time and during the growing season, will work wonders. Occasional applications, when the ground is moist, of liquid manure, made by immersing a bushel of farmyard manure in a twenty-gallon barrel of water, will increase the size of the blooms and intensify the coloring. Dressings of complete fertilizer should also be given when necessary.

The Value of "Maiden" Roses. The really serious exhibitor should learn the art of budding Roses, as it is from maiden plants—those budded the previous year—that the finest flowers are sometimes obtained.

Pruning for Exhibition Blooms. Where bushes two years or more old have to be relied on, the question of pruning is most important. Newly planted Roses can scarcely be pruned too hard the first spring after planting. They should be cut back to two buds from the base of the previous year's growth. In later years all dead and weak shoots should be cut out, together with some of the oldest wood; the best of the previous year's shoots are then pruned back to two buds. This method produces quality flowers on long stems.

Present-day experience is in favor of moderate pruning of established plants, some exhibitors claiming that this method gives better blooms than hard pruning. It is, however, essential to limit the number of shoots.

Thinning the Buds. When the new shoots are growing it will be noticed that most of them bear three buds at the tips. In nearly every case the center one will yield the finest bloom, so the side buds should be removed as soon as possible, thus throwing the whole strength of the shoot into the formation of one fine bloom.

Protecting the Blooms. Hot sunshine often bleaches the colors, and storms of rain cause some of the very full Roses, or those with thin petals, to "ball" or become spotted or stained. To prevent this, English exhibitors use shades

Disbudding, the removal of all buds except the terminal one of each flower stem is practiced to secure the most perfect exhibition blooms of Hybrid Tea Roses.

which are almost never seen in North America. They consist of cone-shaped wire frames covered with thin, canvas-like material which are held in position on stakes and can be adjusted to any desired height. In normal weather they are not brought into use until two days before the show. Most American exhibitors prefer just to cut their flowers as the buds are beginning to open. These are kept cool indoors until show time.

To preserve the freshness of the bloom and to lengthen the central petals, English growers also surround the bloom with thin, greaseproof paper in the form of a funnel, tied just below the flower. In this case protection from rain must be given as soon as the paper is in position.

Tying the Blooms. As the blooms are opening (especially the thin varieties) English exhibitors often press the outer petals gently back and insert a loop of soft, thick worsted over the inner ones, a short distance from the base, and draw them together. The effect of this is to elongate the bud and produce a higher center, so much to be desired in exhibition blooms. It also tends to prevent them from "showing center" or opening prematurely. The tie may be left on until just before the exhibition hall is cleared for judging, and then carefully removed.

Roses make attractive pot plants for forcing into bloom early in greenhouses.

The best time for cutting Roses is the evening before the show, between 5 and 7 o'clock. They should be cut with a good length of stem using sharp shears, and placed immediately in water which reaches almost to the blooms.

Never cut the flowers when wet or they will lose color on the show day and may become stained. If any have been out in the rain, allow them to dry off in a cool, dark, airy room. All blooms must be correctly named. Spare blooms are kept in reserve in case any of those first selected prove unsatisfactory or "show center" before the time of judging. In substituting others, be very careful not to include duplicates in classes of distinct varieties.

Keep the blooms as cool as possible after cutting. In arranging a collection of blooms, see that the colors do not clash, and set those of dark and light colors next to each other. A bright, colorful exhibit will always score over equally good blooms of paler varieties.

Growing Roses in Greenhouses

Reports indicate that in the United States and Canada more space is devoted in commercial greenhouses to the culture of Roses than to any other florists' flower.

Where Roses are grown in quantity, special greenhouses are allotted solely to them. Temperatures, atmospheric humidity, light intensity and ventilation can then be adjusted to meet the particular needs of the Roses. Insect pests and diseases are more readily controlled when Roses are cultivated in a greenhouse by themselves.

The amateur gardener who grows a few Roses in a greenhouse where various other kinds of plants are cultivated is distinctly handicapped, especially if the other plants require different environmental conditions from those most suitable for Roses.

Cultivation in Pots. In small greenhouses, Roses may be flowered most easily during late winter and spring by purchasing bushes for delivery in November and by planting them singly in pots 6 to 8 in. in diameter. Hybrid Tea and Floribunda varieties of Roses should be pruned at potting time to a height of 9 to 10 in. They should then be placed outdoors or in a cold-frame to mature fully before they are brought into the greenhouse about the first of January. A temperature of 55 to 60 degrees at night, with a rise of 5 or 10 degrees permitted in the daytime, is favorable to growth. Rambler and Climbing varieties may be forced into flower by following similar procedures. After potting they may be trained to almost any desired shape by tying their stems to wires or bamboo stakes.

If started into growth about the first of January, the Roses may be flowered for Easter. When Easter is late and the days are sunny it may be necessary towards the end of their growing period to lower the greenhouse temperature somewhat, in order to time the flowers for the date required.

The same plants may be buried to the rims of their pots in a sunny location outdoors for the summer and be brought back to the greenhouse for forcing the following winter. During the summer they must be watered and fertilized regularly, and kept free from disease and insect pests by dusting and spraying.

Roses will not grow well where there is shade, whether this be from trees, buildings or shading material applied to the greenhouse glass. In low-roofed greenhouses, where there is at least 5 to 6 ft. headroom from the soil there is likely to be a constant higher atmospheric humidity than in a very high house. This will be to the advantage of the Roses.

Soil Requirements. Roses grow best in soil that is rich with decayed organic matter and that has perfect drainage. If soil porosity is poor a liberal quantity of sharp sand and peat moss mixed with it will improve it. The addition of half a pint of superphosphate to each bushel of soil mixture will provide necessary phosphorus which is deficient in many soils. When potting, the soil should be of such texture and moistness that if a handful is grasped tightly and the hand is immediately opened the ball of compressed soil will slowly fall apart and will not remain in a tight clod.

When potting, make the soil moderately firm and water immediately. Organic fertilizers in liquid form may be used freely in weak solutions after the plants are thoroughly established and are growing well.

Although Roses grow best under rather moist

conditions, excessive dampness must be avoided when the temperature in the greenhouse is falling. Excessive humidity in the form of free-standing water on foliage, walls and paths in the afternoon and evening is conducive to the spread of black-spot disease, perhaps the most devastating of all diseases to which Roses are subject. Advantage should be taken of sunny days to syringe the plants, by applying water under pressure in the form of a fine spray, to the undersides of the leaves. This helps to keep in check red spider mites, which live on the foliage and are most destructive. Syringing should be done in the forenoon only, so that the foliage dries before dusk.

Ventilate the greenhouse at all favorable opportunities. Guard against cold drafts, for these encourage the development of mildew disease. During winter the temperature may, on sunny days, rise above 70 degrees, which is favorable for growth, provided the greenhouse is ventilated.

Bench and Solid Bed Culture. When Roses are planted directly in soil-filled benches or in solid ground beds in greenhouses their culture is generally similar to that described for potted plants. Good drainage is important. If the greenhouse is located on heavy clay soil, special precautions must be taken when planting ground beds. It may be necessary to lay agricultural drain tiles to carry away excess water.

Benches or raised beds are usually 32 to 36 in. above path level. One-inch wrought-iron pipe is used as a framework. This is tied together with split malleable iron castings secured by set screws and bolts, which may be purchased from greenhouse manufacturers. Pecky cypress boards, 6 in. wide, are most often used for the sides and bottom. Angle-iron plates for the corners and flat iron for the joints may be secured with screws or carriage bolts. These bottom boards should be cut to fit across the bench. If they are arranged in this way, replacements can be more easily made if a board rots or breaks. Since new boards swell when exposed to water, they should be placed at least 1/2 in. apart.

Soil. A satisfactory base for the soil for Rose benches and beds is grass sod from an old pasture, cut 4 to 6 in. thick. This should be stacked outdoors in layers, with alternate layers of cow manure and a generous sprinkling of superphosphate added to each layer. Stacking should be done 3 to 4 months before the soil is needed for the greenhouse, thus allowing sufficient time for it to "break down" or partially decay and be in the best condition at planting time.

Planting. Roses may be planted at almost any season. May to early June is perhaps the best time to do this. They then have sufficient opportunity to make good growth and supply flowers in profusion by fall. Besides, spring-grafted plants obtained in 3-in. pots are ready for planting by May or June and have the sunniest days of the year in which to grow. Hybrid Tea and Floribunda Roses propagated from cuttings are not recommended for greenhouse culture because they do not produce the root growth of plants grafted on Manettii and other favored understocks.

The Rose bushes should be spaced about 15 in. apart each way. Plant so that the union of scion and stock (the graft union) of the Rose is about ½ in. below the soil surface.

As the plants grow, supports will be required. Frames of galvanized iron pipe are fixed at each end of the bed or bench with as many frames located at intermediate points as may be needed to support horizontal wires which are stretched tightly between the frames. A 4-5-ft.-long stake of heavy-gauge wire is inserted in the soil at each plant and is secured to one of the horizontal wires above.

As the crop of flowers develops, generous supplies of water are needed. The water will leach fertilizer elements from the soil, and these should be replaced by applying organic fertilizers in liquid form diluted to a weak solution. Apply such a fertilizer once a week when the plants are in active growth and are producing well; as the flowers become scarcer, reduce slightly the supplies of both water and fertilizer.

Dormant or Resting Period. After a full season of flowering, Roses benefit from being given a rest period. This involves reducing severely the amount of water given and ventilating the house more freely than normal for 3 to 4 weeks. During this time only sufficient water is given to prevent the bark from shriveling. After the soil becomes moderately dry, the top 1½ in. may be

removed and be replaced with a fresh soil mixture of similar nature to that of the original. At this time, too, it is advisable to prune the strong Rose shoots to about half their height and to cut out all weak shoots.

If Rose plants are properly cared for, they last and produce well for several years before they need to be removed and replaced with young plants.

Hybrid Tea Varieties Suitable for Greenhouse Forcing. Aristocrat, clear light pink with petals darker beneath; Better Times, brilliant cerise; Briarcliff, deep rose-pink at center, lighter on outer petals; Double White Killarney, snowy white; E. G. Hill, dazzling scarlet; Golden Rapture, clear golden-yellow; Golden Scepter, deep yellow; Happiness, brilliant red aging to crimson-carmine; Happy Days, geranium-red; Orange Delight, capucine-orange, reverse veined red; President Herbert Hoover, varying orange shades, outside petals much lighter; Rome Glory, inside of petals vermilion, outside cerise; Talisman, golden-yellow and copper; Vanity Fair, cameo-pink; White Pearl, glistening white; Yellow Gloria, golden-yellow, base saffron.

Floribunda Varieties Suitable for Greenhouse Forcing. Garnette, garnet-red, light lemon-yellow base; Goldilocks, deep-yellow; Magic Red, crimson; Marionette, bud clear yellow, white cluster; Pink Bountiful, soft pink; Pinocchio, pink suffused salmon, edge deeper in color; Red Sweetheart, crimson-carmine; Summer Snow, clear white.

Climbers Suitable for Greenhouse Forcing. Climbing Summer Snow, snow-white; Dorothy Perkins, rose-pink; Marie Gouchault, clear red passing to brilliant salmon-rose. Old-fashioned Rose Maréchal Niel also grows exceptionally well in a greenhouse.

Rose Recipes

Rose recipes may be divided into two categories —those dating from medieval, Tudor and Stuart times (these recipes being delightful to read about, but usually too elaborate for these hurried days), and modern recipes.

Our-ancestors used Roses in endless ways. They flavored honey, wine and vinegar with Roses, made Rose conserves and syrups, preserved Roses whole; they made rossoly, Rose drops, "sugar" of Roses; they made Rose wafers, and filled taffety bags with dried petals to scent their linen.

The following are interesting examples of old Rose recipes from England. The first is a recipe used in the royal household in Edward VI's reign to perfume the air; the second the recipe for the Rose-flavored cakes made for Charles I's daughter, Princess Elizabeth; and the third a recipe for preserving Roses whole by Sir Hugh Platt, one of Queen Elizabeth's courtiers.

King Edward VI's Perfume. "Take twelve spoonfuls of bright red Rose-water, the weight of six pence in fine powder of sugar, and boil it on the hot embers and coals softly, and the house will smell as though it were full of Roses, but you must burn the sweet Cypress wood before to take away the gross air." (The "red Rose-water" above is water colored by red Rose petals.)

To make a cake with Rose water, the way of the royal princess, the Lady Elizabeth, daughter of King Charles I., "Take half a peck of Flowre, half a pinte of Rose-water, a pint of Ale yeast, a pint of Cream, boyl it, a pound and a half of Butter, six Eggs (leave out the white), four pound of Currants, one half pound of sugar, one Nutmeg, and a little salt, work it very well and let it stand half an hour by the fire, and then work it again, and then make it up and let it stand an hour and a halfe in the Oven; let not your Oven be too hot."

How to Preserve Whole Roses. "Dip a Rose that is neither in the bud, nor overblowne, in a sirup, consisting of sugar, double refined, and Rose-water boiled to his full height, then open the leaves one by one with a fine smooth bodkin either of bone or wood; and presently, if it be a hot, sunny day, and whilest the sunne is in some good height, lay them on papers in the sunne, or else dry them with some gentle heat in a close room, heating the room before you set them in or in an oven upon papers, in pewter dishes, and then put them up in glasses; and keepe them in dry cupboards neere the fire: you must take out the seeds, if you meene to eat them. You may proove this preserving with sugar-candy instead of sugar if you please."

The following modern recipes are simple and

they will be found to be quite practical.

Rose Petal Jam. About twenty sweet-scented Roses, 3 lb. sugar, 2 pints water, half a teaspoonful citric acid crystals are needed. The Roses, preferably pink or red, must be gathered when fully open, but not overblown. Use best granulated or preserving sugar and put 3 lb. into 2 pints of water and boil gently for half an hour. Pull the Roses to pieces, taking care to cut off all white heels, as they are bitter. Pour half a pint of boiling water over them and, when they are wet through, put all—water and petals—into the boiling syrup. Boil for half an hour, stirring with either a clean wooden or silver spoon.

Rose petal jam is a delicate conserve, so everything used must be scrupulously clean and ordinary metal spoons cannot be used. While boiling, the petals must be frequently pressed down into the syrup, as, being light, they rise. When they are quite tender and transparent, add the citric acid crystals. Lemon juice (4 lemons) is sometimes used, but citric acid brings back the color to the petals better. Then boil for another ten or fifteen minutes. Put in small pots and cover down in the usual way.

Rose Petal Filling for Sandwiches. These are both pleasant and decorative. Pink or crimson sweet-scented petals are the best to use. They must be freshly gathered, and the slices of bread and butter cut extremely thin. Place the petals between the slices and decorate the pile with Rose petals.

Rose Water. Rose water can be freshly made every day during the season and it is very fragrant and pleasant to wash in. Gather at least 2 lb. of Rose petals and cover them with water, preferably rain water. The water should only just cover the petals. Bring slowly to the boil and then simmer for a few minutes. This water keeps good for almost two days.

Candied Rose Petals. This recipe is simple and effective, but must be carefully followed. Beat up the white of an egg and cover the Rose petals on both sides with the beaten-up white of egg. It is best to use a paintbrush, which must, of course, be new and clean. Spread the petals out on a large, flat dish and sprinkle castor sugar over them. Turn them carefully and sprinkle the sugar on the other side of the petals. Dry in the sun. As soon as they are dry, pack them in an airtight jar or can.

ROSE ACACIA. See Robinia hispida.

ROSE APPLE. See Eugenia.

ROSEBAY. Rhododendron maximum, which see.

ROSE CAMPION. Lychnis Coronaria, which see.

ROSE, CHRISTMAS. Helleborus niger, which see.

ROSE, LENTEN. Helleborus orientalis, which see.

ROSELLE. This is the annual Hibiscus Sabdariffa, sometimes known as Jamaica Sorrel. It is a native of the tropics of the Old World and is grown in the tropics and subtropics, including the warmest parts of the United States, for its thickened calyces and bracts, which are acid and are used for making jams, jellies, sauces and beverages.

The plants grow to a height of 4-6 ft. They are usually set in rows about 2 ft. apart. Culture is the same as for Eggplant, which see. The heads or bolls are gathered while they are yet immature and before they turn dry and woody. They are dried or are used in a fresh state. The bolls are red or yellow in color.

ROSE MALLOW. See Hibiscus; Lavatera.

ROSEMARY. Rosmarinus, which see.

ROSEMARY, BOG. Andromeda, which see.

ROSEMARY, WILD. Ledum palustre. See Ledum.

ROSEOCACTUS (Roseocac'tus). A group of Cacti, family Cactaceae, that at one time was included in the genus Ariocarpus. The name is derived from Rose and Cactus, and refers to the appearance of the upper surface of the plants. For the cultivation of these plants, see Cacti.

The kinds grown include R. fissuratus, Living Rock, in which most of the plant body is underground, and which measures at maturity 5-6 in. across and has its upper surface deeply and conspicuously tubercled and roughened. The flowers are pale pink to white. This kind is a native of Texas and adjacent Mexico. R. Kotschoubeyanus, a Mexican native, attains a diameter of not more than 2 in., and has pink to light purple flowers. R. Lloydii, from Mexico, has a rounded top, may be 4 in. in diameter,

and the color of the flowers is reddish purple.

ROSE OF HEAVEN. Lychnis Coeli-rosa, which see.

ROSE OF JERICHO. See Anastatica.

ROSE OF SHARON. See Hibiscus syriacus.

ROSE, ROCK. Cistus, which see.

ROSE, SUN. See Helianthemum.

ROSETTE. A name used in describing radiating clusters of leaves that in form somewhat resemble an open rose flower. They are found in Houseleeks, Saxifrages and plants of similar growth.

ROSINWEED. See Silphium.

ROSMARINUS — *Rosemary* (Rosmari'nus). The only species, Rosmarinus officinalis, is a tender, evergreen shrub which has been cultivated from time immemorial for the fragrance of its evergreen foliage. It is a native of southern Europe. Its name is derived from *ros,* dew, and *marinus,* the sea, owing to its being common on the sea coast.

In old herb gardens Rosemary was generally associated with Lavender, to which it is closely related; both belong to the Mint family, Labiatae. Rosemary was believed by the ancients to have a stimulating effect on the mind, and in consequence it has become a symbol of remembrance.

Deliciously Fragrant Leaves. Rosemary forms a dense branching shrub, up to 7 ft. in height, and has linear (narrow) leaves 1-2 in. in length. They are glossy green above and white below.

Rosemary, Rosemarinus officinalis, is a delightful shrub for growing in herb gardens.

Rosemary is propagated by cuttings of young shoots taken with a "heel," with lower leaves stripped off, in late summer (right). The cuttings root freely in a cold frame and form bushy plants by the following autumn (left).

Pruning. This should be done annually, as soon as the flowers have faded, so that the shrubs have time to make new growth before the winter. The shoots should be cut back by about two thirds; if left unpruned, Rosemary will quickly reach its maximum height in suitable conditions. When given an annual pruning, the bushes are kept compact and are thereby prevented from becoming "leggy" or bare at the base.

When to Take Cuttings. Propagation of Rosemary is by cuttings of firm side shoots in late summer or early autumn. These should be 9 in. in length. In mild climates they are inserted in a trench 5 in. deep out of doors, or in a cold frame. In the following autumn the rooted plants are set out, 1 ft. apart, in a nursery bed. In the following year they may be planted in their permanent positions. The tips of the shoots should be pinched out regularly while the plants are small, in order to make the plants branch out. Cuttings of Rosemary 3-4 in. long root readily in sand in a cool greenhouse or terrarium.

When crushed, they emit a delicious fragrance, and because of this it is good practice to plant this shrub near a pathway where the passer-by may pluck the leaves and inhale their fragrance as they are crushed between the fingers. From the leaves, oil of rosemary is extracted. This is extensively used in hair rinses and perfumery.

When in bloom, in early summer, the Rosemary is doubly attractive, as its small, two-lipped flowers, which are formed in the axils of the leaves, along the whole or greater part of the shoots, are quite decorative.

The Most Suitable Soil and Location. Rosemary thrives best in a sunny location and light, well-drained soil. On heavy clay soil it is more liable to be damaged during severe weather in winter. It is hardy about as far north as Washington, D. C., and thrives in California and in similar climates. It is especially useful for planting near the sea.

In cold climates, where it is not reliably hardy outdoors, Rosemary can be cultivated easily in pots, plunged outdoors in a warm, sunny location from spring through fall, and stored in a light, cool (30-45 degrees at night) greenhouse, cellar or sunroom during the winter.

The best time for planting is in early fall or spring. Beyond deep digging of the soil very little preparation is necessary, except on heavy soil, which should be lightened with compost or leaf mold and sand. After planting, the soil must be made firm, and if it is at all dry a good soaking of water should be given. A Rosemary hedge makes a delightful feature. The variety erectus (pyramidalis) is best for this purpose.

The Low-growing Rosemary. In addition to the ordinary upright form, there is a prostrate variety, R. officinalis humilis. The shoots of this kind sprawl along the ground, and it is therefore seen to the best advantage when planted in a rock garden where the shoots can trail over the face of a large boulder.

Other Kinds. In addition to the regular upright-growing type of R. officinalis, which has lilac-colored blooms, and its variety humilis, with flowers of the same color, there are several other varieties. Variety albiflorus is similar to the regular type but has white flowers; variety angustifolius has very narrow leaves and large blue flowers; variety erectus (pyramidalis) is of even more straight and upright growth than the ordinary type; variety prostratus of gardens is of spreading, prostrate growth but is distinct from variety humilis and is noticeably more tender than R. officinalis and its other varieties listed here. By some botanists it is classed as a distinct species and is given the name R. lavendulaceus.

Rosemary Has an Interesting History. It was probably introduced into northern Europe and in Great Britain in Roman times, if not before, but traditionally it was sent in the fourteenth century by the Countess of Hainault to Phillipa, her daughter, queen of Edward III. In the library of Trinity College, Cambridge, England, there is a manuscript copied by "danyel bain" from the original by "a clerk of the school of Salerno." The manuscript, which was sent by the Countess of Hainault to her daughter, treats of the virtues of Rosemary.

Among other virtues the writer states, "it mighteth the boones and causeth goode and gladeth and lighteth alle men that use it. The leves layde under the heade whanne a man slepes, it doth away evell spirites and suffereth not to dreeme fowle dremes ne to be afearde. But he must be out of deedely synne.

"Lavender and Rosemary is as woman to man and White Roose to Reede. It is an holy tree and with ffolke that been just and Rightfulle gladlye it groweth and thryveth."

The writer records also the tradition that Rosemary never grows higher than the height of Christ during His earthly life, and that after thirty-three years the plants increase in breadth but not in height.

Rosemary Is Associated with Many Old Customs. In Tudor times sprigs of gilded Rosemary were given by the bridesmaids to the bridegroom. Sprigs of it were thrown "for remembrance" into graves. It was among the evergreens used in the Christmas decorations. The aromatic scent was valued as a disinfectant, and it was burned in sick rooms. According to Spanish tradition Rosemary flowers were originally white, but the Virgin Mary, on the flight into Egypt, rested beside a bush of it, throwing her robe over it, and the flowers turned blue in her honor. In Spain a sprig of Rosemary is commonly worn as a protection from the evil eye.

Rosemary was far more commonly grown in the sixteenth and seventeenth centuries than now. Parkinson, in his *Paradisus,* describes the wood being used to make lutes "or such-like instruments," also carpenters' rules. The double-flowered Rosemary is mentioned by Parkinson, but he says of it that it is "more rare than all the other because few have heard thereof, much less seene it, and myself am not acquainted with it but am bold to deliver it upon credit. It hath stronger stalks, not so easie to breake, fairer,

bigger, and larger leaves of a faire greene colour and the flowers as double as the Larkes heele or spurre. This I have only by relation which I pray you accept untill I may by sight better enforme you."

Sir Thomas More's description of Rosemary is famous. "As for Rosemary I lette it runne all over my garden walls, not onlie because my bees love it, but because it is the herb sacred to remembrance and to friendship, whence a sprig of it hath a dumb language."

The Virtues of Rosemary. In Bancke's *Herbal* (1525) there is a list of the virtues of Rosemary. "Take the flowers thereof and boyle them in fayre water and drinke that water for it is much worthe against all manner of evils in the body. Take the flowers thereof and make powder thereof and binde it to thy right arme in a linnen cloath and it shale make thee lighte and merrie. Take the flowers and put them in thy chest among thy clothes or among thy Bookes and Mothes shall not destroy them.

"Boyle the leaves in white wine and washe thy face therewith and thy browes and thou shalt have a faire face. Also put the leaves under thy bedde and thou shalt be delivered of all evill dreames. Take the leaves and put them into wine and it shall keepe the Wine from all sourness and evill savours and if thou wilt sell thy wine thou shalt have goode speede.

"Also if thou be feeble boyle the leaves in clene water and washe thyself and thou shalt wax shiny. Also if thou have lost appetite of eating boyle well these leaves in cleane water and when the water is colde put thereunto as much of white wine and then make sops, eat them thereof wel and thou shalt restore thy appetite againe."

ROSTELLUM. The name given to a third infertile stigma found in Orchids, between the stigmatic surface and the pollinia (masses of pollen). In some Orchids it is hardly discernible, while in others it is greatly modified, particularly in Habenaria, Orchis, Ophrys, Catasetum and Vanda. In Cypripedium it is entirely absent. The rostellum exudes a viscid matter which quickly dries and causes the pollinia to adhere to an insect and thus assists in the transference of the pollen from plant to plant. As Darwin pointed out, no such organ exists in any other plants.

ROT. See Pests and Diseases.

ROTARY TILLER. See Rototiller.

ROTATION OF CROPS. The object of crop rotation is to arrange the order of planting so that crops of a like nature do not follow each other directly. As is well known to gardeners, the soil requirements of any particular kind of plant generally differ from those of others, so if one kind is grown exclusively on a plot of ground it gradually exhausts the available supplies of essential food, with the result that the crop may cease to be profitable. Further, there is often more possibility of disease attacking plants when they are regularly grown on the same plot; this is most marked in plants of the Cabbage group, the Brassicas and their relatives, which are subject to club root disease.

It is obvious that such root crops as Parsnip and Carrot require a deeper soil than Cabbages, Cauliflowers, and Brussels Sprouts, and that their roots break up the lower strata of soil and so release plant food which otherwise would remain locked up. Thus, in a good system of vegetable garden crop rotation, Cabbage, Cauliflower and Broccoli would follow the root crops.

A plan of the garden should always be made, and the cropping of previous years be referred to when making plans for the coming year's crops. In a small garden, a three-years' rotation is usually as much as can be practiced, but the longer the rotation the better will be the crops.

The Permanent Crops. When making the rotation plan of a new vegetable garden, the first things to be considered are the permanent crops, such as Asparagus, Rhubarb, and Globe Artichokes, and perhaps bush fruits and such perennial herbs as Mint. Such crops will normally be left undisturbed for several years, in fact as long as they continue to yield satisfactory results. The remaining crops are mostly grown as annuals and may be rotated (located in a new position) yearly.

In some gardens it is found that Onions and, less often, Carrots, will only thrive in a certain location, so that annual rotation may have to be ignored in the cultivation of these.

The smaller crops—Spinach, Lettuce, Endive and other greens—may be looked upon, in the scheme of rotation, as "catch crops," and fitted in where space permits.

The same principle of changing the crop that is grown on a particular piece of ground should also be followed in the flower garden as far as it is practicable.

ROTENONE. The insecticide Rotenone is of great value in horticulture because it is not poisonous to man but is an effective insect killer when employed under favorable conditions. Because of this combination of properties it is of especial value for use in the vegetable garden and fruit garden in places where there is danger that children or animals may be harmed by insecticides possessed of more deadly properties.

Rotenone kills chiefly by contact but it is also of some importance as a stomach poison. It is used as a spray and in dust form and may be combined with another nonpoisonous insecticide, Pyrethrum, for increased effectiveness or convenience.

Rotenone is derived from a number of tropical trees, shrubs and vines, notably Derris and Lonchocarpus. Most of these plants are used as fish poisons by natives in the tropics.

ROTOTILLER. Rototillers or rotary tillers are power-driven machines designed to loosen the soil to a depth of several inches and, if required, to mix with the soil manures, composts, fertilizers, lime, etc. They greatly lighten the labor of garden soil preparation by effectively performing work that otherwise is usually done with a spade or

Modern rotary tillers make it possible to work garden soils deeply with a minimum expenditure of hand labor.

spading fork. Rototillers disturb the soil by means of a set of tines or blades which are fixed to a power-driven shaft which revolves at right angles to the direction in which the machine is travelling. The shaft and tines are covered with a protective hood to prevent soil, stones, etc. being flung far and wide.

ROUEN LILAC. Syringa chinensis, which see.

ROUGE PLANT. See Rivina.

ROUPALA (Rou'pala). These uncommon, tender trees are found wild in tropical America. The young branches are tomentose (hairy) and the leaves in some kinds are entire (undivided) and others are pinnate (feathery) and average 12 in. in length. Flowers are produced in terminal racemes (loose spikes) of small cylindrical, white or yellowish blooms. These plants belong to the family Proteaceae. The name is a native one in Guiana.

Outdoors and as Pot Plants. In southern California and in the deep South, Roupalas may be grown outdoors. They are also sometimes grown as pot plants for their decorative foliage. They do not bloom in pot-plant sizes.

As young, vigorous plants in 5- or 6-in. pots are the most useful, a constant supply is maintained by raising fresh plants annually. A minimum winter temperature of 50 degrees is required, and the best soil compost consists of equal parts of loam, peat and leaf mold, to which sand is added liberally to make it porous.

Raising Plants from Cuttings. Propagation is by inserting cuttings of firm side shoots in summer. The cuttings are prepared by removing the leaves from their lower halves, and a cut is made just below the bottom node. The cuttings are then set in a close, warm propagating case, which is carefully ventilated until roots are formed, when they are potted into small pots. When they are established in these, a further shift into 5-in. pots is made, and finally they are placed in 7-in. pots.

For small greenhouses plants in 7-in. pots are large enough, so that when they become potbound in these they should be discarded and young plants grown to take their places.

If space can be found for large specimens, they may be repotted annually into larger pots and finally set in large tubs; afterwards they can be maintained in a vigorous, healthy condition by top-dressing them with fresh compost in spring.

Well-rooted plants must be watered freely in summer but moderately at all other times. They need the maximum amount of light during most of the year and need only to be shaded from the fiercest rays of the sun. Syringing of the foliage is not required, but the greenhouse must be kept moderately moist by damping the floor whenever it becomes dry.

The Chief Kinds. R. Pohlii, leaves pinnate and covered with reddish-brown tomentum (felty hairs); R. aurea, leafstalks and upper parts of the shoots covered with golden hairs.

ROWAN TREE. See Sorbus Aucuparia.

ROYAL FERN. Osmunda regalis, which see.

ROYAL PALM. Roystonea, which see.

ROYAL POINCIANA. Delonix regia, which see.

ROYOC. See Morinda.

ROYSTONEA—*Royal Palms* (Royston'ea). A group of handsome, feather-leaved Palms of the American tropics and subtropics; one, R. regia, occurs natively in southern Florida. They belong

The Porto Rican Royal Palm, Roystonea borinquena.

[11—6]
African Violet
(Saintpaulia)

[11—7]
Double-flowered Bloodroot
(Sanguinaria canadensis multiplex)

[11—7a]
Siberian Squill
(Scilla sibirica)

to the Palm family, Palmaceae. The name commemorates General Roy Stone, an American engineer. These Palms are sometimes placed in the genus Oreodoxa.

The Roystoneas are among the most stately and magnificent of Palms, and because of their unique beauty are great favorites for planting in tropical countries. Their straight, clean, tall trunks especially adapt them for planting to form avenues. Such avenues exist in various parts of the tropics, notably at the Botanic Gardens in Ceylon and in Rio de Janeiro.

Roystonea regia is the hardiest kind. It, and some others, are planted for ornament in southern Florida but they do not thrive elsewhere in the United States. They are rarely cultivated in greenhouses. They are propagated by seeds.

The kinds are R. borinquena, the Puerto Rico Royal Palm, 50 ft. or more tall, a native of Puerto Rico; R. oleracea, the Caribbee Royal Palm, 100 ft. or more tall, a native of the West Indies; R. regia, a native of Cuba and southern Florida, 70 ft. or more tall.

RUBBER. A large number of trees and other plants contain latex or sap which, by various means, is converted into rubber or rubber-like substances, but very few are of much commercial importance, owing to the overwhelming superiority of one or two kinds.

The most important rubber-yielding tree of the present day is Hevea brasiliensis, from which Para rubber is obtained. This tree is a native of Brazil, but widely grown in Java, Ceylon and the Malay States. The most important gutta percha-producing tree is Palaquium Gutta, a large evergreen tree of the Malay Peninsula; other kinds have very little commercial use. The Rubber Plant commonly grown in pots, Ficus elastica, produces rubber but is of no commercial importance for that purpose.

RUBBER PLANT. See Rubber and Ficus elastica.

RUBBER VINE. Cryptostegia, which see.

RUBELLUS. A Latin word meaning reddish, used botanically chiefly in identifying the color of flowers.

RUBER. The Latin for red. In one or another of its forms—ruber, rubra, rubrum—it is often used in botanical nomenclature.

RUBESCENS. A word meaning approaching or tending to be reddish, which is used in the botanical descriptions of plants having reddish leaves or flowers.

RUBIA TINCTORUM—*Madder* (Ru'bia). A hardy, perennial, herbaceous plant of little horticultural interest except as a subject to cultivate in collections of economic plants. It is the source of the red dye, madder.

Rubia belongs in the botanical family Rubiaceae, and takes its name from the Latin *ruber*, red; the name refers to the color of the dye which is extracted from the roots.

Madder thrives in a light, well-drained soil and a sunny situation. It is propagated by seeds and by division.

Rubia tinctorum is a native of southern Europe and Asia. It grows to a height of about 4 ft.

RUBRA. Ree Ruber.

RUBUS — *Bramble, Blackberry, Raspberry* (Ru'bus). Erect, arching or trailing, leaf-losing and evergreen shrubs, the branches usually armed with sharp, strong or slender prickles. They are widely distributed, mostly in Europe, Asia and North America. A very large number of kinds have been described. Several bear edible fruits. Of these kinds the most important are the selected and cultivated varieties of R. idaeus or European Raspberry; R. idaeus variety strigosus, the American Red Raspberry; R. occidentalis, the Blackcap Raspberry, Blackcap or Thimbleberry; and cultivated varieties of a number of native species of the group known as Blackberries. Other kinds that have edible fruits are the Dewberries, the Wineberry and the Loganberry. The more important fruiting kinds are dealt with under Raspberry, Blackberry, etc., which see.

Many kinds are distinctly decorative, but most of them grow so vigorously that they require more space than is available in most gardens. As a rule, a very limited number can be grown in an ordinary garden. Rubus belongs to the Rose family, Rosaceae, and the name is the ancient Latin name for the plants.

Soil and Culture. As a group the Rubi are very easy to cultivate. They thrive in any reasonably good soil and many flourish even in soils that are not very fertile. The more exacting kinds give the best results when planted in well-drained, loamy earth that does not dry out to an extraordinary degree. All benefit greatly from having the soil mulched with old manure, compost or similar organic material. All flourish in full sun and some, such as the Flowering Raspberry, R. odoratus, thrive in partial shade.

Most of the deciduous kinds are hardy in the North, but not all of them where winters are very severe. The evergreen kinds are generally less tender than the deciduous (leaf-losing) kinds, but many of them can be grown in parts of the North, although they sometimes do not retain their foliage through the winter when cultivated there.

Propagation can be carried out by means of seeds sown in sandy soil in a frame if desired, but many kinds can be increased by digging up suckers from near the old plants, as in the case of the Raspberry; young plants of the trailing kinds are easily raised by layering the branches, and some by separating pieces that have rooted spontaneously in the earth.

Layering is not carried out in the same way as for most shrubs or trees; the tips of the young branches are pegged down in loose soil. In the course of a few weeks they will form roots and soon become vigorous plants.

How to Prune. Pruning is important. The best results are obtained by cutting out all the old wood as soon as the flowering and fruiting are over. This is very necessary in some kinds, as in the Raspberry, for the flowering branches die after fruiting. In other kinds, of which the fruiting branches do not die, it is wise to thin out a good deal of the older wood in order to keep the plants of manageable size. If the old wood is left for a year or two, old and young branches become so hopelessly intermixed that it is almost impossible to separate them.

However, the gardener must be guided entirely by the condition of his plants as to the amount of pruning required. The time for pruning is between the fall of the fruit and the commencement of growth the following spring, but the earlier in autumn it is done, the better. There is one kind, R. deliciosus, which grows in definite bush form and does not require regular pruning; this is true, too, of the very prostrate Rubus Fockeanus.

The Wineberry, Rubus phoenicolasius, is a native of Japan, Korea and northern China. It has escaped from cultivation and become naturalized in parts of North America. It forms very long, slender branches, covered with stiff glandular bristles, among which are a few prickles. The leaves are more decorative than those of many kinds, but the flowers are small and of no special merit. The fruits, however, are bright red and rather insipid, although edible. They are borne freely and can be used for making jam or jelly.

When cultivated, this plant should be grown on a trellis. If allowed to grow untended, it soon forms vast, impenetrable thickets.

The Ghost or White-washed Brambles. Several kinds are decorative and conspicuous by reason of their white stems. They are called White-washed Brambles or, because of their unusual and quite weird appearance in moonlight, Ghost Brambles.

Good representatives of this type are R. biflorus, a vigorous kind from the Himalayas, and its variety quinqueflorus, from western China; R. lasiostylus, from central China; and R. Cockburnianus (Giraldianus), from northern and central China. All are vigorous growers. These

Avenue of Caribbee Royal Palms, Roystonea Oleracea.

ered kinds, the rose-red R. ulmifolius belli-diflorus, and white R. Linkianus (thyrsoideus flore-pleno), are excellent for the wilder parts of the garden. There is also a variety of R. ulmifolius with variegated leaves (variegatus) and another, inermis, with unarmed branches.

The Rocky Mountain Flowering Raspberry, R. deliciosus, sometimes called the Boulder Raspberry, differs in habit of growth from other forms of Rubus. It is distinctly bushy, has unarmed

Rubus ulmifolius bellidiflorus has very double, rose-red flowers.

The large, white-flowered Rubus deliciosus, the Rocky Mountain Bramble.

kinds are seen to good advantage when planted in front of evergreens. In winter their white stems are very conspicuous. The old stems should be cut out in spring before new shoots appear.

Double-flowered Brambles. Two double-flow-

branches and currant-like leaves. It also sheds its bark in the same way as Neillia, and in a leafless state is difficult to distinguish from Neillia. The large, white, solitary flowers are suggestive of the flowers of a wild Rose; the fruits, which may be orange or purplish, have no value. The flowering time is May. This is one of the loveliest of the Rubi.

The Salmonberry, R. spectabilis, a western North American kind with the habit of growth of a Raspberry, is conspicuous throughout winter by reason of its bright brown stems, in April, and its reddish-purple, nodding flowers; in summer, its foliage is luxuriant. The orange fruits are edible but insipid.

The Strawberry-Raspberry, R. illecebrosus, a native of Japan, is a dwarf plant with sub-shrubby or almost herbaceous shoots, 1½-2 ft. high. The fragrant, white, solitary flowers are an

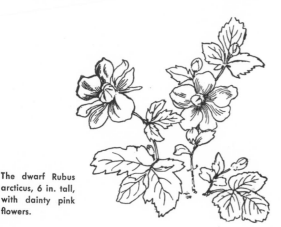

The dwarf Rubus arcticus, 6 in. tall, with dainty pink flowers.

inch or so across, and are followed by large scarlet fruits, 1½-2 in. long. It is of interest in the garden, although the fruits are not palatable unless they are cooked. This kind is sometimes called Balloon Berry.

Dwarf Kinds. R. parvifolius is of dwarf growth with slender, arching stems. It is a native of China and Japan and bears red edible fruits.

The Flowering Raspberry, R. odoratus, is an erect shrub 6-8 ft. high with brown stems, large decorative leaves, and clusters of attractive, fragrant, purplish flowers in May. It is a native of eastern North America.

The flowering Raspberry is well adapted for planting in wilder parts of the garden, especially in partial shade.

Evergreen Brambles. Most of the evergreen kinds of Rubus are less hardy than the leaf-losing ones, but many can be cultivated as far north as Philadelphia or New York. Evergreen and subevergreen kinds are described below.

R. Henryi is a bush with long, slender branches that may grow to a length of 15 ft.; the leaves have three to five lobes, green above and covered with white feltlike hairs beneath. The flowers are pink and the fruits are black, but they are not very attractive. It was received from central and western China in 1900.

R. irenaeus, from the same areas, is an evergreen prostrate shrub suitable for covering stones or tree roots; it has rather large rounded leaves and red fruits.

R. flagelliformis is another Chinese evergreen; it has long, slender, creeping branches and small edible fruits.

Other evergreen or partly evergreen kinds are R. trivialis, the Southern Dewberry, a trailing type with white to pink flowers and edible fruits; R. procerus, the Himalaya Berry, a very vigorous kind with canes 20-40 ft. long that is a native of Europe now naturalized in North America; R. leucostachys, the Broadleaf Evergreen Blackberry, which bears sweetish but rather insipid fruits, and is a native of Europe that is naturalized on the Pacific coast; and R. laciniatus, Cut-Leaf or Evergreen Blackberry, a strong grower with handsome, deeply lobed leaves.

Rubus Fockeanus is an attractive and promising kind that was brought to The New York

Botanical Garden from England in 1952. Five years later it had lived outdoors over four winters and although its leaves, which in milder climates are evergreen, turn brown in winter, the plant makes vigorous new growth in spring and soon becomes green. In fall its foliage assumes beautiful shades of yellow and bronze.

This Rubus is completely prostrate; its stems root freely into the soil. Its leaves are about an inch in diameter, are roundish and rugose or wrinkled. A very decorative ground cover plant, it is of very easy culture. This kind is attractive when grown in pots in a cool greenhouse or window. It is a native of the Himalayas.

A Kind for the Greenhouse. Rubus reflexus is a very beautiful evergreen kind that is sometimes grown in greenhouses, or out of doors in the far South, for the beauty of its foliage. It is a creeping or more or less lax plant, with bright green leaves that are marked with chocolate color along the lower parts of the veins.

This kind thrives best in partial shade. As the leaves on young shoots are always more highly colored than older leaves, everything should be done to encourage the production of these and to prune out older shoots as the plants become crowded. Frequent fertilizing with dilute liquid fertilizer stimulates desirable growth.

This Rubus thrives in a greenhouse. The temperature may range from that of a cool house (night temperature 50 degrees), to that of a warm house (night temperature 55-60 degrees). Any reasonably good soil suits it if well drained. The plant requires reasonable amounts of water; the soil should never be permitted to become really dry. Propagation is very easily carried out by means of cuttings inserted in a sand-filled propagating bench.

RUDBECKIA—Coneflower (Rudbeck'ia). An important group of hardy herbaceous perennial and annual plants which are of considerable decorative value in the garden, more particularly during the late summer and early autumn months. Most of them are tall and vigorous, and all bear flowers with a raised or conelike center, hence the popular name of Coneflower.

The Coneflowers are natives of North America and belong to the Daisy family, Compositae. The name Rudbeckia commemorates Olaf

Flowers of the showy annual Coneflower, Rudbeckia bicolor.

The Best Low-growing Species. The wild kinds of Rudbeckia vary a good deal in height; some grow 5 ft. high, while others are only 2 ft. The best of the low-growing ones is Rudbeckia speciosa, which is known also as R. Newmannii. This kind forms a tuft of long, narrow leaves, and bears golden-yellow, long-stemmed flowers in profusion in July, August and even into Sep-

Perennial Rudbeckias are splendid plants for summer flower borders.

Rudbeck, a Scandinavian professor of botany and his son, also a professor of botany.

The perennial Rudbeckias give no trouble and are first-rate plants for new gardens in one or another of the best kinds or varieties, for they can be relied on to become established quickly and provide a display of bloom the first year.

When to Plant. The perennial Rudbeckias flourish in ordinary well-tilled garden soil; they should, if possible, be planted in a sunny position in the border, although they will flourish in slight shade. The roots may be planted in autumn or in early spring. The earlier the planting is done the better will be the display of bloom during the first season.

The long-stemmed flowers are useful for cutting and Rudbeckia is worth growing on this account alone, especially as it blooms when many of the favorite summer plants are over.

Propagation. The propagation of the hardy perennial kinds is perfectly easy and is most conveniently carried out by division in autumn or spring. The old plants are dug up and separated into rooted pieces, these being replanted where they are to bloom. They can also be raised from seeds sown in spring under glass, or in the open garden in May, to provide flowering plants the following year.

tember. They can be cut with stems 12-15 in. long and are most useful for indoor decoration. This is one of the best hardy herbaceous perennials for the front of the flower border.

Rudbeckia californica, which reaches a height of 4 ft. or more, is a good plant for the back row of the herbaceous border.

The most popular of the tall kinds is Rudbeckia laciniata Golden Glow; this handsome plant reaches a height of 5-6 ft. and bears large, double, rich yellow flowers which make a brilliant display in the garden and are invaluable for cutting for indoor decoration. The botanical name of this variety is R. laciniata hortensia.

R. nitida variety Herbstsonne, 4 ft., with large single yellow flowers in late summer, is also a first-rate hardy herbaceous perennial.

The tall kinds of Rudbeckia are useful plants for grouping in the wild or woodland garden and for the shrubbery border.

Some Garden Varieties. A few especially interesting garden varieties of Rudbeckia have been developed in recent years and are splendid for the perennial border and for providing cut flowers.

R. Goldsturm grows 1-2 ft. tall, is well-branched and bears handsome, deep yellow daisies that may be 3-4 in. in diameter and have a splendid black cone in the center of each. This variety, which blooms continuously over a long period from July onwards, resists heat and drought and grows without trouble.

R. laciniata Gold Quelle grows 3 ft. or less tall and bears its double, clear yellow flowers very freely in the fall.

R. The King is another good kind that is not troubled by heat or drought. Growing to a height

Rudbeckia laciniata Golden Glow, one of the best of the hardy perennial Coneflowers. It has fully double, rich yellow flowers produced in late summer.

Rudbeckia nitida Herbstsonne. This first-rate hardy herbaceous perennial grows 4 ft. or more tall; the flowers are primrose yellow, with greenish centers.

of about 3 ft., this variety produces starlike, crimson-red flowers on stiff stems.

R. White Lustre is a really beautiful perennial with large, white, starlike flowers. These have central cones exhibiting a charming metallic lustre that has been described as a mixture of old brass and old copper. The plants thrive in hot and even dry locations.

All of the four varieties described above need full sun. Apart from that requirement, they make few demands upon the skill of the gardener. They succeed almost anywhere and should find a place in most gardens.

The Purple Coneflower. The plant often grown as Rudbeckia purpurea is correctly named Echinacea purpurea, which see.

Black-eyed Susan and Brown-eyed Susan. Two of the best-loved of our native wild flowers are the Black-eyed Susan, Rudbeckia hirta, and the Brown-eyed Susan, R. triloba. The former occurs naturally from Ontario to Florida and Texas, the latter from New Jersey to Georgia and Labrador.

Both these kinds are biennials in nature; the seeds germinate in late summer and grow into plants which live over winter, bloom the following year, and then die. They may be grown on the same schedule in the garden or they may be raised as annuals and bloomed the first year by sowing them early indoors and transplanting them to the open garden when danger of frost is passed.

Black-eyed Susan grows 2-3 ft. tall, is branched and bears golden-yellow flowers that have dark purple-brown centers. The Brown-eyed Susan grows 3-5 ft. tall and has deep yellow flowers that sometimes have an orange-yellow or brown-purple zone surrounding the black-purple center.

Black-eyed Susan is a fine plant for a sunny, dry position in the border or in the wild garden. The Brown-eyed Susan thrives in sun or partial shade and appreciates a fertile, well-drained soil. It, too, is suitable for wild garden or border, and like the Black-eyed Susan makes a delightful cut flower.

Gloriosa Daisies. In recent years some excellent tetraploid selections and varieties of the Black-eyed Susan have been made and are offered by seedsmen. These are known as Gloriosa Daisies. They have flowers up to 5 in. in diameter in a wide range of yellow, brown, mahogany and bicolor tones and combinations. The flowers are single, semidouble or double.

Gloriosa Daisies are really perennials or biennials but they bloom well the first year from seed and so are often grown as annuals. They thrive in any fairly well-drained garden soil in full sun. Gloriosa Daisies produce a large number of showy flowers over a long period. They are splendid for garden display and for use as cut flowers.

The Annual Coneflowers. Finally there are the annual Coneflowers. These seem to be little

Gloriosa Daisies are a type of annual Rudbeckias that produce enormous flowers in golden-yellow, orange and mahogany shades.

known in gardens, but they are excellent summer flowers, and plants continue gay until well into the autumn months, if care is taken to remove the blooms as soon as they have faded, to prevent the development of seeds. If the dead blooms are left on the plants, these annuals, like all others, will soon cease flowering.

Sowing Seeds Out of Doors. The annual kinds flourish in ordinary garden soil and should be grown in a sunny position. Seeds are sown out of doors in spring, where the plants are to bloom. The best time to sow is as soon as the soil is dry enough to work.

As the plants must be about 6 in. apart, it is unnecessary and wasteful to sow the seeds thickly; they should be covered with ½ in. or so of soil. The plants are unlikely to require support, except perhaps in gardens exposed to exceptionally strong winds, but if support becomes necessary it is best provided by inserting twiggy sticks among them; when the plants have reached their full development the sticks will be hidden, yet give sufficient support to keep the plants upright.

Sowing Annual Coneflowers Under Glass. These annual Rudbeckias can also be raised from seeds sown in a slightly heated greenhouse or frame 6-8 weeks before the young plants will be needed for setting in the garden. The seeds are sown in a flat of light, sifted soil, covered with glass and shaded from bright sunshine. The seeds should be sown thinly so that it will be unnecessary to disturb the seedlings until the time comes to plant them out of doors in May, where they will bloom in late summer and early autumn.

Annual Coneflowers as Greenhouse Plants. These Coneflowers are very pretty when cultivated in cool greenhouses for blooming in late winter and spring; they may be grown in pots or planted in beds. For these purposes seeds should be sown from September to January, in pots or flats containing light, sandy soil. The seedlings are transplanted 2 in. apart in flats or are potted individually in small pots. Later they are set in larger ones (pots 5-6 in. in diameter are suitable for finals) containing rich, well-drained soil. The plants are grown in full sun in temperatures of 45-50 degrees at night and a few degrees higher

by day. After the final pots are well filled with healthy roots the plants benefit from weekly applications of dilute liquid fertilizer.

Good strains offered by seedsmen are Golden Sunset, 18 in., golden-yellow with chestnut markings; Kelvedon Star, 2 ft., yellow-brown and mahogany; Indian Chief, 2 ft., single flowers, deep metallic mahogany red; and Autumn Glow, 18 in., with golden-yellow flowers that are fine.

RUE. See Ruta graveolens.

RUE ANEMONE. See Anemonella.

RUE, GOAT'S. See Galega.

RUELLIA—*Christmas Pride* (Ruell'ia). Free-flowering and ornamental-leaved tender plants from tropical America. They belong to the Acanthus family, Acanthaceae, and are named in honor of Jean de la Ruelle, a French botanist.

Flowers in Midwinter. Ruellia macrantha is the most popular kind. This is a most valuable plant, as it is in full bloom during the midwinter, when flowers are scarce. Although it is possible to obtain large specimens by growing the plants for several years, this method is not

Ruellia rosea, a winter-blooming greenhouse plant with rose-pink flowers.

generally adopted, as plants raised annually in spring are more serviceable. It has semiwoody, bright green stems and ovate leaves, 3 in. in length and 2 in. wide.

The flowers, which are produced in small clusters on short stalks in December and January, are rosy-purple, tubular, two-lipped at the apex and one inch in length. They are short-lived and soon fall, but as they open in rapid succession a continuous display is maintained for many weeks.

Propagation. From cuttings inserted in March, bushy plants 2 ft. in height are obtained in the following winter. To obtain suitable shoots for cuttings, the stems are cut back to within 12 in. of the soil in early March. They are syringed frequently to make them break into growth, and when the new shoots are 2 in. in length, they are removed and inserted in a propagating case having a bottom heat of 65-75 degrees. Roots will form quickly. When sufficient roots have developed, the plants are potted separately in 3-in. pots. The greenhouse in which they are grown in their early stages should have a minimum temperature of 55 degrees. The atmosphere must be kept moist and shade afforded from bright sunlight.

Pinching the Shoots. When the plants are established in the small pots, the tips of the shoots are removed, and as soon as side shoots appear the plants are repotted in 5-in. pots. The side shoots are pinched just above the second joint, and the plants are repotted in 7-in. pots as soon as they break into new growth. No further repotting is required. When well rooted, they must be given cooler conditions and exposed to all but the fiercest rays of the sun, in order to ripen the shoots for the production of flowers. Established plants greatly benefit from occasional applications of liquid fertilizer, but its use must be discontinued as soon as the plants start to bloom.

The best potting compost consists of equal parts of loam, peat and leaf mold with which a liberal amount of sand is mixed. For the first potting the compost should be sifted through a fine mesh sieve; and for the final potting the loam should be broken up into pieces about the size of a walnut.

Winter Management. From October until February a minimum night temperature of 50 degrees is required to make the plants flower freely. After flowering, the water supply is reduced and the soil is kept rather dry until March, when the plants are restarted into growth for the production of cuttings.

In addition to R. macrantha, there are many other kinds in botanical collections: most of these are scarcely worthwhile, however, when plants for decorative purposes are required. They will flourish under the same treatment as R. macrantha and include the following:

R. rosea, a straggling plant with lanceolate leaves, 6 in. in length, and clusters of rosy-pink flowers; R. Portellae, dwarf, with slender stems and small, more or less oval, dark green leaves with pale green veins, and purple undersurface, grown chiefly as a foliage plant; R. formosa, a dwarf kind with upright spikes of scarlet flowers; R. Devosiana, a low-growing plant with white-veined leaves, purple underneath, and small white flowers; and R. fulgida, which grows 2 ft. high, with scarlet flowers.

RUE, MEADOW. See Thalictrum.

RUMEX—*Sorrel, Dock* (Ru'mex). Few of these plants have any horticultural value, most of them being regarded purely as troublesome weeds. There are many kinds found wild in North America as well as in most temperate regions of the globe. They are closely related to Rhubarb (Rheum) and Polygonum, and belong to the family Polygonaceae. The name Rumex is an ancient Latin one. See also Sorrel.

Troublesome Weeds. The plants have thick, thonglike roots which penetrate deeply into the soil, and are difficult to eradicate. The leaves are mostly lanceolate (lance-shaped) and vary in length from a few inches to several feet, according to the kind. Some have bright green leaves, those of others are streaked or flushed with

Ruellia macrantha is a popular greenhouse plant.

red, and one kind, **R.** sanguineus, has blood-red veins. The flowers, although freely produced on long panicles (branching spikes), are not sufficiently attractive for garden decoration.

Seeds are scattered far and wide by the winds, so that Docks are found springing up in all parts of the garden, especially on lawns, where they quickly become a nuisance. Docks growing on a lawn can be eradicated by piercing the centers with a skewer dipped in weed killer and by use of 2, 4D weed killer. Liming eliminates some kinds that grow only on acid soils. When spading vacant ground, make certain that every particle of root is removed, as the smallest pieces are capable of forming new plants.

For the Water Garden. R. Hydrolapathum, the Great Water Dock, which grows 7 ft. in height and has leaves averaging 2 ft. in length, is sometimes planted in shallow water on the edges of large ornamental ponds for the beauty of its massive leaves.

Sorrel as a Salad Plant. R. Acetosa (Sorrel) in improved garden varieties is sometimes grown in gardens for the leaves, which are used in salads. They have an acid flavor and are not very popular. The seeds are sown in drills, 1 in. deep and 12 in. apart, in early spring, and the seedlings are thinned out to 6 in. apart. In the following autumn the plants are set out 18 in. apart on a well-manured plot, and from the following spring onwards the leaves are gathered as required.

As soon as they appear, the flowering shoots are cut out, as they rob the plants of nourishment and prevent the leaves from reaching their maximum size. A top-dressing of manure annually, in spring, is sufficient to keep the plants growing vigorously for four or five years. Afterwards they should be lifted and divided and the pieces replanted in freshly prepared ground.

A Substitute for Spinach. R. Patientia (Herb Patience), a tall-growing plant, the leaves of which are used as a substitute for Spinach, is grown in the same way as Sorrel.

RUNNER. Many perennial plants produce horizontal shoots which run along the surface of the ground. These are called runners. Along the runners one or more young plants develop, usually some distance apart, and adventitious roots

grow in bunches at the nodes or joints. In time the horizontal stem decays, leaving a large number of small plants all firmly rooted around the original one. The Strawberry affords a familiar example.

RUSCHIA (Rus'chia). A group of South African succulent plants that at one time were included in Mesembryanthemum and that require the same cultural treatment as Mesembryanthemum, which see.

The Ruschias are branched, spreading or erect plants, with three-angled leaves. Their flowers are daisy-like in general appearance, pink, violet or white. They vary in height from 2-3 in. to 2-3 ft.

These plants belong to the botanical family Aizoaceae.

The kinds of Ruschia are numerous. Among those likely to be found in cultivation are R. acuminata, R. dichroa, R. crassa, R. impressa, and R. uncinata.

RUSCUS—_Butcher's-Broom_ (Rus'cus). Evergreen plants that are usually referred to as shrubs for want of a better term, although they cannot be regarded as true shrubs. They belong to the Lily family, Liliaceae, and are related to the Asparagus, but are of stiffer habit of growth than the garden Asparagus, and have not the

Fruiting branch of Ruscus aculeatus, the Butcher's-Broom.

trailing or climbing habit of the decorative kinds of that plant. Rather fleshy stems are produced from a rootstock; they last for a period, then die, and are replaced by new shoots.

Plants Which Have No True Leaves. They bear leaflike bodies which are not true leaves, but cladodes, which function as leaves, and bear flowers and fruits from the center. In this article they are referred to as leaves for the sake of convenience. Male and female flowers are borne on different plants, and if plants of the two sexes are grown together an ample crop of attractive fruits is borne. Ruscus is the old Latin name for the Butcher's-Broom.

Propagation is usually carried out by division of the clumps in spring, although seeds can be used. Every small piece bearing roots, detached from an old plant, will grow. Propagation by division has one defect: it tends to increase the plants of one sex only in a garden, therefore many growers never see the fruits. Plants should be examined once or twice a year and worn-out shoots cut out to the ground line.

Will Thrive Under Trees. The several kinds of Ruscus thrive in moist, loamy soil in semi-shade and sun; they should not be planted in sunny places where there is a possibility of their becoming very dry. They form excellent plants, in mild climates, for covering ground beneath taller shrubs or for forming undergrowth in shady places. They are not hardy in the North.

The Common Butcher's-Broom. R. aculeatus, the Butcher's-Broom, grows 1½-3 ft. high and bears small, ovate, spiny "leaves"; the flowers are very small and produced from the center of the "leaf"; the scarlet fruits, from ⅓-½ in. in diameter, are attractive. It is found wild in Europe. The variety angustifolius has narrow "leaves," and latifolius has broad "leaves." The name Butcher's-Broom originated from the custom that butchers once had of using small bundles of the branches to sweep their cutting-up blocks.

R. Hypoglossum is a native of southern Europe; it grows 8-18 in. high, in compact masses. The "leaves" are not spiny. The red berries are produced from the middle of the "leaves."

R. Hypophyllum, a native of southern Europe, the Canary Islands and North Africa, is more

dwarf than the last-mentioned kind. It grows 6-12 in. high, bearing white flowers and red fruits. The flowers appear from the undersides of the "leaves."

RUSH. See Juncus.

RUSH, CLUB. See Scirpus.

RUSH, FLOWERING. Butomus umbellatus, which see.

RUSH-LEAVED DAFFODIL. Narcissus juncifolius, which see.

RUSSELIA—*Coral Blow* (Russel'ia). Free-flowering, tender shrubs with slender, rushlike, pendulous branches. The small ovate leaves are few in number and are reduced to tiny scales on the older branches, giving them an almost leaflike appearance. During the summer months the flowers are produced freely along the whole length of the slender side shoots; they are bright red, tubular, ½ in. in length and terminated by five rounded lobes. These plants are found growing wild in tropical America and Mexico, and belong to the Figwort family, Scrophulariaceae. They were named in honor of Alexander Russel, a botanical author.

Outdoor Culture. In southern Florida and similar mild climates Russelias are easy to grow outdoors. R. equisetiformis, the Coral Plant or Fountain Plant, a native of Mexico, is naturalized in Florida and the West Indies.

For Pots or Hanging Baskets. When grown in greenhouses, these plants require a minimum winter temperature of 55 degrees and a soil compost of equal parts of loam, peat and leaf mold, with which sand is mixed to make it porous. They make excellent pot plants and are also suitable for cultivating in hanging baskets, in which the pendulous shoots of scarlet flowers are displayed to the best advantage.

Repotting and Pruning. Early in February the plants are lightly pruned to make them shapely, and then syringed frequently to induce new shoots to form. They are removed from the pots and, after all loose soil has been removed from the roots with a pointed stick, the plants are repotted in slightly larger pots. The new pots are well drained with crocks and the soil is made firm.

To assist the plants to recover quickly from the repotting, the shoots are lightly syringed two or three times a day, the atmosphere is kept moist by damping the floor and benches and the plants are shaded from strong sunlight. Care must also be exercised in watering until the plants are well rooted; afterwards the soil should be kept moist for the remainder of the summer. During the autumn and winter, water should only be given when the soil is quite dry.

If the plants are to be grown in hanging baskets, these are lined with moss and filled with the prepared compost. One or more plants, according to the size of the baskets, are then set in position. The baskets are suspended from the roof of the greenhouse and the treatment is as advised for pot plants.

Propagation. Young plants are obtained by cuttings or layers. Cuttings are made from the small side shoots, which are removed with a heel in spring. They are inserted in sand in a propagating case with a bottom heat of 70-75 degrees.

When rooted, the young plants are potted in 3-in. pots, and afterwards into larger pots, or placed in hanging baskets.

To obtain rooted layers, the shoots are notched just below a joint, about 3 in. from the ends, and are pegged down in a pan of sandy soil which is kept moist. Layers root most quickly in a humid atmosphere.

The chief kinds are R. elegantissima, R. equisetiformis (Coral Plant), and R. sarmentosa. All have red tubular flowers and grow 3-4 ft. in height.

RUSSIAN ALMOND. Prunus tenella, which see.

RUSSIAN MULBERRY. Morus alba variety tatarica, which see.

RUSSIAN OLIVE. Elaeagnus angustifolia, which see.

RUSSIAN WORMWOOD. Artemisia sacrorum, which see.

RUST. See Pests and Diseases.

RUSTIC WORK

The woods commonly used for rustic work are Black Locust, Red Cedar, Redwood, Hickory and Oak. The wood for rustic furniture is sometimes used with the bark on, but is better peeled, the wood in the latter case being varnished with or without staining. Some people prefer the natural color of the wood, while others like the shades produced by applying various stains and preservatives. Varnish is applied if a shiny finish is desired. In this case, plenty of time must be allowed for the surface to dry out, before finishing off with varnish. Waxing also provides a good, somewhat glossy finish.

The Necessary Tools. The tools required are few. A good saw and hammer are enough for most purposes; for some of the more elaborate work a chisel and brace and bits are useful. There is also a type of saw known as a bow saw, having a thin blade kept in tension by twisted string, and capable of being twisted at an angle by the handle at each end. Such a saw will be found very handy where curved joints have to be cut, and for working green wood, where an ordinary carpenter's saw would be-

come stuck by the sap and the resin in the wood.

Eight useful joints are shown in the sketches, and a brief description of the application of each may be found helpful; some of them are only used for special work. The joint shown at A is used when making a right-angle corner, and may be used in a modified form for other angles. The ends are cut as shown, overlapped, and nailed together. B is a mitered end, for use when two ends are to be butted together at a corner. C

Rustic bridge, with part of the floor cut away to show details of construction.

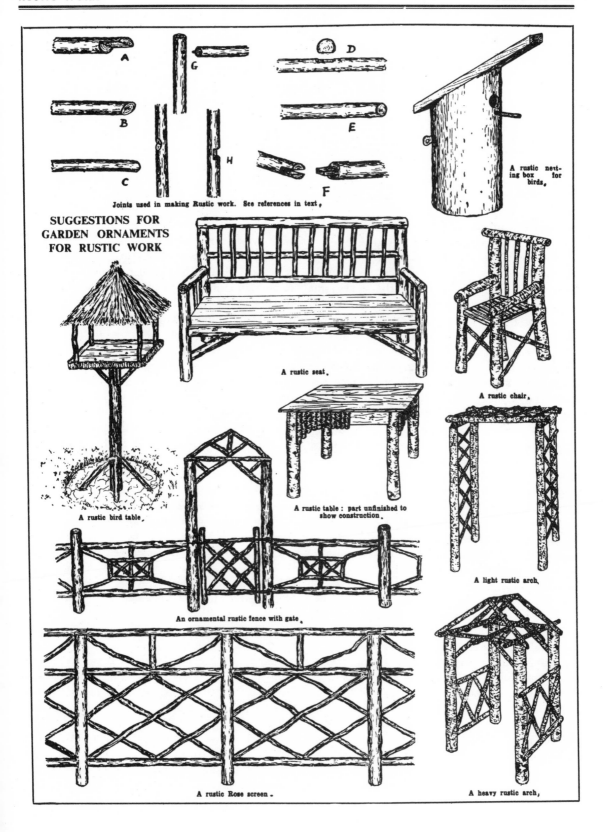

Joints used in making Rustic work. See references in text.

A rustic nest-ing box for birds.

SUGGESTIONS FOR GARDEN ORNAMENTS FOR RUSTIC WORK

A rustic seat.

A rustic chair.

A rustic bird table.

A rustic table : part unfinished to show construction.

A light rustic arch.

An ornamental rustic fence with gate.

A rustic Rose screen.

A heavy rustic arch.

Design for an ornamental pergola made of rustic timber.

illustrates a simple notched joint, which is very useful for joining crossrails to uprights.

D shows a small recess cut in a crossbar to receive the end of another which rests on it. The rested end is cut as in E, the same joint being used when resting the end of a bar on top of an upright. F is an open mortise and tenon, needing a chisel for its cutting out, and the joint A can generally be substituted. G shows a doweled joint, for fixing rails to uprights. The latter have a hole bored to receive a peg, the other end of which fits into a hole in the end of the rail, the latter being cut off on a curve for good fitting. Joint C may be used instead.

H is used when crossing two rails in the same plane, when a very neat finish is necessary; otherwise the rails are laid across each other and a nail is driven through both at the intersection. Another use of the joint A is for connecting the ends of rails in the same line, as for example, on the top of a screen or pergola.

Rose Screens, Arches, and Pergolas. The application of some of these joints can be seen in the illustration of the Rose screen, which is easily made. On similar lines is the rustic fence with gate, the two gate posts being higher than the rest and arched at the top. This arrangement is suitable for the entrance to a pergola. A solid and easily built pergola is also shown, and a heavy and light type of arch are illustrated, as well as a rustic arbor.

When erecting this type of work, measure out the pieces and cut the necessary joints, then put the uprights in the ground first, after scraping their lower part and giving it a coat of asphaltum, paint, tar, creosote or other wood preservative. From 18 in. to 2 ft. of the post

should be below the soil, and the area treated with preservative is extended a little way above, as decay takes place chiefly at ground level. It is a good plan to bed each post on stones, and to ram in stones when filling up the hole.

After the uprights are firmly set, the crossbars are added; filling in with thin, latticed pieces is best left until the end.

Making a Garden Bridge. Another attractive feature is a rustic bridge; it is constructed in this way. The decking, which takes all the weight, is placed in position first, and is made by nailing sawed planks 1½ in. thick, on the main side bearers. The latter can be made from 10 in. by 6 in. outside roughs from the timberyard. These are sawed planks with bark edges, and should be 2 in. or more thick. The side bearers are spiked at each end on cross-bearers. The posts for the parapet should be about 4 ft. high and 4 in. through, with side supports as shown in the sketch.

For the top runners use curved pieces, if possible, but straight ones will do, of smooth, non-splintering wood; these runners or rails should be of nearly the same thickness throughout their length.

The sides are filled in with cross bracings of rustic work, which may be of almost any pattern. Triangles are a good choice, as these give great rigidity and are easily made. The wood may be used with the bark on, but it is preferable to peel and treat it as described below, for greater durability.

Garden Furniture. Designs for a seat, table and chair are given in the sketches. The seats and table top are made of sawed wood, but the rest of the framework is generally made in rustic work, the notched joint, or a modification there-of, being very useful in this connection. The sizes are not given in the various illustrations, because individual requirements vary.

A rustic bird table makes a useful as well as an attractive feature in the garden, and looks well if thatched. The post should be stayed with thin pieces, the top being supported on struts as shown. The base is made from thin boards and a rustic post is nailed in each corner, the roof being made of thin wood, well tarred or creo-soted. Holes are drilled in the base for drainage and a rim of cork bark is nailed around the edge for decoration and to prevent the food from being scattered. It is a good plan to fix a hook in the roof so that lumps of suet can be suspended.

Birds' Nesting Boxes. These are attractive when made from old logs; the insides of these are hollowed out by burning or gouging, and a small roof is fixed on top to project over the entrance. Make the boxes about 10 in. high and 5 or 6 in. wide, with an entrance of about 1½ in., a small perch being placed just beneath. The lid is best hinged at the back and held down by a catch so that the old nests can be taken out each year. Means are provided for fixing the boxes to a fence or on trees, by screwing on a metal piece at the back or by driving in large staples and hanging the boxes by wire.

Treating the Wood. The following hints as to general methods of treating the wood and erect-ing it will be found helpful when building rustic work.

The wood with bark on is best used for arches and other similar work; it needs little beyond tarring or creosoting of the cut ends and parts below the soil level. For the garden furniture the wood is best used peeled, as the preserva-tives which can be applied will keep it in good condition for many years.

After peeling, the wood is made smooth with coarse sandpaper and the prominent knots are rasped or planed down level. The pieces may be treated with wood dyes and varnished, or with Cuprinol or other wood preservative, and varnished as well if desired; a good result can be obtained by using a dark brown copal var-nish.

For joining the various pieces, use galvanized wire nails for the thinner ones and cut nails for the heavy work, as these have strong holding power. The uprights must be quite straight be-fore the others are put in. Every winter, rustic work should be examined and replaced where necessary; it is well worth while to revarnish peeled work as a means of saving money in the long run.

If a post has started to decay below ground level, the soil should be dug out and the post scrubbed clean, fresh tar or asphaltum being applied to the surface; the soil is then replaced and rammed down. Another method is to bore an auger hole into the heart of the post and fill the cavity with Cuprinol, afterwards plugging the hole with a wooden peg. The preservative soaks into the heart of the wood and prolongs the life of the post.

RUTA—*Rue, Herb of Grace* (Ru'ta). Dwarf, evergreen, shrubby plants of minor horticultural value. Ruta graveolens, the Common Rue, has medicinal properties for which it was held in high esteem by the ancients. This shrub, which grows about 3 ft. in height, has pinnate (feathery) smooth, glaucous (blue-gray) leaves, which emit a very pungent odor when bruised. It produces small clusters of yellow flowers in summer. Ruta belongs to the family Rutaceae. The name is the ancient Greek one for this plant.

Although an attractive shrub, Rue is not much planted nowadays, except in herb and medicinal gardens. At one time it was extensively used in Europe to form low dividing hedges in the kitch-en gardens of large estates. There is a variety variegata, with white-edged leaves, and Jackman's Blue is a good form with glaucous-blue foliage.

Planting and Pruning. Rue succeeds best in light, well-drained soil. Heavy soil requires lightening with sand, cinders, and compost, leaf mold or humus. Planting is done in October or spring, in a sunny position. Pruning is carried out in April, when the shoots are cut back hard to make them break from the base.

Propagation. Rue may be propagated from seeds or cuttings. The cuttings are made from side shoots, inserted out of doors, or in a cold frame or greenhouse, in late summer or early autumn.

In the following autumn they are lifted and planted in their permanent positions.

Seeds are sown out of doors in spring, in drills ½ in. deep, the seedlings being thinned or pricked out to 6 in. apart and set in their permanent positions when large enough to transplant.

Other kinds of Ruta, sometimes met with in botanical collections, are: R. patavina, 12 in., yellowish-green flowers, suitable for a sunny position on the rockery; and R. suaveolens, which is scented like the English Cowslip, Primula veris. These kinds are not quite so hardy as the Common Rue.

RUTABAGA OR SWEDISH TURNIP. Botanically the Rutabaga is named Brassica Napobrassica, a fact which proclaims its close relationship to several other well-known vegetables, including Cabbage, Cauliflower, Brussels Sprouts, Kale, Kohlrabi, Mustard and Turnips. It belongs to the Mustard family, Cruciferae.

Rutabagas, when well grown, provide a fine table vegetable and are especially valuable because they can be stored so easily for winter use. In addition to their use for human food, they are grown in large quantities for feeding stock, particularly sheep and cattle.

The Rutabaga is hardier than ordinary Turnips and requires a longer season of growth. It needs a mellow, fertile soil that does not become excessively dry, and that does not contain fresh manure. A neutral or slightly alkaline soil is better than one decidedly acid.

Rutabagas are primarily cool-climate crops that can be grown to best advantage north of Washington, D. C. The seeds are sown from the middle to the end of June or at the beginning of July in rows 2-2½ ft. apart, and the young plants are thinned to 9-12 in. apart. During the summer they are kept cleanly cultivated.

Those that are to be stored for winter should be harvested after frost but before the roots have been subjected to serious freezing. They may be stored in a root cellar or buried in sand in a shed or other cool place, or buried in storage pits outdoors; the essentials are to keep them cool but safe from hard freezing.

In seedsmen's catalogues several varieties are offered, some with yellow, some with white flesh.

The seeds of Winter Rye are large. They are sown by scattering them over the soil surface and raking them in.

RYE, WINTER. This is a form of the important grain, Rye (which is botanically Secale cereale). Winter Rye is of importance horticulturally because it is employed as a cover crop and green manure.

Winter Rye is valuable for sowing in late summer or fall and for turning under in early spring. By doing this, erosion on slopes and other places is prevented or minimized, the texture of the soil is improved, loss of soluble fertilizers from the soil by leaching is greatly

A crop of young Winter Rye.

reduced, and valuable humus, formed by the decay of both the tops and the roots of the Winter Rye, is added to the soil.

RYE GRASS. Annual and perennial grasses that belong to the genus Lolium and are used as pasture and meadow grasses, as "nurse" grasses in lawn-seed mixtures, and for making temporary lawns. For the last two uses, Lolium multiflorum, the Italian Rye Grass, is favored. Rye Grass is not to be confused with Winter Rye. (See Rye, Winter, above.)

RYE, WILD. See Elymus.

S

SABAL—*Palmetto* (Sa'bal). These New World Palms vary greatly in height. Some kinds, especially S. minor (Adansonii), the Dwarf Palmetto, have short stems and, as these are buried beneath the soil, the plants appear at sight to be stemless. At the other end of the scale is the lofty S. Palmetto, the Cabbage Palm, with a stem sometimes 80 ft. high.

A young plant of the Texas Palmetto, Sabal texana.

The treelike trunks of these Palms are covered with the stumps of the dead leafstalks, and the leaves, which are fan-shaped, are borne on the ends of long petioles (leafstalks). When they are first formed, the leaves are upright, but they become pendulous with age and are split into ribbon-like segments by the wind. Sabals, which belong to the family Palmaceae, are natives of the southern United States, the West Indies, Central America, and northern South America. The origin of the name is obscure, but it is probably a South American native name.

Outdoor cultivation of the Sabals in climates suitable to their growth presents no difficulties, for they are all of simple culture. They thrive in moist and in fairly dry soils and succeed admirably in sandy soil. They do well near the sea.

Sabals are among the hardiest of Palms; one, S. Palmetto, is found as a native as far north as North Carolina. They are much planted for ornament in the far South.

For a Large Greenhouse. Most Sabal Palms, when cultivated under glass, are only suitable for a large greenhouse or conservatory; they require a minimum winter temperature of 45 degrees. For potting, a compost of two parts of loam and one part of leaf mold is the most suitable. In the small state the plants are repotted annually in larger pots, but later on they are set in large tubs or planted out in a prepared bed of soil in the greenhouse.

Good drainage is required in the pots or tubs, as well as in the prepared bed of soil, because Sabals require abundance of water in the summer, but will not withstand a waterlogged condition of the soil. The compost must not be allowed to become very dry in winter, but much less water is needed then than in summer. Established plants greatly benefit by occasional applications of dilute liquid fertilizers during the summer months.

To clean and freshen the foliage, the plants should be syringed forcibly daily in summer; the atmosphere is kept moist by damping the floor and benches frequently.

The leaves of S. Palmetto and other species which grow up to 8 ft. in length are used for making baskets, fans and hats, and the thick fibers are used in the manufacture of brushes.

Propagation Is by Seeds. These must be fresh, as they quickly lose their power of germinating. As Palm seeds have extremely thick and hard seed coats, the shells are notched deeply on one side, with care being taken not to damage the embryo; they are then soaked in tepid water for two or three days. They are sown 1 in. deep in a pan of sandy soil, which is plunged in a propagating case with a bottom heat of 75-80 degrees until germination takes place.

As soon as the first leaves have formed, the seedlings are potted separately in small pots, and are replaced in the glass case. When well rooted, they are placed on the open benches and eventually potted in larger sizes. Care must be taken in repotting young Palms, as their roots are very susceptible to damage; they need only a slightly larger pot, as the roots are liable to decay if surrounded by a large mass of soil.

The Chief Kinds. Among Sabals likely to be cultivated are: S. Beccariana, native locality unknown, a tall tree; S. bermudana (sometimes called S. Blackburniana), Bermuda Palmetto, 30-40 ft., trunk stout and often inclined or crooked, occurring naturally only in Bermuda; S. causiarum, Puerto Rican Hat Palm, 40-50 ft., a native of Puerto Rico; S. exul, Victoria Palmetto, planted in Texas, probably a native of Mexico, a large tree with bright green leaves;

S. louisiana, 15 ft., native to the lowlands of Louisiana; S. minor, Dwarf Palmetto, an apparently stemless kind often found in swamps, from Georgia to Florida and Texas; S. Palmetto, the Cabbage Palmetto, 50-80 ft. or even more, occurring from North Carolina to Florida, chiefly near the coast; S. texana, Texas Palmetto, 50 ft., found in the lower Rio Grande valley and in Mexico; and S. umbraculifera, a sturdy, tall Palm to 50 or 60 ft., a native of Haiti; and S. uresana, 30 ft., a native of Mexico.

SABATIA—*Rose Pink* (Sabat'ia). Low, hardy flowering plants that are natives of North America and belong to the Gentian family, Gentianaceae. From a rosette of small, lanceolate leaves, they send up smooth, slender stems which bear, at intervals, small, opposite, sessile, ovate leaves

Sabatia campestris. It grows 15 in. tall, with rose-colored flowers in summer, and is suitable for a moist position in a rock garden or bog garden.

and are terminated by cymes (widely branching flower spikes) of roundish, white, rose or purple, many-petaled flowers, 1 in. in diameter. The name Sabatia commemorates Liberatus Sabbati, an Italian botanist of the eighteenth century.

These plants are not widely grown in gardens. One reason, no doubt, is that they are mostly biennials, and have to be perpetuated by sowing seed each year. Also, although the individual flowers are pretty, they do not provide sufficient masses of color to make them popular. They are best suited for cultivation in wild gardens and in rock gardens. Their native habitats are swamps and marshes, often brackish.

As these plants are of low growth and are moisture-loving, the ideal location for them is toward the base of the rock garden or in a moist spot in the wild garden. Equal parts of loam and leaf mold, with sand added, form the best compost in which to grow them.

When to Sow Seeds. The seeds are sown in May, in a well-drained flower pan filled with a finely sifted compost of loam, leaf mold and sand. To saturate the soil thoroughly, the pan is immersed nearly to its rim in water until bubbling ceases; the seeds are scattered thinly on the surface and covered with fine, sandy soil. The seed pan is then covered with a pane of glass and placed in a cold frame.

When the seedlings are large enough to handle, they are transplanted, 2 in. apart, into seed pans or flats of light soil and kept in the cold frame until the following April, when they are planted out in their permanent positions. For the remainder of the time, and until the flowers wither, the soil must be kept constantly moist.

The Chief Kinds. Among kinds worth cultivating are S. angularis, 1-3 ft., flowers rose-pink with greenish central part; S. campestris, 8-15 in., flowers lilac; S. dodecandra, 1-2 ft. tall, flowers pink or white; S. paniculata, 2-3 ft., flowers white; S. stellaris, 1-2 ft., flowers pink or white.

SACCHARUM — Sugar Cane (Sacch'arum). Mostly tender perennial plants which belong to the Grass family, Gramineae. The name is derived from saccharon, an old Greek name for sugar. They are of little horticultural interest, but S. officinarum, the Sugar Cane, is of great economic importance as a source of sugar.

S. officinarum has reedlike stems about 15 ft. in height, with long, broad, deep green, recurved leaves, and bears large feathery plumes of white flowers. It is a native of the tropics and is widely grown in many tropical countries.

When mature, the stems are cut down and crushed between rollers to extract the juice; this undergoes the various processes of boiling, crystallizing and refining, to make it fit for domestic uses. The substance which runs from the sugar during the process of crystallization is known as molasses.

Some varieties of S. officinarum are grown outdoors in the far South, but these are not the best sugar-producing kinds. For its best development Sugar Cane needs a really tropical climate.

A Hardy Sugar Cane. S. spontaneum, a native of the Mediterranean region, is suitable for growing out of doors except in climates where very severe winters occur. It is not so tall as S. officinarum, but is more graceful. It should be planted in early summer by the margin of a pond or in some other moist position. Propagation is effected by dividing the roots and replanting them early in summer.

SACCOLABIUM (Saccolab'ium; Sacco'labium). Most of the members of this group of Orchids, as seen in our greenhouses, are of low growth, but remarkable for the beauty of their small flowers. All are evergreen and epiphytal, and are found wild from northern India to the Philippines, New Guinea and Java. They have more or less erect stems with fleshy leaves, from the axils of which the usually short flower spikes are produced, generally in spring and summer. The flowers are brightly colored; in some kinds they are clustered, in others in short spikes, while some have pendent spikes. The name is derived from the Latin saccus, a bag, and labium, a lip, and alludes to the shape of the lip.

Orchids for a Hothouse. All these Orchids come from localities in which the temperature is high, and accordingly they require a greenhouse with a tropical temperature in the summer, and a winter temperature of not less than 60 degrees. They must be watered throughout the year, abundantly in summer, carefully in the winter.

Shading is required during the spring and summer; it must be adjusted with care in the autumn, particularly for the small growing kinds, admitting enough light to harden them, but not enough to turn the leaves yellow.

The small-growing kinds—for example, S. acutifolium and S. bellinum (Gastrochilus bellinus)—are grown in small pans suspended from the roof. The larger kinds do better in Orchid baskets. They may be planted in cut osmunda fiber, in Tree Fern fiber or in chips of bark of Redwood, Fir or other kinds which have proved satisfactory for Orchids. If repotting is not carried out every spring, the compost should be renewed in places if necessary. Drainage must be free.

S. bellinum (Gastrochilus bellinus) has flowers over an inch across, with yellow sepals and petals blotched with dark purple-red, and a lip which is almost white. S. acutifolium is of similar color, but has smaller flowers; while S. ampullaceum (Ascocentrum ampullaceum) and S. curvifolium are bright rose and cinnabar red respectively. S. gemmatum has small white and purple flowers and can be grown on a suspended wood block. Other notable kinds are S. calceolare, yellowish with red-brown markings; and S. giganteum (Anota densiflora), white and mauve, very fragrant.

SACRED BEAN. See Nelumbium.

SADLERIA CYATHEOIDES — Tree Fern (Sadler'ia). A tropical Tree Fern, from the Hawaiian Islands, with a treelike trunk, 6 ft. in height, which is surmounted by a tuft of large, feather-shaped fronds. It is sometimes grown in greenhouses, but for this purpose is not a popular Fern, as it requires a good deal of space. Sadleria belongs to the family Polypodiaceae, and is named after Joseph Sadler.

For a Shady Hothouse. A shady hothouse with a minimum winter temperature of 60 degrees is necessary and, for potting, a compost of equal parts of peat, loam and sand should be used. This Fern is grown in a large, well-drained pot or tub, in which it is planted in spring. It may remain undisturbed for many years, and can be kept growing vigorously by an annual top-dressing of fresh compost in spring. During the summer months it should be shaded from bright sunlight. The soil must be kept moist and the stems syringed daily. The air should be humid.

Young plants are obtained by sowing spores (see Ferns), but it is a slow process, and it is therefore more usual to procure imported plants.

SAFFLOWER. See Carthamnus tinctorius.

SAFFRON CROCUS. See Crocus sativus.

SAFFRON, MEADOW. See Colchicum.

SAFFRON, THISTLE. See Carthamus.

SAGE. This southern European herb, Salvia officinalis, is an evergreen shrubby plant which is hardy, though it is liable to perish during a severe or excessively wet winter, especially if it is planted in clayey soil. It thrives best in well-drained, rather light soil in a sunny place. Planting is done early in spring, the plants being set 12 in. apart, in rows about 15 in. from each other. The plants last for several years, but when they begin to lose vigor a fresh stock should be raised by sowing seeds or by taking cuttings or slips. The latter two are the usual means of propagation.

Taking Slips and Cuttings. In May or June, slips (side shoots, with a heel of older wood attached) may be taken from the old. plants, or cuttings can be made from the top 3-4 in. of the shoots. The slips or cuttings, if set in a bed of well-firmed sand in a cold frame that is shaded, soon root. The slips or cuttings are planted about 4 in. apart, and the young plants are ready

The Garden Sage, Salvia officinalis, is a favorite herb.

for setting outdoors in their permanent locations the following spring. If the weather is dry after transplanting, the plants must be watered.

When the young plants are growing freely, the tops should be cut off to make them branch out. A very attractive variety of Sage, Salvia officinalis variety tricolor, has foliage variegated with creamy-white and pink. Variety aurea has yellow leaves. Variety purpurascens has reddish purple foliage.

SAGE, AZURE. Perovskia atriplicifolia, which see.

SAGE, BLUE. See Salvia patens.

SAGE, JERUSALEM. See Phlomis fruticosa.

SAGE OF BETHLEHEM. Pulmonaria officinalis, which see.

SAGE, SCARLET. Salvia splendens, which see.

SAGINA—*Pearlwort* (Sagi'na). Hardy herbaceous creeping plants, natives of North America, Asia and Europe; a few kinds are found growing wild in the Arctic regions. They are mostly weeds, especially in lawns on light, sandy soil, but a few are used for various purposes in the garden, such as planting in the crevices between random paving, draping rockery ledges and for carpet bedding designs. They belong to the Pink family (Caryophyllaceae).

The Saginas have slender, creeping stems which bear tiny, narrow, bright green, mosslike leaves and small, white, roundish flowers in summer. The name Sagina, which means fatness, was given to these plants because of the supposed value of one kind as food for sheep.

Plants for the Rock Garden and Paved Paths. S. glabra, which forms a dense carpet of greenery, starred with miniature white flowers in summer, and its variety, S. glabra aurea, which has golden-yellow leaves, are useful for planting in rock gardens and in the crevices of stone paving.

Light, well-drained soil and a sunny position are required. Small tufts are planted 3 in. apart in spring. These spread quickly and need little attention; small portions are apt to die off and must be replaced with fresh plants.

For paved paths the same conditions as to soil and position are required. Small clumps are inserted in the crevices and watered until established, when they quickly run along the joints.

For Carpet-bedding Designs. The golden-leaved variety, S. glabra aurea, is grown in flats and planted in carpet-bedding designs where lines or patches of a golden color are required. Little tufts are set closely together and watered when necessary. Being dwarf in habit, they require little attention beyond an occasional trimming to restrict them to their allotted space.

Propagation is principally by division in spring. The golden-leaved variety, used for summer bedding, is lifted in autumn and pulled into small tufts which are planted closely together in flats and set in a cold frame for the winter. Sagina is also easily raised from seeds, which should be sown in April in the positions in which the plants are to grow.

S. glabra has been tried in England as a substitute for grass on lawns where the soil is poor and sandy. When rolled and frequently mowed, it has a grasslike appearance, but as it is liable to die off in large patches during severe weather, it has never become popular.

The chief kind is S. glabra, which has white flowers; S. glabra aurea is a golden-leaved variety. S. subulata is a hardy perennial, a native of Corsica. It forms a mosslike growth and has white flowers. S. procumbens is the kind usually found as a weed on lawns.

SAGITTARIA — ***Arrowhead* (Sagitta'ria). Hardy and tender bog and aquatic flowering plants suitable for the margins of pools out of doors, and tanks or tubs in a greenhouse. They belong to the family Alismaceae. The name Sagittaria is derived from the Latin, *sagitta*, an arrow, and refers to the shape of the leaves.

These plants usually have tuberous rootstocks and leaves of the shape of an arrowhead, which are overtopped by tall spikes of attractive, white flowers, $\frac{1}{2}$-1 in. in diameter. The plants vary in height from 2-4 ft. and flower from June to October.

For Planting in Shallow Pools. S. sagittifolia, the Old World Arrowhead, is a native of Europe and Asia, and produces underground tubers which are eaten in the Orient. This and its double-flowered variety, flore-pleno, sometimes called S. japonica, are well worth cultivating. The double variety is the more popular, as the flowers remain longer in bloom. Another hardy kind is S. latifolia, of North America, which grows about 4 ft. in height, the flowers being larger than those of S. sagittifolia. The double variety of this is sometimes grown in gardens as S. variabilis flore-pleno.

How and When to Plant. A sunny or semi-shaded position at the edge of a pond, where the water is not more than 18 in. in depth, is required. The tuberous roots are planted in October or early spring, in a compost of loam en-

A plant of the double-flowered Arrowhead Sagittaria sagittifolia florepleno.

A flower spike of the double-flowered form of the Arrowhead, Sagittaria sagittifolia flore-pleno, a good plant for the margins of pools or other moist locations.

riched with well-decayed manure. The tubers are enclosed in a piece of burlap containing the compost, together with a large stone, and dropped into the water. Instead of burlap a wicker basket may be used, or, in small cemented pools, the tubers may be planted in a wooden tub, which can be lifted out during cleaning operations. Once planted, they need no further attention, except that they should be prevented from exceeding their allotted space. This is accomplished by pulling out the straggling shoots in early summer.

Tender Kinds. The principal tender kind is S. montevidensis, a native of South America, which grows 6 ft. high and bears white flowers blotched at the base with crimson. S. lancifolia, also from South America, is slightly taller and bears whorls of white flowers.

These kinds are planted in a tank or tub in a greenhouse with a minimum winter temperature of 50 degrees or, in the far South, may be planted outdoors permanently. In the North they may be set in outdoor pools in summer and transferred inside before winter.

When the plants are grown permanently in tubs indoors, a soil mixture of loam and decayed manure is placed in the bottom to a depth of 12 in., the tuberous roots are inserted just below the surface, and the soil is covered with an inch of sand. The tub or tank is filled with water and the plants are not disturbed until they become overcrowded; then they are removed, and a few of the strongest tubers are replanted in fresh compost.

Propagation is by the division of the plants in October–November, or March–April.

SAGITTATE. A botanical term, derived from *sagitta,* an arrow, and used to describe leaves having blades shaped like an arrowhead.

SAGO PALM. The common name of a number of Palms and Cycads. See Metroxylon and Cycas.

SAHUARO. Carnegiea gigantea, which see.

ST. ANDREW'S CROSS. Ascyrum hypericoides, which see.

ST. AUGUSTINE GRASS. Stenotaphrum secundatum, which see.

ST. BERNARD'S-LILY. Anthericum Liliago, which see.

ST. BRUNO'S-LILY. See Paradisea.

ST. DABOEC'S-HEATH. See Daboëcia.

ST. JOHN'S-BREAD. Ceratonia Siliqua, which see.

ST. JOHN'S-WORT. See Hypericum.

ST. JOSEPH'S-LILY. See Hippeastrum Johnsonii.

SAINTPAULIA—*African Violet* (Saintpaul'-ia). Tender, flowering plants which were introduced into cultivation from central Africa in 1894. They form rosettes of leaves close to the soil, the leaves being ovate or almost round, deep green, fleshy and hairy on the upper surface. The undersides of the leaves are greenish-

A single-flowered African Violet, Saintpaulia ionantha.

white and the leafstalks are hairy and succulent.

The flowers resemble large Violets in shape and color, and have conspicuous yellow stamens. They may be had in bloom at any season of the year. These plants, which belong to the Gesneriaceae, the same family the Gloxinia belongs to, were named after Baron Von Saint Paul-Illaire, the discoverer of the plant. In recent years they have become very popular as house plants, and numerous varieties have been raised and named.

For a Warm Greenhouse. These dainty and compact plants require a minimum temperature of 55-60 degrees, and a soil compost of equal parts of loam, leaf mold and peat moss, with sand added. Although they are perennial, young plants are generally raised annually in spring

African Violets, Saintpaulias, are favorite house plants.

Varieties of African Violets that bear double flowers are especially charming. The flowers of this one are pale blue.

The leaves are cut from a healthy African Violet plant for use as leaf cuttings.

The leaf cuttings are planted with their stems in a mixture of peat moss and sand or some other suitable rooting medium.

If kept in a humid warm atmosphere, the leaves develop roots and new shoots from the bases of their leafstalks.

When new growth is well started, the young plants are potted individually in a loose soil mixture.

The soil is pressed loosely about the roots and the newly potted plants are then watered with a fine spray.

Under favorable conditions the rooted leaf cutting soon develops into a sturdy new plant.

from seeds or leaf cuttings, or by plant division.

Taking Leaf Cuttings. The most popular method of propagation is by leaf cuttings. Mature leaves are detached with the leafstalks intact, and dibbled in a well-drained pan filled with sand, a mixture of sand and peat moss, or vermiculite. They are watered and placed in a propagating case in a warm greenhouse in a terrarium, or under a bell jar or an inverted Mason jar. They are shaded from direct sunshine and are kept moist and close, being ventilated only sufficiently to prevent moisture from collecting on the inside of the glass. When roots are formed, and young shoots appear above the soil, the plants are potted in small pots and, when well rooted, in 4-in. pots in which they will bloom.

Raising Seedlings. From seeds sown in Febru-ary, plants are obtained which begin to bloom in late summer. The seeds are sown in a well-drained pot filled with finely sifted compost. Being extremely fine, the seeds are not covered with soil; a sprinkling of sand is sufficient. A pane of glass is laid over the pot, which is then set in a propagating case, temperature 60-70 degrees, and is shaded from direct sunshine.

As soon as the seedlings are large enough to handle, they are transplanted, being set 1 in. apart in a well-drained pan of finely sifted soil. In their early stages the seedlings require careful watering to prevent them from damping off (a diseased condition). As soon as they show signs of overcrowding, they are potted separately and treated as advised for plants raised from leaf cuttings.

Propagation by Division. A simple method of

African Violets can be divided by pulling apart the old plants in spring.

Each division is potted individually in a loose soil mixture that contains an abundance of organic matter.

obtaining a stock of young plants is by carefully dividing the old ones in spring. They are knocked out of their pots and pulled apart to form separate pieces, each with some roots attached; the divisions are planted individually in small pots.

Watering, Fertilizing and Shading. While young, the plants are watered moderately; when they are well-rooted, the soil is kept always evenly moist, and liquid fertilizer is applied once a week until the flowers open. After the plants have passed out of bloom they benefit from being partially rested by keeping the soil somewhat drier than normal. During this period the soil is watered only when it becomes nearly dry. From spring through early fall the plants need shade from bright sun, but for the remainder of the year no shading is required.

Syringing and wetting the foliage by other means are undesirable, but the atmosphere must be kept moist by damping the greenhouse floor and benches at suitable intervals.

As House Plants. During the last decade or so the popularity of African Violets as house plants has increased tremendously. Thousands of amateurs throughout North America cultivate these charming plants, and nursery greenhouses specializing in raising plants to supply the market are numerous.

A vigorous national society, the African Violet Society of America, Incorporated, has been formed to stimulate interest in the plants, to carry out research on them, and to disseminate information about them. A large number of local African Violet Clubs and African Violet Societies are affiliated with the national body.

Amateur interest exists chiefly in growing the plants, in exhibiting them at flower shows, and in raising new varieties. Hundreds and perhaps thousands of new varieties have been raised and named within the past few years, many by amateurs. These new kinds show great variation in flower color, form, foliage appearance, and habit.

African Violets, when grown in houses, seem to succeed under a wide variety of conditions. For the best results, good light, but with shade from strong sunshine, is necessary. A temperature of 60-70 degrees, an evenly moist soil, avoidance of wetting the foliage, and freedom from the baking, dry heat of a nearby radiator are other requirements.

It is not always easy to provide the desired atmospheric humidity in the house, but this may be appreciably increased in the vicinity of the plants by standing the pots on shallow trays filled with sand, cinders, gravel or moss kept constantly moist.

Under Artificial Light. Because African Violets thrive in subdued light, they are excellent subjects for cultivation under artificial illumination. They can be grown without difficulty without any daylight at all, and many amateur gardeners grow them successfully in basements.

Fluorescent light provided by daylight-type tubes suspended 12-15 in. above the growing plants and kept burning about 14 hours each day gives good results. Some little experimentation is

African Violets and other plants are grown in this dark basement under fluorescent light.

Under artificial light supplied by fluorescent bulbs African Violets thrive and bloom freely.

necessary to determine the best height for the source of light above the plants in any particular case; a difference of an inch or two often affects flowering. Trials with different period-lengths of illumination to be given each day should also be made; 14 hours daily is usually satisfactory, but longer or shorter periods may prove more satisfactory under some circumstances.

Plants grown in locations in the house where they receive insufficient natural light for their well-being will benefit from having this supplemented with artificial light.

Kinds of African Violets. The species, or kinds of African Violets that occur in the wild in their native country, are not many. Chief among them, and the first to be introduced to cultivation, is S. ionantha, which is sometimes called the Usambara Violet. This kind natively has violet-colored flowers, but in cultivation it has given rise to innumerable varieties and color forms. S. ionantha inhabits limestone cliffs at slight eleva-

tions above sea level in its native variety.

S. amaniensis is a trailing kind with violet flowers that grows at elevations of 3,000 ft. in the Usambara Mountains of East Africa. S. diplotricha has pale green leaves and blue or violet flowers. It grows at elevations of 1,000-3,000 ft. This is the plant that was formerly grown under the name S. kewensis. S. Grotei has shiny, nearly round leaves and pale violet-blue flowers. It produces long, trailing stems. S. magungensis is similar to S. Grotei but has violet-blue flowers of darker shade. S. pusilla is similar to S. ionantha but smaller in its parts. S. tongwensis resembles S. ionantha but has glossier leaves.

In addition to these wild species, there are a great many garden varieties, chiefly of S. ionantha. These have white, pink, lavender-blue, and violet flowers (but no yellow). The flowers are single or double. Some kinds with cream-variegated leaves are grown.

SAINTS. There are two patron saints of gardening and one saint (Maurille) who, though not a patron saint, was a gardener for at least part of his life.

Saint Phocas lived in the third century, and his retreat was near the city of Sinope, in Pontus. He divided his time between prayer and his garden, where he cultivated vegetables for the poor people of the district, and also grew flowers.

During a period of persecution, Phocas was visited by two strangers, to whom he offered hospitality. Before nightfall they told him that they were searching for one Phocas, a Christian, and that they had orders to kill him.

The saint said nothing, but went into his garden and dug himself a grave, prayed, and then, returning, told the strangers he was Phocas. They were horror-struck, but he told them to do as they had been ordered. They cut off his head and buried him among the flowers he had tended.

Saint Fiacre, the other patron saint, was an Irish prince who lived in the seventh century. He became a hermit and went to Gaul to preach to the heathen near the river Marne. First, he built himself an oratory (chapel) in the midst of a great forest, and near his oratory he made a garden. He was sought out by so many that he asked the bishop for more land, and the bishop told him he could have as much land as he could enclose in one day.

The saint, on his return, marked out far more than one man could enclose and prayed for help. By a miracle his plot was enclosed. A woman who observed this told the bishop that the saint had enclosed his garden with the help of the Evil One, and that she had seen it with her own eyes. The bishop visited Saint Fiacre, and a curse was put on any woman who ventured to come near his plot.

The belief in Saint Fiacre's curse persisted throughout the Middle Ages, and it is historical fact that when Anne of Austria visited Meaux in 1648, she declined to enter his chapel in the cathedral lest the curse should overtake her.

The Confraternity of Saint Fiacre used to hold their meetings at the house that formerly belonged to De la Quintinye, head of Louis XIV's vegetable gardens, and when carriages for hire were first established in Paris, they used to congregate outside this house. Hence French cabs are to this day called "fiacres," and Saint Fiacre is regarded as the patron saint of cab drivers as well as of gardeners.

Saint Maurille was a native of Milan, and studied under Saint Ambrose, a great religious figure of the fourth century. He accompanied Saint Martin to Tours and was ordained by the saint. The bishop of Angers sent Maurille to Chalons to preach to the heathen there, and ultimately Maurille became Bishop of Angers. Feeling this was too great an honor, he fled and took refuge in Britain. According to another version of the legend he was overwhelmed with grief because Saint René died without the chrism. He took the keys of the relics with him, but the powers of evil, the legend says, caused him to drop them overboard.

Maurille offered himself as a gardener to a British prince, but after a time a stranger visiting the court recognized him and, he was persuaded to return to Angers. Tradition does not say which British prince, but this would have been at the time the Roman legionaries were being withdrawn, a period about which there is little information.

Two scenes from this legend are depicted in one of the famous Angers tapestries, which date from the fifteenth century. There is an illustration from the tapestry which shows the saint working in his garden, and presenting the fruits of his labor to the prince and princess. To this day Saint Maurille is specially venerated in Anjou.

SALAD BURNET. Sanguisorba minor, which see.

SALICIFOLIA. A botanical term used in the description of plants that have leaves which resemble those of the Willow or Salix.

SALIX or WILLOW

Ornamental Trees and Shrubs for Moist Ground

Salix (Sa'lix). Numerous leaf-losing (deciduous) trees and shrubs are included in this genus. Most are hardy. They occur as natives in Europe, Asia, northern Africa, North America and, a few, in the Southern Hemisphere. Some grow wild in arctic and alpine regions. Salix belongs in the botanical family Salicaceae and is the old Latin name for a Willow.

Growth Habits and Foliage. Most Willows are fast growers and are comparatively short lived. Their young stems are pliant and strong and in some cases are used for basket making and as ties to bundle nursery plants together for shipping, but the wood of the older branches and trunks is soft and brittle and is very subject to breakage and storm damage.

Willows vary considerably in their habits of growth and the appearance of their foliage. Some are prostrate shrubs, others large bushes; some are trees of moderate size and of somewhat for-

The Weeping Willow, Salix babylonica, is a graceful tree especially suited for planting by the water side.

mal outline; others have pendent branches and are among the most graceful of all trees. Between the several extremes there are all sorts of intermediates.

Although the leaves vary a good deal in size and shape, those of most kinds are narrow in comparison to their length, the peculiarity being so characteristic that leaves of certain other plants are often referred to as willowlike. In some instances, however, they, are more broadly elliptical or ovate. There are two stipules (appendages) at the base of each leafstalk; these may be very small and fall early, as in Salix viminalis, or they may be well developed and remain in good condition throughout the greater part of summer, as in S. amygdalina.

Flowering Habits. The flowers of Willows are borne in compact catkins which are carried erectly on the branches and thus differ from those of the nearly related Poplars, which are in drooping catkins. Most Willows bloom in early spring before their leaves appear; a few flower later.

Male and female flowers are usually borne on different plants. The male catkins are more conspicuous than the female and are usually yellow when they mature, but in some kinds are reddish. The female flowers are usually green or gray-green. In a few instances male and female flowers are borne together on the same catkin. This phenomenon may sometimes be noticed in natural hybrids between S. Caprea and S. cinerea.

The seeds of many kinds ripen during late May and June. They are whitish in color, small, and sparingly produced among cottony fiber.

As Ornamentals. Very few of the 300 or more species of Willows and of the many hybrids between them are sufficiently decorative to plant in gardens, although a few kinds have attractive flowers and are worth growing for that reason, and some others have brightly colored twigs which are especially attractive during winter. Dwarf Willows are of interest for planting in rock gardens and several taller shrub and tree kinds are suitable for planting at the sides of lakes and streams. Those with weeping branches and those that have attractively colored bark are especially desirable for such waterside locations.

Because Willows have extensive root systems, they are well adapted for using to bind the banks of rivers and streams to prevent erosion, but this same character makes them unsuitable for planting near drains or septic tanks, where the roots may cause trouble by clogging pipes.

Culture of Willows

Willows are among the easiest of plants to grow. For the best results they require exposure to full sun.

Trees and Shrubs for Moist Ground. Willows thrive in a variety of soils, that of a moist, loamy character being particularly suitable. They do well in damp places, such as the banks

The Crack Willow, Salix fragilis, is naturalized in North America. It thrives near the sea. This specimen is located on Long Island, New York.

of lakes and streams, and are not harmed by occasional flooding. Many Willows will grow in marshy ground, but the best results cannot be expected by placing most kinds in permanently waterlogged land.

When Willow trees are planted for decorative purposes they should be widely spaced, and this is especially desirable with the kinds that have weeping branches. They should be set so far apart that there will be space between the trees at maturity; trees that are well isolated are more effective than those that are crowded. Willows of shrubby types may be planted closely together to form more or less dense colonies. Planting may be done in spring or fall.

Propagation is almost invariably by cuttings of ripened wood; the usual length of a cutting is 9-12 in., although cuttings 12 ft. or more in length may, in some cases, be used.

Division can be effected with some of the dwarf kinds, and plants are sometimes raised from seeds. Seeds, however, need care, and they must be sown in moist soil as soon as they are ripe, when germination will take place within a few days.

Cuttings may be made from the time the leaves fall until late winter. They are planted in nursery rows, the bush kinds about 6 in. apart in rows 12 in. from each other, the tree kinds 12 in. apart in rows 15-18 in. apart. They are set at such a depth that only the upper 3 in. shows above the ground.

Cuttings may be planted where the future trees are to grow. That is usually done when beds of Willows for basket-making purposes are formed, and tree kinds are often raised in this way when long cuttings are obtainable.

In England, the Cricket-bat Willow, S. alba variety calva (S. coerulea), is often raised from polelike cuttings, 12 ft. or more long, planted where the trees are to grow. Willow cuttings are very easy to root and young plants grow rapidly the first year; tree kinds may form shoots 6-9 ft. long.

Training and Transplanting. Each young plant of the tree kinds should be restricted to a single main shoot. All Willows raised in nursery beds should be transplanted at the end of the first season, and bush kinds may be cut back to within a bud or two of the base when replanted; this treatment will result in vigorous growth the following year. Tree kinds that have produced only a weak shoot may also be cut back to the base to encourage the development of a strong stem the following year.

Pruning. When Willows of bushy or shrubby types are overgrown, they may be cut down to the ground in spring and they will soon renew themselves by means of new shoots from their bases. The tree kinds require some annual attention to pruning while they are young. The object should be the gradual clearance of branches from the lower part of the trunk, the maintenance of a central leading shoot until the trees have attained their normal height, and the development of a shapely head of branches.

Pollard Willow Trees. These are often grown in Europe in fields along the margins of streams, the heads being cut off at about 8 ft. from the ground. Young erect shoots are formed which are removed at intervals of 4 or 5 years, according to the use to which the wood is to be put. Years ago much of this wood was used for charcoal; now it is used for making fences, crates and other purposes. The kinds most often planted for this purpose are the Crack Willow, S. fragilis, and the White Willow, S. alba.

Kinds of Willows

The Willows mentioned below are of most general interest. They are grouped according to their forms and uses.

Weeping Willows. These are good decorative trees with weeping branches. S. babylonica, the common Weeping Willow, a Chinese tree, often 25-35 ft. high, is of very graceful outline, with long, slender, wandlike branches clothed with dainty leaves. A female form is common in cultivation, but it has no value as a flowering tree. The variety ramulis-aureis has golden shoots; so also has the variety aurea, which indeed may be identical with variety ramulis-aureis.

S. blanda, also known as S. pendulina, the Wisconsin Weeping Willow, is a hardier and

rather more vigorous tree of very graceful outline. It is regarded as being a hybrid between S. babylonica and S. fragilis. A closely related and equally elegant and hardy kind is S. elegantissima, the Thurlow Weeping Willow, which may grow 40 ft. high. Another useful weeping kind is S. Matsudana pendula, from northern China and Korea.

The Golden Weeping Willow, S. alba tristis, is a very elegant weeping variety with bright golden yellow bark. It is beautiful at all seasons of the year, even when it is leafless.

Other Tree Willows. In addition to those Willows which are distinguished by their weeping habits of growth, other tall-growing kinds are of importance. Among the best of these are the following: The Crack Willow, S. fragilis, which makes a spreading tree up to 60 ft. high and is a native of Europe and Asia, naturalized in North America; S. alba, the White Willow, a native of Europe, Asia and northern Africa, which is naturalized in North America, has whitish leaves and attains a maximum height of about 75 ft.; S. pentandra, the Bay-leaved Willow, a native of Europe and northern Asia, which is naturalized in eastern North America, has conspicuous, dark green leaves, flowers in May and June and grows about 60 ft. high.

S. nigra, the Black Willow, is a graceful tree that occurs natively from New Brunswick to western Ontario, and southward to Florida and California. It attains heights of 30-60 ft.

S. Scouleriana is a handsome western North American tree that grows commonly from Alaska to California and New Mexico. It grows up to about 30 ft. high and bears attractive catkins in late winter or early spring.

A curious and interesting tree is S. Matsudana variety tortuosa, which has been whimsically called the Permanent Wave Tree. This variety is distinguished by having its branches and twigs twisted in spiraling fashion. It grows to a height of 30 ft. or so.

Pussy Willow is a name applied to more than one species of Salix. The true Pussy Willow is S. discolor, a native of eastern North America from Nova Scotia to Virginia and Missouri. A few-stemmed shrub or small tree, in nature it prefers wet soils, but under cultivation grows

The Pussy Willow, Salix discolor, a native of eastern North America, is a favorite for cutting for indoor decoration.

satisfactorily in any fairly good soil that is of average moistness. In early spring it produces its silky "pussies," which are the male catkins.

S. Caprea and S. cinerea provide shoots furnished with equally decorative male catkins, and these are the kinds that are often sold by florists in spring under the name of Pussy Willow. S. Caprea is more correctly known as the Goat Willow or Sallow, and S. cinerea is the Gray Willow. Both are natives of Europe, and the Gray Willow is also found in Asia.

S. Caprea is much like the American Pussy Willow, and grows as a tree about 25 ft. tall. Its variety pendula, known as the Kilmarnock Willow, has drooping, crooked branches. Its variety variegata has its leaves variegated with white.

S. cinerea is closely related to S. Caprea, and hybrids between the two species are common. A variety of S. cinerea named tricolor has leaves variegated with yellow and white and sometimes pink or red. S. cinerea and its variety are shrubs about 15 ft. tall.

S. Medemii grows to a height of about 12 ft. One of the earliest Willows to bloom, it is a beautiful kind for gardens but is rare in them.

For early bloom indoors, branches of these Pussy Willows may be cut and stood in containers of water in a sunny window in a warm room any time after the middle of January. In a very short time the "pussies" develop; they remain attrac-

tive while displayed for a considerable period.

Willows with Colored Twigs. The red- and yellow-stemmed kinds, S. alba variety vitellina, yellow, S. alba variety chermesina, red, and the one known as S. cardinalis, red, are excellent for grouping near water. Left unpruned, they grow to be sizable trees, but for the most colorful results they should be cut down to the ground each spring, and thus kept to a height of 4-5 ft. The color of the young stems is most vivid and persists all winter. Provided the ground is moderately moist, these Willows can be grown away from water, but they are seen to best advantage when associated in the landscape with water.

Attractive Dwarf Willows. S. Bockii is a graceful bush a few feet high, native to China. It bears very small leaves and flowers in October. A good rock-garden kind is the prostrate S. herbacea. The most dwarf forms of S. repens are rock-garden plants, as also is the stiff-branched S. lanata, which has large leaves covered with white down; it is called the Woolly Willow and is found in cold regions of northern Europe and Asia.

S. purpurea variety nana, sometimes called Dwarf Blueleaf Arctic Willow, is a low shrub with gray blue-green leaves. It stands clipping well and may be used as a low, formal hedge.

Basket Willows. A large number of named varieties of Willows are grown abroad and to a lesser extent in North America for basket making, but most of them can be traced to a few species. The most important are S. amygdalina, the Almond-leaved Willow, a native of Europe and Asia, which, if unpruned, grows into a tree 30 ft. tall; S. purpurea, the Purple Osier, a native of Europe, Asia and northern Africa, forming a shrub 8-9 ft. high; and S. viminalis, the Common Osier, a native of Europe and Asia, naturalized in eastern North America, which, when unpruned, grows 30 ft. high.

SALLOW. Salix Caprea, which see.

SALMONBERRY. See Rubus spectabilis.

SALPICHROA RHOMBOIDEA (Salpichro'-a). A climbing representative of a group of South American shrubs, subshrubs and herbaceous plants that is planted to some extent in southern California and similar mild climates. It belongs to the Nightshade family, Solanaceae. Its name is derived from *salpinx,* a tube, and *chroos,* skin, and refers to the form and texture of the flowers.

This plant grows rapidly and has tuberous roots. It is suitable for covering trellises and similar supports, and as a ground cover. Its small, white, edible berries are sold in Paraguay under the name of Cock's-Eggs. They are of inferior eating quality.

Salpichroa rhomboidea thrives in full sun and in a variety of soils, including those that are of the type known as alkali. It is usually propagated from cuttings but may also be raised from seeds. The plant is very susceptible to frost damage.

SALPIGLOSSIS SINUATA (Salpigloss'is). A handsome annual which reaches a height of 2-3 ft. and bears somewhat tube-shaped flowers, the petals expanding at the apex, in spring or summer, according to whether the plants are grown under glass or out of doors. It is a native of Chile and belongs to the Nightshade family, Solanaceae. The name is derived from *salpinx,* a tube, and *glossa,* a tongue, and refers to the shape of the style of the flowers.

There are numerous varieties and strains of Salpiglossis bearing flowers which exhibit a wide range of coloring—purple, crimson, yellow, violet, blue and rose; the flowers of some varieties are marked with golden-yellow, which adds considerably to their beauty. They are among the

Salpiglossis, one of the most aristocratic of annual flowers.

most striking flowers of all garden annuals.

For Summer Flower Beds. To provide plants which will be ready to be set out of doors in May, seeds are sown in a flat of light soil early in March, in a greenhouse having a temperature of 55-60 degrees. The soil is kept moist and shaded, and covered with glass to ensure satisfactory germination of the seeds. Before the seedlings become crowded, they should be transplanted, either singly in 3-in. pots, or 2 in. apart in flats 4 in. deep filled with a compost of loam, two thirds, and leaf mold, one third, with a scattering of sand.

The seedlings must be kept in a warm greenhouse until well established after the transplantation, and subsequently be hardened off in a cold frame for planting out of doors when danger of frost is over. They should be set 10-12 in. apart. A sunny and fairly sheltered position must be chosen for them, and the stems need supporting by thin sticks to prevent their being damaged in windy weather. They will be in full beauty during July and August.

Seed may also be sown directly outdoors in a finely prepared bed of soil in spring, and the young plants thinned to 6-9 in. apart. They do not thrive in very hot summer weather.

For the Greenhouse. The Salpiglossis makes an admirable plant for the decoration of the greenhouse and conservatory in the spring and early summer months and for using as a cut flower. To provide plants for this purpose, seeds are sown towards the end of August or early in September, in the way already described. When the seedlings are 2 in. or so high, they should be potted separately in 3-in. pots of loam, leaf mold and sand. During the winter months they must be safe from frost, but it is unwise to grow them in a high temperature or the plants will become weak and will not bloom satisfactorily.

A minimum winter temperature of 45-50 degrees at night is high enough. In early spring, when the plants are well rooted in the small pots, they should be repotted in 5-in. or 6-in. pots, in which they will bloom in April and May. The compost for the final potting consists of loam, two thirds, with leaf mold, humus or peat moss and thoroughly decayed manure, one third. When the flower buds are developing, the plants

[11—8]
Scarlet Sage
(Salvia splendens)

[11—8a]
Salpiglossis

[11—9]
Weeping Willow
(Salix babylonica)

[11—9a]
Umbrella Pine
(Sciadopitys verticillata)

A bed of Salpiglossis in early summer.

may be placed in a higher temperature to advance their flowering and thus provide a succession of bloom.

If Salpiglossis is grown for cutting, good results may be had by transplanting the young plants from 3-in. pots to soil-filled benches or beds, spacing them 8-12 in. apart.

Under glass, Salpiglossis will reach a height of 4-6 ft.; out of doors, it grows 2-3 ft. high. Seeds can be purchased of a dwarf type of which the plants do not grow more than 15 in. high.

SALSAFY. See Salsify.

SALSIFY. A vegetable grown for the sake of its roots, which are in season in winter. Its botanical name is Tragopogon porrifolius. This plant grows wild in Europe, and is naturalized in parts of North America. The name is sometimes spelled Salsafy. It is commonly called the Vegetable Oyster because of its fleshy roots.

Salsify is of simple cultivation. It is a hardy biennial; that is to say, it will flower in the year following that in which seeds are sown. The flowers are of rose or purplish shade of color. It belongs to the Daisy family, Compositae.

The gardener is concerned only with the edible roots; these are long, rather narrow, white

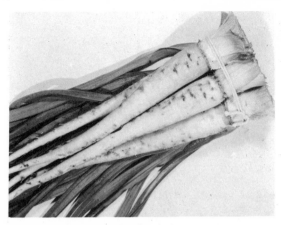

Roots of Salsify or Vegetable Oyster, an excellent root crop of simple cultivation.

and fleshy, and provide a welcome change from the commoner kinds of winter root vegetables.

When to Sow Seeds. Salsify is raised from seeds every year. It should be grown on land that has been deeply prepared and is free from fresh manure or lumps which would interfere with the development of the roots. The seeds are sown in early spring in drills about ½ in. deep. They should be scattered thinly, for the seedlings must eventually be thinned out until they are about 10 in. apart. The rows should be 12-15 in. from each other.

During the summer months the only attention required is to thin out the seedlings gradually until those remaining are at the correct distance from each other, and to cultivate the soil frequently to keep down weeds and to stimulate the growth of the plants.

The roots will be ready for use in late autumn and winter. When the leaves have changed color, and before the ground freezes hard, the roots may be lifted and stored. The best method of storing, where winters are not very severe, is to set the roots at the foot of a wall or fence and cover them with fine soil or sand, these materials and the roots being set in alternate layers. Where severe winters occur, the roots should be stored in a root cellar.

SALT HAY. This is hay made from grasses that inhabit salt marshes. It is a valuable material for using as a winter protective mulch on garden plants, and also as a mulch for Strawberries, to prevent the berries from becoming soiled by rain-splashed earth. It is easily removed after it has served its purpose.

This hay's particular virtues for these purposes are due to the fact that it is firm-stemmed and does not mat down or rot so quickly as ordinary hay or straw, and also to the fact that it is free of weed seeds that will grow in ordinary, non-saline garden soils.

SALT MARSH HAY. The same as salt hay, which see.

SALT TREE. See Halimodendron.

SALVIA OR SAGE, TENDER AND HARDY PLANTS FOR GREENHOUSE AND GARDEN

Salvia (Sal'via). A large and important group of hardy and tender perennials, annuals and shrubs, some of which are of great decorative value in the garden. Many of them are wild in South America, others are found in southern Europe, northern Africa and North America. Salvia belongs to the family Labiatae. The name is derived from *salveo,* to save, and refers to the medicinal value the plants were considered to possess.

Some Salvias are very handsome tender perennials valued for filling summer flower beds and for growing in greenhouses; others are hardy herbaceous perennials suitable for planting in borders, and one is a hardy annual. The common Sage, S. officinalis, a well-known herb, is dealt with under Sage, which see.

Tender Salvias

Of the tender kinds, the favorite is the Scarlet Sage, S. splendens, which is much used in summer flower beds, window boxes, porch boxes and for similar purposes. S. leucantha is an attractive winter-flowering kind, useful for growing in cool greenhouses and for outdoor cultivation in very mild climates, and S. farinacea is much grown to produce summer bloom outdoors. The best time to set them outdoors is after the weather is warm and settled, about the time it is safe to plant Tomatoes. The plants may be spaced 12-18 in. apart.

Taking Cuttings of Scarlet Sage. The Scarlet Sage may be propagated by cuttings taken in late summer or fall. The cuttings are inserted in a bed of sand or vermiculite in a greenhouse or cold frame, shaded during bright sunshine and watered with a fine spray. Subsequent watering should be sufficient to keep the rooting medium moderately moist. As soon as the cuttings are well rooted they are potted separately in 2½-in. or 3-in. pots in a porous soil mixture and are kept over winter in a greenhouse in which a minimum temperature of about 50 degrees is maintained. When the young plants are 3-5 in. tall, their tips are pinched out to induce branching. In February or March the plants are potted in 5-in. pots. They are kept growing in a sunny location in the greenhouse until shortly before they are to be planted outdoors, and are then placed in a cold frame to be hardened off for a week or two preparatory to being planted in their flowering locations.

Raising the Scarlet Sage from Seeds. Most commonly the Scarlet Sage is raised from seeds sown in a greenhouse in February or March, in a temperature of 60 degrees. The seedlings are transplanted in flats or individually in small pots. Subsequently, if necessary, they are re-

potted in pots 4-5 in. in diameter. Later they are hardened off as recommended above for plants raised from cuttings.

Scarlet Sage for Winter Bloom. This plant may be had in bloom in pots in winter in a sunny greenhouse where a minimum temperature of 55-60 degrees is maintained. For this purpose cuttings should be taken during June or July. Through the summer the plants are grown in a cold frame or are plunged (buried) to the rims of their pots in a bed of sand or ashes outdoors. The shoots are pinched occasionally to make them branch and all flower buds which form during summer should be picked off before they open. The plants may eventually occupy 6-in. or 7-in. pots. As soon as the pots in which they are to flower are filled with roots, weekly applications of dilute liquid fertilizer should be given.

Salvia Dorisiana, a native of Honduras, is one of the loveliest of tender kinds. It has very large pink flowers.

The **Gentian Sage,** S. patens, is a tender tuberous-rooted perennial; it reaches a height of 18-24 in. and bears in summer flowers of exquisite blue coloring. This kind is well suited for growing only where summers are comparatively cool. The tuberous roots, which are stored in a dormant condition over winter, are started into growth in March in a greenhouse having a temperature of 50 degrees. They are set separately in 3-in. pots of sandy soil. They must be watered carefully until leaf growth is seen, then more freely. The plants are kept in a cool, sunny

The Scarlet Sage, Salvia splendens, can be grown in pots to provide winter bloom.

greenhouse until all danger from frost is past, and then, after being hardened off in a cold frame, are set out of doors.

This Sage needs a sunny position and well-drained soil. It blooms from July to the first frost. When, in late autumn, the leaves change color, the plants are lifted and laid in the greenhouse for a few days to dry. The dead stems and leaves are then removed and the tubers are stored in sand in a cool frostproof place for the winter. In mild climates the roots may be left in the ground over winter.

Taking Cuttings of Gentian Sage. This Sage can be propagated by taking cuttings of the young shoots in early summer; the cuttings should be about 3 in. long; they are inserted in a greenhouse or cold frame which is kept close until the cuttings have formed roots. The sand or vermiculite in which the cuttings are planted should be kept moist but not wet, and shade from sunshine is necessary. When the cuttings are well rooted, they should be potted separately in small pots of soil, and subsequently planted out of doors.

Raising the Gentian Sage from Seeds. S. patens is easily raised from seeds. These may be sown in a greenhouse in February or early March, in a temperature of 50-55 degrees. The seedlings are transplanted to flats or small pots and are later planted outdoors, to bloom in summer.

The Pineapple-scented Sage, S. rutilans, is a shrubby kind which has fragrant pineapple-scented leaves and bears small scarlet flowers chiefly in summer. It is suitable for permanent planting outdoors where little or no winter frost is experienced, and for cultivation in a greenhouse or as a window plant. Plants of this kind may be had in bloom in a 50-degree greenhouse in December from cuttings taken in mid-May and repotted until they occupy 6-in. pots, without pinching the plants at any time.

S. Grahamii (S. microphylla) is a beautiful shrubby kind, 2-3 ft. high, which is suitable for planting out of doors in mild climates, in a warm sunny corner in well-drained soil. It reaches a height of about 3 ft. and bears flowers of rose-scarlet color in summer. It is a native of Mexico and requires the same culture as S. rutilans.

S. Greggii, a native of Texas and Mexico, attains a height of 1-3 ft. and bears spikes of red or purplish red flowers in summer. It requires the same culture as S. rutilans.

The Texas Sage, S. coccinea, native from South Carolina to Florida and Texas, grows to about 2 ft. high and has scarlet flowers 1 in. long. It is easily raised from seeds sown indoors in spring. The young plants are set in the open garden when the weather is warm and settled.

S. farinacea, sometimes called the Mealycup Sage, is a great favorite. Although a tender perennial, it is most commonly cultivated as an annual, except in mild climates, where it persists over winter outdoors.

This Salvia is a native of Texas. It grows 2-4 ft. high, branches freely and in summer and fall bears an abundance of slender, erect spikes of blue-purple or violet-colored flowers, each of which has a conspicuous white-mealy calyx.

The plants are easily raised from seeds sown in a greenhouse in a temperature of 55-60 degrees in February or March, and the seedlings are transplanted 2 in. apart in flats of porous soil. They are grown in full sun in a minimum night temperature of 50 degrees and are planted outdoors as soon as all danger of frost is past. They need a sunny location and any ordinary well-drained soil. They succeed well in dryish soils, and may be spaced 10-15 in. apart. As they grow, they need staking to prevent them from being damaged by summer storms.

This Salvia may also be raised by sowing seed directly outdoors as soon as the soil has warmed up in spring. A variety called Blue Bedder is dwarfer and more compact than the typical kind. In variety alba, the flowers are white.

For Fall and Winter Bloom. S. leucantha is a favorite kind for growing in cool greenhouses to provide pot plants to flower in fall and winter. It is a native of Mexico, of shrubby habit, 2-4 ft. high, and bears slender, erect spikes of small flowers, the conspicuous parts of which are the densely hairy lavender or violet-colored calices rather than the insignificant white petals.

This Salvia is propagated by cuttings planted in a bed of sand or vermiculite in a shaded location in a cool greenhouse from February to June. The cuttings are transplanted individually to small pots of sandy soil as soon as they are well rooted. Later the young plants are repotted in larger containers, and usually a third transfer to a larger pot is desirable. Plants raised from cuttings rooted early in the season may be flowered in 8-10 in. pots; those rooted later, in pots of 5-7 in. diameter.

S. leucantha requires essentially the same culture as the Chrysanthemum (which see), but the plants are not disbudded. Except during the time that the cuttings are rooting, exposure to full sun is important. The plants should be pinched occasionally until late July to induce bushiness. A rich, loamy soil suits this plant well, and after the final pots are filled with roots the application, once or twice a week, of dilute liquid fertilizer is highly beneficial. Good drainage is essential, but at no time must the soil be allowed to become dry.

The minimum greenhouse temperature is 45-50 degrees. On all favorable occasions the greenhouse should be ventilated freely.

A New Salvia. One of the most magnificent of tender Salvias is a newcomer from Honduras which was first described and named in 1950. Salvia Dorisiana is its name and it promises to be a fine addition to the winter and spring-blooming plants that are grown in pots in greenhouses and permanently out of doors in frostfree and nearly frostfree climates. Salvia Dorisiana is an herbaceous or subshrubby kind that has very large, rich rose-pink flowers. It can be propagated by seeds and by cuttings without difficulty and requires the same care as the Scarlet Sage, Salvia splendens.

Hardy Kinds

Of the many herbaceous Salvias that are hardy, several are very ornamental plants well worthy of being cultivated in gardens. They are chiefly suitable for perennial borders and for use in naturalistic plantings. Most are perennials, a few are biennials.

Cultural Requirements. These plants thrive best in well-drained, loamy soil and need a sunny location. In heavy clayey soil they are apt to perish during the winter months. Such soil can be made more suitable for them by spading deeply and mixing in liberal amounts of organic matter, such as decayed manure, compost or humus and some sand or coal ashes. On heavy land, planting should be done in spring. On light land, the plants may be put in during early autumn.

Propagation can be done by lifting and dividing the plants into rooted pieces in October or in early spring, by taking cuttings in early summer, and by sowing seeds. It is, however, unwise to disturb Salvias unnecessarily; they do best when left alone, and are slow to recover after transplanting.

Taking Cuttings. Cuttings will form roots if set in a bed of sand packed firm in a frame kept close, or covered with a bell jar. They should be taken when the fresh shoots are 3-4 in. long in early summer.

Raising Seedlings. Seeds may be sown in a greenhouse or frame, in spring; they are sown in a pot or flat containing a porous seed soil, kept moist and shaded, and covered with a piece of glass until germination has taken place. When the seedlings are about 2 in. high, they should be set in a nursery border, 6 in. apart; there they will remain until they are large enough to be planted permanently. They may also be raised from seeds sown in a bed of fine soil in a cold frame or outdoors in May.

The Best Hardy Salvias. S. azurea is native from South Carolina to Florida and Texas. It grows 3-4 ft. tall and in summer bears attractive blue, or more rarely white, flowers in racemes (spikes). The plant usually grown in gardens as S. azurea is S. Pitcheri.

S. Jurisicii, a perennial, is a native of the Balkans, grows 9-15 in. high and has semi-procumbent hairy stems and finely divided leaves that are covered with white hairs on their undersurfaces. The lavender-blue flowers are borne in long, erect racemes (spikes) in June. This is a pretty plant, well suited for planting in sunny, well-drained locations in rock gardens. Its white-flowered variety alba is very fine.

S. Pitcheri (S. azurea grandiflora) is a beautiful perennial plant, a native of the central United States, which reaches a height of 4 ft. and bears long racemes (spikes) of exquisite blue flowers in September. It must have well-drained soil and should be planted in a sunny position.

S. pratensis, a European plant, grows 2-2½ ft. high, and bears purple flowers; it is suitable for planting towards the front of the perennial border. There are several varieties with white, pink and deep purple flowers. It is a perennial.

S. Sclarea, Clary, and its variety turkestanica are vigorous plants, among the most attractive of the hardy kinds, with bold leaves and white or pinkish flowers. Their display value is increased by the pink and white leafy bracts that accompany the flowers. They are biennials and need to be raised fresh each year from seeds sown in May. Clary grows 4 ft. tall and is a handsome plant for grouping in borders.

S. uliginosa, a perennial kind that reaches a height of 4 ft., bears rich blue flowers in August–September. It needs well-drained soil and a warm, sunny position. This Salvia is a native of South America.

One of the loveliest of all the hardy Sages is S. haematodes, a short-lived perennial, about 3 ft. tall, producing whorled spikes of blue-violet flowers with great freedom throughout summer. It is a native of Greece.

S. superba, wrongly named S. nemorosa and S. virgata nemosa, is one of the best of the hardy Sages; it thrives in ordinary well-drained soil, is

Salvia leucantha is often cultivated as a pot plant. It blooms in late fall and winter.

perfectly hardy, grows to a height of about 3 ft., and bears a profusion of purple flowers accompanied by reddish bracts. A well-grown plant is very handsome, and provides brilliant color in the herbaceous border in July and August. This Salvia is supposedly of hybrid origin.

A Beautiful Hardy Annual

The annual Sage, S. Horminum, is a charming hardy plant which is grown for the sake of its colored bracts, the true flowers being small and inconspicuous. There are several varieties, and these differ in the colors of their bracts, which are rose-pink, purple, purple-blue or white. The most striking, called Blue Beard, has violet-blue bracts. This species is a native of the Mediterranean region.

These plants make a pretty display in the summer and early autumn months. They are raised from seeds sown out of doors in April in the position where the plants are to grow; the seedlings are thinned out to 6 in. apart. Alternatively, they may be raised from seeds sown indoors in early spring and grown in flats until it is time to plant them in the garden. They reach a height of 18-24 in.

S. farinacea and S. splendens, (see under Tender Salvias, above) are often cultivated as annuals, although actually they are tender perennials.

SALVINIA (Salvin'ia). Tender aquatic plants which float on the surface of the water. They have slender stems bearing leaves in threes. Two of the leaves are ovate, ½ in. in diameter, light green, and covered with fine whitish hairs, and the other, submerged and colorless, consists of a large number of fine rootlike fibres.

The spores are borne on special bodies called sporocarps, which are found on the submerged leaves, and give rise to two kinds of spores. These fall to the mud below, germinate, and give rise to male and female organs. The latter, when fertilized by the males, produce fresh plants.

The Salvinias, which are closely related to the Ferns and belong to the family Salvinaceae, are natives of the tropics, and were named in honor of Antonio Salvini, an Italian botanist of the

The Rain Tree or Monkeypod Tree, Samanea Saman.

eighteenth century. They are of little horticultural value, but are sometimes grown in small tanks or aquaria in a warm greenhouse.

They do best in an acid medium. A few inches of peat or decayed leaf mold is placed at the bottom of the tank, which is then filled with rain water and set in the greenhouse. After a period has been allowed for all sediment to settle, the small plants are laid on the surface of the water. No further attention is required, except that the water must be replenished as it evaporates; when growth becomes unsatisfactory, the tank is cleared out and replenished with fresh compost.

The chief kind is S. auriculata (often grown as S. natans), a spore-bearing, floating aquatic that is a native of South America.

SAMANEA SAMAN—*Rain Tree, Monkeypod, Saman, Zaman* (Samane'a; Saman'ea). This member of a group of tropical American trees and shrubs is grown in southern Florida and is popular in the tropics as a shade tree. It belongs to the Pea family, Leguminosae. Its name is a modification of the Spanish name for this tree, Zaman. It is sometimes called Pithecellobium or Inga Saman.

Samanea Saman forms a very wide-spreading specimen and reaches a maximum height of 60-80 ft. It is a rapid grower. Its leaves are twice or thrice divided and its ball-like clusters of yellow flowers, with light red stamens, are followed by long pods which contain seeds that are enclosed in pulp. This pulp is rich in sugar, and the pods are eagerly eaten by cattle and horses.

The name Rain Tree refers to the fact that the leaves fold at the approach of cloudy weather and at night. This is a response to diminished light rather than to any other factor that is connected with the coming of rain.

Samanea Saman grows in a variety of soils, including sands, without difficulty or special care. It is propagated by seeds. In moist climates it is apt to become top-heavy with age and it characteristically produces a large expanse of spreading surface roots.

SAMBUCUS—*Elderberry* (Sambu'cus). Chiefly leaf-losing hardy shrubs or small trees, though one or two kinds are of herbaceous habit of growth. They are natives of Europe, Asia and North America, and are distinguished by rather coarse, opposite, pinnate leaves, large heads of usually white or cream-colored flowers, and small black, bluish or red fruits.

Leaves and flowers are accompanied by a rather disagreeable odor, although that from the leaves is not noticed until the leaves are bruised. The young strong shoots contain a large amount of pith, but the wood of old plants is hard and compact. The varieties with finely cut or variegated leaves are most suitable for decorative planting.

Sambucus belongs to the Honeysuckle family, Caprifoliaceae, and the name is said to be derived from an old type of musical instrument known as Sambuca. The vigorous young shoots from which the pith has been extracted are still sometimes used for whistles, and Italian peasants are said to make a musical instrument called a zampogna from the shoots.

Propagation of the wild species of Sambucus may be effected by means of cuttings but is best carried out by means of seeds sown as soon as ripe in pots or flats of loamy soil placed in a greenhouse or cold frame. The young plants, if set out in nursery rows, grow large enough for permanent planting in the course of one summer. Varieties of species, which cannot be increased by means of seed, can be increased by cuttings of firm shoots, 9-12 in. long, set in a cold frame or in a sheltered border out of doors in fall.

As a Windbreak Shrub. All the Elderberries thrive in ordinary garden soil. The common Elderberry, Sambucus canadensis, grows well almost anywhere; as a windbreak, it does well even when exposed to strong sea winds. A good point about the plant is that it succeeds in sun as well as shade.

Pruning. There are varieties with golden leaves. These do well only in good soil, and the color is often most satisfactory when the growths are cut well back each year in early spring. This results in the development of vigorous young shoots that produce fine and well-colored leaves. Other bushes do not need regular pruning but, when overgrown, they may be cut back in winter or spring.

The fruits of the Elderberries are used for making Elderberry syrup, wine and pies, and the flowers are also used for making wine. The American Elderberry, S. canadensis, is sometimes cultivated for its fruit. (See Elderberry.)

The bruised leaves of Elderberries were once used in summer for keeping away flies.

The European Elderberry, S. nigra, is a shrub or small tree 15-25 ft. high, with a considerable

Sambucus nigra, the European Elderberry. Leaf, flower and fruit are also shown.

spread of branches. It is common in woods and on banks, where it is very effective when in flower and fruit. Birds are very fond of the fruits, and these are soon taken after they are ripe. This shrub will often grow where others fail.

Varieties with Colored Leaves. There are several varieties of European Elderberry with distinctive names. Albo-variegata has white-margined leaves; in aureo-variegata the leaves are margined with yellow; in heterophylla the parts of the leaves are divided into fine segments; alba has whitish fruits; pendula has weeping branches, and pyramidalis has stiff, erect branches.

The European Red Elderberry, S. racemosa, is a very attractive shrub, 12 ft. high, in central and northern Europe. The flowers are white, in dense clusters, and are followed by bright red fruits. There are several attractive varieties, notably plumosa, with finely cut leaves; plumoso-aurea, with golden, finely cut leaves; and laciniata and tenuifolia, with much-divided leaf segments.

The Golden-leaved American Elderberry. S. canadensis variety aurea produces large and attractive golden leaves. This kind is often grown for color effect. It grows vigorously and gives little trouble.

S. pubens is a red-fruited kind native to North America, and S. Sieboldiana is a small tree or shrub, 15-18 ft. high, from China and Japan.

S. Ebulus, from Europe and the Orient, sometimes called Danewort, is the best-known of the herbaceous kinds. It is a vigorous, spreading plant, 3-4 ft. high, with coarse, dark green leaves and white flowers.

SAMOLUS — Water Pimpernel (Sam'olus). Dwarf, hardy, herbaceous perennials which belong to the Primula family, Primulaceae. One kind, S. Valerandi, a native of Europe, is sparingly naturalized in North America and is found growing in moist soil on waste ground. It forms a small rosette of obovate to oblong green leaves and bears a slender spike, 6-8 in. high, consisting of miniature white flowers, in late summer. It is not cultivated in gardens, as the flowers are inconspicuous.

A native American kind, S. floribundus, is a larger plant but has smaller flowers.

The Australian kind, S. repens, is sometimes grown as a rockery plant under the name of S. littoralis. This is a pretty, trailing plant with small evergreen leaves and tiny pink blossoms. It does best in a moist position at the base of the rockery.

Preparations for planting are made by taking out a hole to a depth of 1 ft. and filling it with sandy peat. No drainage is required, as this plant is found growing wild in boggy ground. Planting is done in spring, and the plants are watered freely in dry weather. Propagation is by division in April.

SAMPHIRE. This herb, seldom used now but popular in Shakespeare's day, is a European seaside plant found wild on cliffs; its leaves, because of their piquant flavor, are used in salads and pickles. It thrives best in seaside gardens, in warm, well-drained positions, and is raised from seed sown when ripe in autumn. It may also be propagated by division in spring.

This plant's botanical name is Crithmum maritimum. It belongs to the Parsley family, the Umbelliferae.

SAMUELA — *Date Yucca* (Samuel'a). Tall, yucca-like small trees belonging to the Lily family, Liliaceae. The name honors the American botanist Sam Farlow Trelease. The Date Yuccas are planted for ornament to some extent in the Southwest.

These plants are suitable for desert gardens, where they thrive under the same conditions as Cacti and other dry-climate plants. They are propagated by seeds.

Kinds cultivated include S. carnerosana, a native of Mexico that attains a height of 18 ft. and is usually unbranched. Its white flowers, borne in dense clusters, are each about 4 in. wide. Both they and the fruits are eaten by Mexicans. In Mexico this kind is known as Palma Samandoca.

S. Faxoniana forms a trunk to 15 ft. tall that often branches towards the top. It is a native of western Texas and bears white flowers, each about 4 in. wide, in large clusters.

SANCHEZIA NOBILIS (Sanche'zia). Tender shrubs and subshrubs with ornamental leaves and conspicuous flowers. They belong to the Acanthus family, Acanthaceae, and were named after

Sanchezia nobilis is a beautiful ornamental foliage plant that is suitable for planting outdoors in the far South and in greenhouses.

J. Sanchez, professor of botany at Cadiz, Spain.

Sanchezia nobilis is the only kind in general cultivation. It has woody, winged stems, oblong-ovate leaves, 6-9 in. in length, with crimson midribs, and bears large terminal panicles of yellow, tubular flowers in summer. The blooms are 2 in. long and are terminated by five rounded lobes. The variety glaucophylla has yellow-veined leaves. This plant is a native of Ecuador. It may be grown outdoors in the far South; it also is an attractive greenhouse plant.

Plants with Colored Leaves. Sanchezia is principally grown for its ornamental foliage and, as small plants in 5-in. pots are most useful for greenhouse decoration, it is usual to raise young plants annually from cuttings. The tops of the shoots are removed and prepared by trimming off the lower leaves and making a cut just below the bottom joint.

Propagation. Cuttings are inserted in a propagating case with bottom heat. They will soon form roots. The rooted cuttings are potted separately in 3-in. pots and later on in 5-in. pots. In these they remain for the first season and are used as ornamental foliage plants to decorate the greenhouse or house.

If desired, they can be "grown on" for several years to produce flowers, but after the first year or two they become bare at the base and straggling. Plants which are grown in pots or tubs to form large specimens are pruned fairly hard in March, to make them bushy. When new shoots appear, the plants are taken out of their pots, the masses of soil are slightly reduced, and the plants are then repotted in large pots. The best compost consists of equal parts of loam and peat, with one part of well-decayed manure and a scattering of sand.

Summer and Winter Treatment. The Sanchezia revels in abundance of heat and moisture. The minimum temperature of the greenhouse in winter should be 55 degrees. Damping the floor and benches and syringing the foliage should be done twice a day in summer and once a day in winter, and the leaves should be frequently sprayed to keep them free from insect pests.

During the summer months, when the plants are growing freely, the soil must be kept moist, and a weekly application of dilute liquid fertilizer assists them to make vigorous growth. Much less watering is required in winter, but the soil should not be allowed to become very dry. They should be shaded from bright sunlight in the summer.

SAND. In horticulture the word sand is generally used to denote loose granular rock of all kinds, in the form of small particles. Common sand, however, is entirely siliceous, and consists of quartz or silica, with feldspar, mica, and other mineral impurities. It is obtained from powdered rocks, seashores, river beds, valleys and great sand beds that must have been deposited in early geological history.

Sandy soils quickly lose all soluble plant foods, since the water which percolates through them so readily takes these foods away. For that reason it is not advisable to leave sandy soils long without a crop; this holds the plant foods. If no garden crop is required, sow down with Rape, Buckwheat, Rye Grass, or Winter Rye, to be dug in later; this changes the plant foods into herbage and prevents their loss. Sandy soils should be manured in spring.

In order to make them porous, sand is used in potting composts for plants grown in pots, tubs and flats and in greenhouse benches. The best sand to use is a gritty sand which is said to be "sharp." Ordinary washed sand, as used by builders, is found to answer very well if it feels "sharp" when rubbed between finger and thumb (see Sharp Sand).

Cuttings root readily in sand that is kept moist; as the sand is deficient in plant foods, however, the cuttings must be potted in a soil compost soon after roots are formed.

Seashore sand should be spread out to be washed by rain for a few weeks before being used in composts.

SAND CHERRY. Both Prunus Besseyi and P. pumila are known by the name of Sand Cherry. Prunus Besseyi, a Great Plains native, is a low, gracefully spreading shrub 3-4 ft. high, that bears heavy crops of cherry-like fruits. It has been improved by Great Plains fruit breeders and hybridized with Plum species, so that there are a number of Sand Cherries and hybrids that are useful fruits in that area where few other fruits will tolerate the harsh climate. The fruits of the Sand Cherry are inferior to those of the Sweet Cherries, and in humid regions the twigs and fruits are subject to brown rot disease.

Sand Cherries make good jelly, jam, sauce and pies, and the best varieties are fairly palatable for eating fresh.

Some of the improved varieties are Sioux, Brooks, and Black Beauty. Sand Cherry hybrids are Opata, Sapa, Zumbra, Compass, St. Anthony, Nicollet, Tom Thumb, Oka and others.

Propagation of the species is by seeds sown as soon as ripe. The varieties are budded on Sand Cherry seedlings.

Sand Cherries fruit better on poor, sandy soils than on fertile soils and do well on gravelly embankments. Pruning is limited to thinning out some of the older wood. See also Prunus.

SANDERSONIA AURANTIACA (Sanderson'ia). A tuberous-rooted, tender plant, from South Africa, which belongs to the Lily family, Liliaceae. The only kind, S. aurantiaca, forms a stem 2 ft. in height which is clothed with linear, sessile (stalkless), alternate leaves 3 in. in length. The flowers, which are borne singly in the axils of the leaves in July and August, are urn-shaped and about 1 in. in length. The name Sandersonia commemorates John Sanderson, a horticulturist of Natal.

For a Greenhouse. The tubers are potted in February. One tuber is set in a 5-in. pot, or several tubers are placed in a larger pot. The pots are well drained with crocks and half-filled with a compost of equal parts of peat, loam, and leaf mold, to which sand is added. The tubers are set in position and covered with 2 in. of the compost.

Very little water is given until the shoots appear, then the quantity is gradually increased, and when the plants are in full growth, liberal quantities of water are applied. As the flowering shoots elongate they should be tied lightly to canes.

After flowering, water is gradually withheld, and when the foliage has died down the pots are stored on their sides under the benches until potting time in spring.

The stock of plants is increased by removing the offsets at potting time. These are potted separately and "grown on" until they reach flowering size.

Sandersonia can be grown as a window-garden plant or out of doors in the same way as Gloriosa. (See Gloriosa.)

SAND LILY. Leucocrinum montanum, which see.

SAND MYRTLE. See Leiophyllum.

SAND PEAR. Pyrus pyrifolia, which see.

SAND PINK. See Dianthus arenarius.

SAND VERBENA. See Abronia.

SANDWORT. See Arenaria.

SANGUINARIA CANADENSIS—*Bloodroot* (Sanguina'ria). A dwarf, hardy, free-flowering perennial plant which is a native of eastern North America and is one of the prettiest of wild flowers. It belongs to the Poppy family, the Papaveraceae. Sanguinaria has a fleshy rootstock

Sanguinaria canadensis, the Bloodroot.

which contains a blood-red juice, hence the common name, Bloodroot. The flowers, which appear in early spring before the leaves unfold, are borne singly on slender stems, 6 in. in length, which rise straight from the rootstocks. They are poppy-like, 2 in. across, and white or tinged with pink. The leaves quickly follow the flowers and are heart-shaped, deeply divided at the margins, and tinged with red. The name Sanguinaria is derived from *sanguis,* blood, and refers to the color of the sap.

Will Thrive Beneath Trees. This pretty spring-flowering plant, which grows wild in the woodlands, is suitable for the front of the partially shaded border, for carpeting beneath deciduous trees, for rock gardens and woodland gardens. It will grow in ordinary garden soil, but does best in light sandy loam, and is planted in early fall or early spring.

After planting, the roots should not be disturbed for many years, as the plants flower best when firmly established. An occasional top-dressing of leaf mold, applied in spring, is sufficient to keep the plants growing vigorously.

Propagation is by taking up the roots in spring or in August and dividing them into small sections, each of which contains a few buds. The pieces are then planted separately in sandy soil containing an abundance of organic matter. Unless the primary object is to obtain as many plants as possible, it is best to leave the plants undisturbed and raise fresh ones from seed.

The seeds are sown in fall or in early spring in a well-drained pan filled with light soil that contains generous amounts of leaf mold. The pan is covered with a pane of glass and set in a shady part of a cold frame. The seedlings, when large enough, are planted in a bed in a cold frame or in a shaded nursery bed, 6 in. apart; there they remain until they are large enough to be planted in their permanent locations.

The only species is S. canadensis, 6-8 in., white, blooming in early spring. A beautiful double-flowered variety named multiplex is also cultivated.

SANGUISORBA—*Burnet, Japanese Bottle-Brush Flower* (Sanguisor'ba; Sangui'sorba). Hardy perennial and annual plants, few of which are of value in the garden. They are

The American Burnet, Sanguisorba canadensis, is a good plant for moist soils.

found wild in Europe, North America and Japan. Sanguisorba belongs to the Rose family, Rosaceae. The name is derived from *sanguis,* blood, and *sorbere,* to soak up, and refers to the plants' supposed styptic properties. A more commonly used name for this genus is Poterium.

The most decorative kind in the garden is Sanguisorba obtusa, a hardy herbaceous perennial from Japan, which reaches a height of 2-3 ft., has pinnate leaves, and bears curious bottle-brush-like inflorescences of rose-pink coloring which are in full beauty in July. It thrives in ordinary, well-cultivated garden soil in a sunny situation and needs no special treatment; it also looks well by the waterside, where it will reach its maximum height, when in bloom, of 3 ft. There is also a white-flowered variety, alba.

This is one of the most distinct of hardy herbaceous plants, but it is very leafy and takes up a good deal of room; for this reason it is scarcely suitable for planting in a small flower border, for the long leaves are likely to smother smaller neighboring plants. It is suitable for grouping in the less formal parts of the garden or even in open spaces among shrubs; it must be kept moist in dry weather.

The American Burnet is S. canadensis, a kind that grows in wet meadows, moist prairies and marshes from Labrador and Newfoundland westward to Manitoba and southward to North Carolina, Ohio and Indiana. It is a stout perennial, 5-6 ft. tall, with abundant leafage and whitish flowers in cylindrical heads. It blooms from July to September.

S. canadensis is worthy of a place in the mixed perennial border and is a good plant to use in wild gardening, being especially suitable for moist soils.

The Great Burnet, S. officinalis, is a native of Europe and Asia that is naturalized in North America and might be considered for planting in a wild garden. It grows to 3 ft. tall and resembles S. canadensis in habit of growth and foliage. The flower spikes are brownish-red.

The simplest method of propagation is by lifting the plants, separating them into rooted pieces, and replanting these where they are to be grown. Plants which are divided in autumn will yield a finer show of bloom the following year than others which are not dealt with until spring.

The Salad Burnet, S. minor (Poterium Sanguisorba), is occasionally grown for a supply of leaves which may be used, like Borage, in the preparation of claret cup and other cooling drinks, and for flavoring purposes. It is easily grown in well-drained garden soil and may be planted in autumn or spring. If an increased number of plants is required they are provided by lifting and dividing the old ones in early spring. It is usual to cut off the flowers, as they are of no value.

SANSEVIERIA — *Bowstring Hemp, Snake Plant* (Sansevie'ria). These ornamental-leaved, somewhat succulent, evergreen plants are natives of tropical Africa and of the East Indies. They are cultivated as greenhouse and house

Well-established plants of Sansevieria produce spikes of greenish-white, fragrant flowers.

Sansevieria tri-
fasciata variety
Laurentii, the Bow-
string Hemp, is
a popular house
plant because of
its handsome foli-
age.

plants. The principal kind, S. zeylanica, has a short, thick rhizome from which the leaves spring direct, in the same manner as those of the bearded Iris. The leaves are sword-shaped, 1-2 ft. in length, 2-3 in. broad, thick, fleshy and smooth, and variegated with grayish-white markings. The long, slender spikes of greenish-white flowers are actually of little decorative value

Sansevieria Hahnii is a popular dwarf, rosette-forming plant.

but provide a gentle and pleasant fragrance.

The leaves contain tough elastic fibers which were used by the ancient Hindus in making bowstrings, hence the common name. Mats and ropes are also made from the fibers of the plants.

Sansevieria belongs to the Lily family, Liliaceae, and was named in honor of Raimond de Sangrio, Prince of Sanseviero.

Pot Plants with Ornamental Leaves. Providing they are grown in a minimum winter temperature of 50 degrees or more, the cultural requirements of the plants are very simple. They are repotted every few years in spring or early summer. The pots should be exceptionally well drained, and a porous compost, consisting of two parts of loam and equal parts of leaf mold and sand, should be used.

Owing to their thick, leathery leaves, these plants are capable of withstanding dry atmospheric conditions, and they also withstand dry soil conditions for considerable periods. The best results are obtained by keeping the soil moist during the summer and only watering it in winter when it becomes quite dry. The plants require little shading.

Propagation by Division. Young plants are easily obtained by division. The old plants are removed from their pots in spring, and the rhizomes are severed into several portions, each containing one or more leaves.

Leaves and sections of leaves may also be inserted as cuttings. They are set in sand and plunged in a bottom-heated propagating case. Eventually young plants will form at the bases of the cuttings. These are potted separately in small pots.

It must be remembered that at least some of the kinds of Snake Plants which are variegated with vertical bands of yellow or cream, such as the popular S. trifasciata variety Laurentii, produce only plain green plants from leaf cuttings. To perpetuate and increase these variegated kinds it is necessary to propagate by division.

Kinds of Sansevieria. The number of species of Sansevieria in cultivation is not great but in recent years a number of horticultural varieties have been introduced and, because of the superior forms and appearance of many of these, they are becoming popular.

Among the kinds grown are S. arborea, a stemmed kind with dull-green leaves that have a white edge; S. cylindrica, a species with leaves that are 3-5 ft. long and round in section; S. Ehrenbergii, tall, leaves bluish with red and white penciled stripes on upper surfaces; S. Hahnii, a low, dense rosette of dark green leaves that have gray-green crossbands; S. Hahnii aureo-striata, a low rosette with 2 or 3 broad bands of yellow and several narrow, lengthwise yellow stripes; S. Kirkii, leaves to 6 ft. long and with wavy margins, grayish-green mottled with pale green; S. parva, stiff, spreading leaves 1-1½ ft. long; S. thyrsiflora, leaves to 1½ ft. long, flat and broad, margined with yellow; S. trifasciata variety Laurentii, the common Snake Plant, with erect green leaves that are mottled and horizontally banded with light green and are marked lengthwise with stripes of golden yellow; S. trifasciata variety Craigii, leaves with a narrow central band of green and broad marginal stripes of yellow; S. zeylanica, leaves similar to those of S. trifasciata variety Laurentii, but without the golden-yellow stripes.

SANTOLINA—*Lavender Cotton* (Santoli'na). A small group of hardy and nearly hardy shrub-like perennial plants which are natives of the south of Europe. They belong to the Daisy family, Compositae. The name is from *Sanctum linum,* holy flax, an earlier name for Santolina virens. Some of these shrubs have silvery gray

Santolina virens is a bright green-foliaged bush that bears heads of cream-colored flowers.

leaves; in summer they bear yellow or white flowers.

These plants thrive best in well-drained or rather light soil, and should be planted in a sunny position. They may be grown in a large rock garden, in a border at the foot of a sunny house wall, or in the form of a low hedge in the flower garden. They are improved by being pruned as soon as the flowers are over.

Propagation is by means of cuttings set in a cold frame in August. The frame must be kept close and shaded from bright sunshine for a few weeks until the cuttings are rooted. They should

The silvery-gray Santolina Chamaecyparissus is planted to form a sinuous pattern in this herb garden.

be potted separately in small pots, kept in the frame for the winter, and planted out of doors in spring.

The favorite and hardiest kind is Santolina Chamaecyparissus, which reaches a height of 18-24 in.; it has silvery gray leaves and in summer bears small yellow flowers. This shrubby plant makes a most attractive low hedge; when grown for that purpose, it is usual to cut off the flowers, for the charm of the hedge lies in the silvery foliage. The hedge should be pruned in August. The variety named nana, which is of dwarf, compact growth, is sometimes used in summer bedding.

Other kinds are S. neapolitana (rosmarinifolia), green leaves and yellow flowers, and S. virens, green leaves and cream-colored flowers.

SANVITALIA PROCUMBENS (Sanvital'ia). A hardy annual which grows wild in Mexico and belongs to the Daisy family, Compositae. The name commemorates an Italian family, Sanvitali. This pretty little plant grows only 6-8 in. high, and bears small, yellow, daisy-like flowers in summer. It is useful for sowing towards the front of the flower border, or may be used to fill spaces in the rock garden. It thrives best in a sunny place and in light or well-drained soil.

To provide flowers in early summer, seeds are sown, in mild climates, out of doors early in September, where the plants are to bloom; for a display from July onwards, and in severe climates, seeds are sown in early spring. The seedlings should be thinned out to 2-3 in. apart.

Sanvitalia procumbens is a low annual from Mexico that produces an abundance of small, yellow, daisylike blooms.

It is not advisable to try to transplant them.

Those raised from a sowing in September are not thinned finally until spring, for there are likely to be losses among them in the winter months. Seeds of a double-flowered variety can be purchased and they produce flowers that are decidedly pleasing.

SAPINDUS—*Soapberry* (Sapin'dus). Tropical and subtropical trees and shrubs, some of which are native to the South and some of which are grown there as ornamentals. They belong to the Sapindaceae or Soapberry family. The name is derived from *sapo-indicus,* Indian soap. This name refers to the fact that the fruits contain saponin and are used for washing purposes in some parts of the world.

The Soapberries grow well in rocky and sandy soils. They are propagated by seeds and by cuttings.

Kinds of Soapberry include S. Drummondii, 50 ft., a leaf-losing tree, native from Missouri to Mexico; S. marginatus, a leaf-losing tree, native from Florida to South America, 30 ft. high; S. Mukorossii, a native evergreen tree of Asia that is planted in southern Florida; S. Saponaria, a South American evergreen tree, to 30 ft. tall.

SAPIUM SEBIFERUM — *Chinese Tallow Tree, Vegetable Tallow* (Sap'ium). This member of a group of tropical trees and shrubs is a native of China and Japan that is both naturalized and is cultivated as an ornamental in the South. It is a member of the Euphorbiaceae or Spurge family. The name Sapium was applied by Pliny to a resinous Pine tree. Sapium sebiferum, which belongs to a family of plants completely different from Pliny's Pine, exudes a greasy sap.

The Chinese Tallow Tree grows 30-40 ft. tall and is useful as a shade tree and ornamental specimen. Its juice, like that of other kinds of Sapium, is poisonous. This tree grows in a variety of soils and is propagated by seeds and by cuttings.

In China and elsewhere the wax that covers the seeds of S. sebiferum is used for making candles and soap and for dressing cloth.

Other kinds of Sapium are good sources of rubber, certain of these being natives of South America. Some of the "Jumping Beans" are seeds of certain kinds of Sapium that contain insect grubs which supply the motive power that causes the beans to jump.

SAPODILLA. Sapota Achras, which see.

SAPONARIA — *Soapwort* (Saponar'ia). A group of free-flowering hardy annual and herbaceous perennial plants, most of which are natives of Europe. Saponaria officinalis, the Soapwort or Bouncing Bet, is found wild in western Asia and occurs plentifully in Europe, principally on waste ground, and near habitations, where it is thought to be an escape from cultivation. It is a common naturalized plant in North America.

Saponaria belongs to the Pink family, Caryophyllaceae. The plants are rather diverse in habit; some kinds have stout upright stems, 3 ft. in length, others creep along the ground or trail over rocks and a few are of a tufted growth. The name is derived from *sapo*, meaning soap. The bruised leaves produce a lather, like soap, when stirred in warm water.

The Double-flowered Bouncing Bet. S. officinalis flore-pleno, the double variety of the common Soapwort, is a late summer-flowering plant, suitable for a sunny or semishaded position in the perennial border, or in the front of a shrubbery. It is a hardy perennial, with semiwoody

Saponaria officinalis, flore-pleno, a double-flowered Bouncing Bet.

stems, alternate ovate-lanceolate leaves 3 in. in length, and bears large spreading spikes of double pink flowers. It is a showy plant, and lasts in flower for many weeks, but it is not popular for the mixed border, as it spreads so rapidly by means of its underground rhizomes.

Almost any kind of soil is suitable. Planting may be done in fall or spring, when the soil is sufficiently dry. As it has double flowers, it is propagated vegetatively, by means of pieces of rhizome, with a few buds attached.

For Summer Bedding. S. calabrica, deep rose, and its variety Scarlet Queen, scarlet, are ideal carpeting or bedding plants. These free-flowering annual or biennial plants grow 6 in. in height, are of tufted habit, and produce their small, star-shaped flowers in great profusion. The best results are produced by sowing the seeds in a deep seed pan in September. When 1 in. in height, the seedlings are transplanted to flats of sandy soil, and wintered in the cold frame. In May or early June they are planted as an edging or carpeting for the summer flower beds.

An Easily Grown Annual. The annual S. Vaccaria or Cowherb grows 2-3 ft. in height and produces graceful sprays of small pink flowers in great profusion. It is an easily grown kind. A European native, it is naturalized in North America. There is a variety of S. Vaccaria with white flowers.

To provide a succession of flowers outdoors, it is desirable, where conditions favor the procedure, to make two sowings, one in the autumn and the other in the spring, in a sunny position and light soil. The seeds are sown in irregular patches in the flower border, or in the garden for cut flowers, in early spring or, in mild climates, in fall. When 2 in. high, the seedlings are thinned to 6 in. apart. During dry weather the soil should be kept moist by watering.

Pot Plants for the Greenhouse. S. Vaccaria also makes an excellent pot plant. Five or six seedlings are placed in each 5-in. pot, filled with a light, fertile soil. Autumn-sown plants are grown in a cool, sunny greenhouse for blooming in late winter and spring.

For the Rock Garden. The Rock Soapwort, S. ocymoides, a hardy perennial, is a charming rock-garden plant, and also does well in a dry

[11—10]
Scilla pratensis

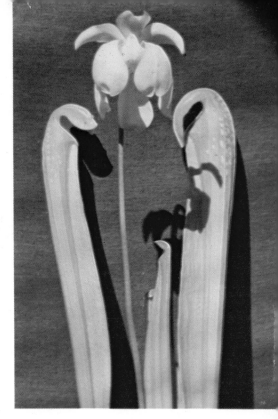

[11—10a]
Pitcher Plant
(Sarracenia)

[11—10b]
Figwort
(Scrophularia nodosa variegata)

[11—10c]
Schomburgkia

[11–11]
Sanvitalia procumbens

[11–11a]
Sedum compressum

[11–11b]
Sedum album

[11–11c]
Cobweb Houseleek
(Sempervivum arachnoideum)

wall. Its flowering is so profuse that the small ovate-lanceolate leaves are often hidden. There are several varieties, notably albiflora, white; splendens, deep rose; and versicolor, white, then pink. S. calabrica may also be grown in the rock garden.

Saponaria caespitosa, of tufted habit, with small linear leaves, and bearing clusters of rose-pink flowers from June to September, is a hardy perennial; so also is S. bellidifolia, which grows 4-8 in. high, has spathulate (spoon-shaped) leaves and terminal clusters of cream-white flowers. They require a sunny position, and a compost of sandy loam with which a liberal proportion of grit is incorporated. Planting may be done in fall or early spring.

Seeds are sown in pans of sandy compost in March or April. They are set in a warm greenhouse and the seedlings transplanted to flats of light soil. When established, they are hardened off in a cold frame, and planted in their permanent positions in autumn.

SAPROPHYTE. A plant which obtains all its nourishment from decaying matter; this may be of vegetable or animal origin. Saprophytic flowering plants usually have no green color in their leaves, and the leaves are mostly reduced to mere scales, so that the plants appear leafless.

The roots of these plants are generally covered by a fungus mycelium (fine cobweb-like growth). This is not harmful to the plant, but enables it to obtain nourishment from the decaying matter.

There are but few native flowering plants which are saprophytic: Monotropa, which belongs to the Heath family, Ericaceae, is represented by the Indian Pipe, M. uniflora, which is a succulent herbaceous plant, to 10 in. tall, waxy white or sometimes pink or red, that is found in rich woods in leaf mold; and the Pinesap, M. Hypopithys, a yellowish, brownish, pink or red plant that grows to a height of 1 ft. in moist or dry woods, usually in acid soil.

A Saprophytic Orchid. Coralroot, Corallorrhiza maculata, is a slender plant of light brown or purple-brown color. It grows in open woods. There are several other species of Corallorrhiza native to North America.

In addition to these saprophytic flowering plants, there are many saprophytic bacteria and fungi. These obtain their nourishment from decaying matter and assist in the process of decay. The rotting of leaves and manure is due chiefly to the action of saprophytic bacteria. They transform the substance in the manure and leaves into a form in which it can be used by the green-leaved plants.

The cultivated Mushroom is a saprophyte, as it obtains all its nourishment from decaying manure. The majority of Toadstools are also in the same class (an exception is the Honey Fungus, Armellaria mellia, which is often parasitic on Privet and other shrubs).

A few saprophytic fungi are also the causes of disease in plants. The Coral Spot fungus, which is found on dead Pea and Bean sticks, often affects dead branches on living trees. Once it has obtained a foothold on the tree it is capable of attacking the living portion.

SAPWOOD. A term used to describe the more recently formed wood of dicotyledonous trees. This wood is usually much lighter colored and softer than the wood nearer the center of the trunk, which is known as heartwood. The width of sapwood in a tree trunk in comparison to heartwood is greater in young than in old trees.

SARCANTHUS (Sarcanth'us). Most of the plants included in this group of epiphytal (tree-growing) Orchids are of botanical interest only. All are found wild in the Orient, chiefly in India and China. They vary considerably, but all are without pseudobulbs, and have erect stems with thick leaves arranged in opposite rows. The flowers are small and rather fleshy, and the lips terminate in short spurs. The majority are summer-flowering. The name is derived from the Greek sarkos, flesh, and anthos, a flower, and alludes to the substance of the flower.

Large plants are very rarely seen under cultivation. Small ones are best grown in pans suspended near the roof in a greenhouse with a tropical atmosphere in the summer and a winter temperature of 60 degrees. In summer, shading is required, and the plants may be watered freely. In winter, water must be given carefully. The potting compost may be osmunda fiber cut into small pieces, Tree Fern fiber, or Fir bark or Redwood bark. The best time to attend to repotting is in spring.

The following kinds, though small-flowered, are attractive: S. erinaceus, white, suffused with rose; S. Williamsonii, lilac-pink; and S. paniculatus, a strong-growing kind often mistaken for a Vanda, with many-flowered, branched panicles of dull yellowish-brown flowers.

SARCOCHILUS (Sarcochil'us; Sarcoch'ilus). Orchids which are found wild from northern India to Australia. All are epiphytes without pseudobulbs, and the greater number are evergreen. Some have attractive flowers; in other kinds the flowers are small and dull. The name is derived from the Greek *sarkos*, flesh, and *cheilos*, a lip, and refers to the fleshy lip.

These Orchids may be grown in cut osmunda fiber, in Tree Fern fiber, or in Fir bark or Redwood bark. S. luniferus and the other leaf-losing kinds should be placed on pieces of cork, the stronger-growing kinds in pots, and the smaller ones in pans. A tropical atmosphere suits the majority, and a winter temperature of about 60 degrees, but S. Fitzgeraldii and S. Hartmannii, two beautiful kinds from Australia, require careful shading, a moist atmosphere throughout the year, and not too high a temperature. For these a suitable corner can often be found in a tropical or subtropical house, the winter temperature being kept at about 60 degrees.

The following are the principal kinds. S. Hartmannii is dwarf-growing with narrow leaves and several-flowered racemes, the flowers being white marked with red. S. Fitzgeraldii has larger but fewer flowers, more densely spotted, and a yellowish front lobe to the lip. S. unguiculatus, from the Philippines, which resembles a Phalaenopsis when out of flower, produces a succession of cream-white flowers which only last a few hours.

SARCOCOCCA (Sarcococ'ca). Evergreen shrubs bearing small, fragrant, white flowers; several hardy kinds are found wild in western and central China and the Himalayas. Male and female flowers are in different parts of the same inflorescence, and the latter are succeeded by small fleshy fruits. They are allied to Buxus, but in foliage bear a resemblance to some kinds of Ruscus or Butcher's-Broom.

Sarcococca belongs to the Box family, Buxaceae. The name was taken from the Greek

Sarcococca Hookeriana variety humilis, a low-growing, hardy evergreen shrub, produces clusters of white, very fragrant flowers in late winter or early spring

sarkos, flesh, and *kokkos*, berry, and alludes to the fleshy fruits.

Evergreen Shrubs for Shady Places. Numerous stems are produced from the rootstock and the development of new stems is continued throughout the life of the shrubs. As the old stems deteriorate, they should be removed to make way for young ones. The shrubs are better as evergreens than as flowering plants, particularly as they thrive in shady places.

These shrubs thrive in ordinary garden soil; it is advisable to reserve them for shady places where more attractive flowering plants do not succeed.

Propagation is by means of cuttings of side shoots, 4-5 in. long, dibbled into a cold frame in July or August or in a greenhouse in October. Or the rootstocks may be divided in spring.

The Chief Kinds. S. Hookeriana is a Himalayan shrub, 4-6 ft. high, with narrow, lance-shaped leaves, white flowers in March and black fruits. Its varieties digyna and humilis are varieties of much dwarfer habit, and are native to China. S. ruscifolia is a bush 2 ft. high, native to central China; its rounded leaves are 1-2½ in. long, and its fragrant white flowers, borne in March, are followed by dark red fruits. S. Hookeriana humilis rarely exceeds 1½ ft. in height; it has narrow, lanceolate leaves, and the white, fragrant flowers are produced in short clusters in early spring; the fruits are blue-black. It was introduced from western China in 1907 and is the hardiest kind, living outdoors in the vicinity of New York City, which other kinds will not do. S. saligna, a native of both the Himalayas and

China, grows 2-3 ft. high; it has narrow leaves, greenish-white flowers, and purple fruits.

SARMENTOSE. A botanical term used to describe plants which produce long runner-like growths like the Strawberry and Violet.

SARMIENTA REPENS — *Chilean Pitcher Flower* (Sarmien'ta). An uncommon plant, from Chile, which belongs to the Gesneria family, Gesneriaceae. It has long, slender, smooth stems clothed with small, ovate, fleshy leaves. The flowers, which are produced singly in the axils of the leaves, are tubular, spreading out at the tips into five lobes. The name Sarmienta commemorates Sarmiento, a Spanish botanist.

A Greenhouse Plant for Hanging Baskets. This plant has scandent (viny) shoots and is seen to the best advantage when grown in hanging baskets. It is not an easy plant to grow. The best compost consists of equal parts of fibrous peat (from which all fine particles have been shaken out) and sphagnum moss. In addition a small quantity of lump charcoal should be added. This keeps the soil sweet and prevents the roots from decaying. The baskets are lined with sphagnum moss, and half-filled with compost. The plant is set in position, and the remainder of the compost is added.

Until they are well rooted, the plants must be carefully watered, but afterwards the soil is kept moist throughout the summer. For the remainder of the time they are watered very moderately, sufficient water only being given to prevent the leaves from shriveling. A minimum winter temperature of 55 degrees is suitable. Other essential conditions are shade from strong sunlight and a moist atmosphere.

The plants are grown in the baskets until they deteriorate in vigor, when they are replaced by young plants.

Propagation. New plants are obtained from cuttings, which are rather difficult to root. Pieces of shoot tips, 3 in. in length, are taken off in spring, trimmed below a joint, and inserted in vermiculite or sand. They are kept in a propagating case with slight bottom heat, until roots are formed, care being taken to keep the vermiculite or sand moist.

The young plants are potted separately in 3-in. pots. These should be half-filled with crocks and the compost used as recommended above, but in a finer state. When established in the small pots, they are set in their final positions in the baskets.

SARRACENIA—*Sidesaddle Flower, Pitcher Plant* (Sarrace'nia). These curious, yet attractive, insectivorous plants (see Insectivorous Plants) are found wild in the swamps of North America. They are grown in bog gardens and sometimes in greenhouses for the sake of their handsome pitcher-like leaves. These are of various sizes and shapes and are colored. In some kinds, the pitchers are but 2 in. high, whereas others are more than 2 ft. Some are cup-shaped; others are cylindrical or shaped like trumpets. The coloring of the pitchers varies from green to yellow, red, crimson and purple, and most of them are streaked or blotched with contrasting colors.

The pitchers are stemless and rise up from below the soil, where they are attached to slender creeping rhizomes. Flat, winglike appendages run from the bases to the tips, which are terminated by hooded or flap-shaped structures.

The pitchers catch insects which are attracted by the vivid coloring. Alighting insects are enticed to explore by minute drops of honey-like

The insect-catching plant named Sarracenia purpurea. Its pitcher-leaves are purplish and they and the greenish-purple flowers are curiously attractive.

substance secreted by the glands on the lids. Intermingled with the honey glands are downward pointing hairs, which lead the victims to a slippery area. This offers them no foothold and they are thus precipitated into the water at the base of the pitcher. From this, their exit is barred by downward pointing hairs and they soon perish.

The Flowers of the Sarracenia Are Ornamental. They are borne on slender leafless stalks which rise straight up from the crowns of the plants. The tip of each bends over and bears one large nodding flower. The flowers are cup-shaped and five-petaled; they vary from 1-3 in. in diameter and are either greenish-yellow, lemon-yellow, crimson, greenish-purple or purple. Flowers are not produced until the plants are several years old.

Sarracenia belongs to the family Sarraceniaceae and was named in honor of D. Sarrazin, who introduced S. purpurea into Europe 300 years ago.

The chief requirements of these plants, when grown indoors, are moist soil and atmosphere, and shade from strong sunlight. A greenhouse in which a minimum winter temperature of 40 degrees can be maintained is required. The plants may either be grown in flowerpots or deep pans, or they may be planted in a bed of prepared soil in the greenhouse bench. Good drainage is necessary to enable the liberal quantities of water which the plants require to pass freely away. The best compost consists of three parts of fibrous peat from which all fine particles have been shaken, and one part of sphagnum moss, together with a small quantity of lump charcoal.

Planting or Potting Is Done in March. The soil and atmosphere are kept constantly moist at all times of the year, although less watering and damping are required during the winter. Unless the plants are not doing well, they must not be disturbed, as they resent root interference. If growth is not satisfactory repotting should be done in spring. The plants are knocked out of their pots and all the old compost is removed from the roots; they are then repotted in fresh compost.

Established plants can be kept growing vigorously by top-dressing them in spring with fresh compost and watering them in summer with dilute liquid fertilizer.

Outdoor Cultivation. Sarracenias are not always easy to establish in gardens. They need acid soil and bog conditions. The soil should be mostly black organic matter and sand. A sunny location is necessary.

Planting may be done in early spring. Established plants that are thrifty should be left undisturbed as long as possible.

The hardiest kind is S. purpurea, which in nature is found from Labrador to Florida and the Rocky Mountains. The other kinds are mostly not hardy in the North, although S. flava and S. Jonesii have been successfully grown in the vicinity of New York City with a little winter covering with evergreen branches.

The principal method of propagation is by division. This is done in early spring, when the plants are lifted, split into smaller pieces and repotted or replanted. After division they recover more quickly if they are kept in a close propagating case until they are established.

The various kinds of Sarracenia cross-fertilize readily one with the other, so that many hybrids have been obtained. These must be propagated by division to keep them true to type.

The species or wild types can be increased by seeds. The best method of raising seedlings is to sow the seeds in soil obtained from around the growing plants, or the seeds may be scattered on the compost surrounding the plants. The seedlings should be left undisturbed until large enough to handle and then potted separately in 3-in. pots, which should be half-filled with crocks.

The Chief Kinds. S. Drummondii, 48 in., pitchers green and purple mottled with white, flowers greenish-purple; S. flava, 36 in., pitchers green with purple veins, flowers yellow; S. purpurea, 10 in., pitchers purple, flowers greenish-purple; S. Claytonii, pitchers purple, flowers purplish; S. rubra, 20 in., pitchers green with purple veins, flowers crimson; S. psittacina, 6 in., pitchers green with purple-white veins, flowers greenish-purple.

SARSAPARILLA. A term used for the rhizomes or roots of various kinds of Smilax. The soil is removed from above the roots of growing plants, and the roots are cut off near the rootstock. They are dried, tied into bundles, and exported from Mexico and various Central American sources for use in medicine. The medicinal action of the roots is tonic, alterative and diuretic. Sarsaparilla is often used in making up tonic medicines and as a flavoring ingredient in root beer and other carbonated beverages.

East Indian Sarsaparilla is an entirely different product, for it is the root of Hemidesmus indicus, which belongs to the family Asclepiadaceae, whereas Smilax belongs to Liliaceae. Indian Sarsaparilla is also known as Hemidesmus Root.

SARSAPARILLA, WILD. See Aralia nudicaulis.

SASA (Sa'sa). Dwarf and fairly low Bamboos that belong in the Grass family, Gramineae. The name is a Japanese one for dwarf Bamboos. Numerous species of Sasa occur wild in the Orient.

Only a few of the Sasas are in cultivation. Of these the following are most important: S. chrysantha, 6 ft., often variegated with yellow; S. senanensis, 6-8 ft.; S. senanensis variety nebulosa, similar but with purple stems; S. tessellata, 4-6 ft.; S. Veitchii, 2-3 ft., spreads rapidly.

Sasas are hardier than many Bamboos. Many will live outdoors as far north as Philadelphia, and some in sheltered positions as far north as New York City.

They require the same cultural conditions as Arundinaria and Bambusa, which see.

SASH. This is the name given by gardeners to the movable, window-like, glazed tops of cold frames and hotbeds.

SASKATOON. See Amelanchier alnifolia.

SASSAFRAS. A small group of leaf-losing trees, one of which is a native of North America. Another occurs in Formosa and one on the mainland of Asia. They belong to the Laurel family, Lauraceae. The name is an adaptation of salsafras, which is the Spanish vernacular name.

The American kind, S. albidum, previously known as S. variifolium, occurs naturally in woods, along roadsides and in fields from Massachusetts to Ontario and Michigan and southward to Florida and Texas. It sometimes attains a height of 90 ft., but usually is lower and often is more or less shrublike. It is of pyramidal growth.

The American Sassafras is distinct among native trees by reason of its mitten-shaped leaves of varied outlines, which in fall assume handsome and brilliant hues of red and orange-yellow.

All parts of the tree are aromatic and it was at one time prized because of its reputed value as a medicine. From the bark of the roots a pleasant beverage is made.

The Sassafras thrives best in light, fertile soils. It is readily increased by seed and by suckers which spring up freely in the vicinity of established trees. In the North the Sassafras thrives best in warm, sheltered locations exposed to full sun; these requirements are of less importance in the South.

Because of their long taproots and rangy root systems, Sassafras trees are very difficult to move when they are large. New plantings should always be made of young vigorous specimens.

The American Sassafras, S. albidum, is hardier than the Chinese S. Tzumu, a kind which can be expected to grow only in the South.

SATINFLOWER. Lunaria, which see.

SATUREIA (SATUREJA)—*Savory* (Saturei'a). These hardy, aromatic-leaved herbs are planted in flower gardens, and some are used for flavoring soups and stews. Two kinds, S. hortensis, Summer Savory, and S. montana, Winter Savory, are commonly cultivated for this purpose. Both are natives of southern Europe and belong to the Mint family, Labiatae. Satureia, sometimes spelled Satureja, is an old Latin name used by Pliny. Several native Satureias occur in North America. S. hortensis is naturalized.

Summer Savory, S. hortensis, is a hardy annual with slender, erect, branching herbaceous stems, 12 in. in height, which are covered with small, narrow, pale green leaves. The small flowers, which are produced in the axils of the leaves in July, are lilac in color. This plant is raised annually by sowing seeds in drills, 1/2 in. deep and 12 in. apart, in spring. It requires a sunny position and does well in ordinary cultivated soil. When the seedlings are 2 in. high they are thinned to 6 in. apart.

The soil is watered in dry weather and, when the plants are coming into flower, they are ready for harvesting. This process consists of pulling up the plants, tying them in bundles and hanging them in a cool, airy room or shed until quite dry. The leaves are then picked off and stored in airtight bottles that keep them for future use.

Winter Savory, S. montana, is a perennial shrubby plant. It grows 12 in. or more in height, has small, narrow, pointed leaves and pale lilac flowers in summer. To obtain a stock of plants, seeds are sown and the seedlings treated as for the Summer Savory. They are planted out, 15 in. apart, when about 3 in. high; when the plants are established, the tips of the shoots are removed to make bushy plants. The shoots are cut off and harvested like Summer Savory.

In autumn the shoots are trimmed closely. Every third year the old bushes should be pulled up and discarded and replaced by young plants. These may be obtained by sowing seeds as described above, or cuttings can be taken from the old bushes. Side shoots 3 in. in length are removed with pieces or "heels" of the old stems attached, and inserted to half their depth in sandy soil in a semishaded border. They are kept moist until well rooted, when they are transplanted to their final positions.

If desired, the Winter Savory may be treated as an annual by sowing seeds each spring and discarding the plants as soon as the crop is gathered.

Other Kinds. A number of Satureias, most of which have also been known at one time by the name Calamintha, are suitable for rock gardens and flower gardens. They all thrive in well-drained soils, in sunny locations. All are readily propagated by seeds, and the perennial ones also by division in spring and by cuttings in summer.

Among the most popular of decorative kinds are S. alpina, Alpine Satureia or Alpine Calamint, 4-6 in., flowers purple, June; S. Calamintha, Calamint, 1-2 ft., flowers lavender; and S. grandiflora, 1½ ft., flowers purple-rose.

SATYRIUM (Satyr'ium). Terrestrial, leaf-losing and tuberous-rooted Orchids which are found wild in Africa, particularly South Africa, but also in India and other eastern countries. The flowers vary in size and color, and may be set densely or loosely on stout or slender spikes, which are erect and often bracteate (leafy). Most kinds bloom in summer. The name Satyrium is said to be derived from the Greek satyr; Satyrion was a Greek name for a kind of Orchid.

These Orchids are rather difficult to cultivate. The tubers should be placed in well-drained pots, just below the soil surface, in a compost consisting mainly of fibrous loam mixed with leaf mold and sand. During growth, abundance of water is given, and light shading is necessary; but as the foliage decays, water should be gradually withheld and as much exposure to light as possible given. In winter the plants are kept dry until growth recommences.

Some of the South African kinds can be grown in a cold frame in the summer, but, on the whole, a greenhouse with a winter temperature of about 50 degrees is most suitable. Those from warmer countries require the same compost and similar treatment, but a higher temperature.

The Chief Kinds. S. coriifolium has yellow and red flowers; S. carneum has flesh-colored flowers shading to white; S. erectum has orange and purplish-tinted blooms; and S. candidum produces a spike nearly 2 ft. high, with fragrant white, but rather small flowers.

SAUROMATUM GUTTATUM — *Monarch of the East* (Sauro'matum). Tender plants which are grown for their curious flowers and ornamental foliage. They are natives of the Orient and belong to the Arum family, Araceae. These remarkable plants are grown chiefly as curiosities because their large, flattish corms or tubers will produce flowers without being planted in soil or given any water. This is the plant sometimes called Voodoo Lily.

The name of this plant is derived from the appearance of the flowers; Sauromatum is from *sauros,* a lizard, and refers to the spotted spathes.

Blooms Without Soil or Water. The corms need not be potted, but may be placed on the mantelpiece or window sill in a warm room. Without further attention, they produce their conspicuous blooms. From the center of the fleshy corm rises the large, arumlike flower, which is tubular at the base, spreading out into a large spathe above. This is greenish-yellow, with purple spots, and is about 12 in. in height.

After flowering, the corms are potted in 6- or 7-in. pots. The pots are well drained with crocks, and a soil compost of two parts of loam and one part of peat moss or leaf mold, with the addition of a little sand, is used. The pots are placed on a

The curious Monarch of the East, Sauromatum guttatum.

window sill in a warm room or in a greenhouse. No water is given until growth commences, and then the soil is kept moist throughout the summer. The summer growth consists of large, deeply divided, palmlike green leaves on stalks 3 ft. in length.

Good results are obtained by planting the corms out of doors in May. The soil is enriched with well-decayed manure or rich compost and kept moist throughout the summer. When the foliage dies down the roots are lifted, kept dry, and again placed indoors to flower. In mild climates the corms may remain in the ground all through the year.

Propagation may be effected by detaching the small corms (bulbs) that form around the parent corm, potting them, and growing them until they reach flowering size. This is not generally done, however, as they take several years to reach their full development; since most people grow but one or two plants as curiosities, it is far more satisfactory to purchase large corms.

SAURURUS — *Lizard's Tail* (Saurur'us). Hardy, aquatic perennials of North America and Asia. They grow 12 in. to 2 ft. in height; the slender stems bear heart-shaped leaves and are terminated by long, slender spikes of small white or yellowish-white flowers in midsummer. The tips of the flower spikes arch over and point downwards. The name Saururus was suggested by the appearance of these inflorescences, and is derived from *sauros,* meaning a lizard, and *oura,* a tail. Saururus belongs to the family Saururaceae.

For Planting in Shallow Water. The cultural requirements of these plants are very simple. They should be planted in October or March in sandy loam in shallow water by the margin of a pond or in the bog garden. There they can be left to themselves for several years, or until they show signs of deterioration, or of exceeding their allotted space. They are then lifted, divided and replanted. Division is the principal method of propagation.

The chief kinds are S. cernuus, 5 ft., white, fragrant, and S. chinensis (Loureiri), 15 in., yellowish-white. The American kind, S. cernuus, grows naturally from Connecticut to Florida and Texas.

SAUSAGE TREE. Kigelia pinnata, which see.

SAUSSUREA — *Sawwort* (Saussu'rea). Hardy perennial plants, few of which are of value in the garden. They are found wild chiefly in central Asia; a few inhabit the mountainous regions of Europe. Saussurea belongs to the Daisy family, Compositae, and was named in honor of Horace B. de Saussure, a Swiss botanist.

These plants are thistle-like in appearance and grow 6 in. to 3 ft. in height. The leaves are lanceolate, sessile (without leafstalks), with prickly edges, and the tufts of thistle-like purple flowers are borne at the tops of the stems in summer.

They thrive in ordinary garden soil and need no special treatment. The dwarf kinds are planted in the rockery and the taller kinds in the herbaceous border. They may be planted at any time from October to March and need a sunny, well-drained position.

These plants are grown chiefly in botanic

gardens or in private plant collections, as they are not sufficiently showy for garden decoration.

Propagation is by sowing seeds in drills, 1 in. deep, out of doors in April. The seedlings, when 2 in. high, are transplanted 4-6 in. apart in a nursery bed. Later they are transplanted to their flowering locations.

The chief kinds are S. alpina, 6 in., purple; S. pygmaea, 12 in., purple; S. japonica, 2 ft., purple; and S. elegans, 2 ft., pink.

SAVANNAH FLOWER. See Echites.

SAVIN. The common name of Juniperus Sabina, which see.

SAVORY. The common name of two herbs which are grown in the vegetable garden for the sake of their aromatic leaves. The Summer Savory (Satureia hortensis) is an annual, and the Winter Savory (Satureia montana) is a perennial; the latter may, however, be grown as an annual. Full details of cultivation are given under Satureia, which see.

SAVOY CABBAGE. A type of hardy Cabbages (Brassica oleracea bullata) which have large, wrinkled leaves and form big, solid hearts. Cultivation is similar to that for other types of Cabbage (see Cabbage).

Savoy Cabbages do best on ground that was manured well for the previous crop. Seed is sown in a specially prepared seedbed outdoors in April–May; the seedlings are transplanted, very

Savoy Cabbages.

firmly, in late June or early July, preferably in showery weather, otherwise they should be watered in well. They are set 24 in. apart each way. A light dressing of sulphate of ammonia in the early stages will stimulate growth, but any feeding should cease by the end of August, otherwise growth will be too soft to stand the winter well.

SAW CABBAGE PALM. See Paurotis.

SAWARA CYPRESS. Chamaecyparis pisifera, which see.

SAWDUST. Contrary to common belief, sawdust is an excellent source of humus for the soil, although it is most valuable after it has been used as bedding for animals, owing to its power of absorbing ammonia.

For direct application, sawdust is most satisfactory when used as a mulch, for if dug in in a fresh state it will temporarily reduce the available nitrogen in the soil. Applied as a surface mulch in spring and early summer, it will help to conserve moisture in the soil, and by autumn it will be well weathered and in suitable condition for digging in.

Sawdust may be mixed with other garden material for composting.

Whenever sawdust that is not thoroughly decayed is used for digging into the soil or as a mulch, an application of sulphate of ammonia or other nitrogenous fertilizer should be made at the same time. This provides the nitrogen that the bacteria of decay need to reproduce themselves and grow; if nitrogen is not so provided, they will take it from the soil, to the possible detriment of the plants or crops being grown.

SAWFLY. See Pests and Diseases.

SAW PALMETTO. See Paurotis.

SAWWORT. Saussurea, which see.

SAXATILIS. A term meaning found on rocks; it is used in plant names, as, for example, in Alyssum saxatile.

SAXEGOTHAEA CONSPICUA—*Prince Albert's Yew* (Saxegothae'a; Saxego'thaea). An evergreen tree with yewlike leaves, native of Chile and western Patagonia, where it grows about 40 ft. high. Male and female flowers are on the same tree, the male flowers in stalked clusters from the leaf axils, the female flowers from near the tips of the shoots. The ripe fruits are small, with fleshy scales containing a few seeds;

rarely as many as six are found in one fruit.

In the South and on the Pacific coast it grows into a large bush or small tree sometimes 20 ft. or more high, but it is not hardy in the North and not common.

Cuttings of short shoots, 4-5 in. long, taken in July and inserted in a close frame or greenhouse, can be rooted, and good plants can be raised in this way.

The young plants should be placed in a sheltered position in loamy soil which contains a little peat or leaf mold. The ground should be permanently moist without being waterlogged. During the early years it will probably be necessary to tie the leading shoot to a stake to encourage upward growth. At the same time, the side branches may need some cutting back. That can be done in summer. Unless this care is given the plants may develop into unsymmetric specimens.

Saxegothaea belongs to the Yew family, Taxaceae, and the name was given in honor of Prince Albert of Saxe-Coburg-Gotha, consort of Queen Victoria, and a patron of horticulture. S. conspicua is the only kind known.

SAXIFRAGA or SAXIFRAGE
A Fine Group of Plants for Favored Climates

Saxifraga is a big group of mostly hardy perennial plants belonging to the Saxifrage family, Saxifragaceae. Only a few are annuals or biennials. The name is an old Latin name used by Pliny, and is derived from *saxum,* a rock, and *frangor,* to break, the plant having been supposed to break stones in the bladder. Rockfoil is a common name applied to Saxifrages.

Saxifrages are principally natives of north and south temperate and arctic regions. A few are found in Asia; they are rare in South America, and are absent from Australia, South Africa and the islands of the Pacific.

The Saxifrages are an extremely varied group of plants. For convenience, botanists have divided them into a number of sub-groups or "sections," each distinguished by a special name.

In gardens Saxifragas are chiefly valued for planting in rock gardens, but one, S. sarmentosa, is frequently grown in greenhouses and as a house plant. As a group they are notable for their lovely flowers and their fine foliage. They have a remarkably long flowering season. The earliest sorts, those of the Kabschia, the Engleria and the Porphyrion sections, in favorable climates, open their dainty blossoms in January and February, apparently quite unperturbed and unharmed by somewhat inclement weather.

The Silver Saxifrages (section Euaizoonia) are best grown in raised positions among rocks or in the dry wall, where their handsome clumps of silver-encrusted rosettes of foliage make an extremely beautiful feature all the year round. From such raised, rocky positions, too, the sprays of white, pink, or yellow flowers can arch outwards in a natural and graceful manner, exactly as they do in Nature.

The Mossy Saxifrages (section Dactyloides) should be grown in cool, half-shady places, and given ample room to spread, as they are rapid growers. After flowering, it is a good plan to topdress the clumps of Mossy Saxifrages heavily with a fine mixture of sifted loam, leaf mold, and sand. This may be poured over the plants in a perfectly dry state, and then, with the fingers, delicately worked down between the rosettes. If the top-dressing soil is dry and fine, it will work down between the leaves quite easily. A good overhead watering, in the form of a fine spray, will complete the work and settle the soil.

Mossy Saxifrages tend, with age, to become brown and patchy, but this top-dressing serves to keep the plants in a healthy state for a long time. Eventually, however, it will be found necessary to renew the plants. They should be dug up, pulled to pieces, the ground dug over and enriched with fresh soil and leaf mold or peat moss; then the divided tufts may be replanted a few inches apart. This may be done either in spring or early autumn. It should be remembered that the red-flowered Mossy Saxifrages develop their color best when planted in a shady or half-shady

A lovely drift of Mossy Saxifrages in full bloom in the rock garden in early spring. They like a cool location and moisture-holding but well-drained soil.

Ideal Alpine House Plants. Cultivating the Kabschia Saxifrages in pots and pans in an alpine house is a fascinating branch of rock gardening. They flower in earliest spring, and their exquisite, jewel-like flowers develop under glass to perfection, and are particularly welcome at that time of year. The plants may be potted singly in small pans, and repotted as becomes necessary until they are large specimens. Single plants may be started in pans three or four inches in diameter, or three or five small plants may be grouped in a larger pan; in a year or two they will join up and form a large specimen in a comparatively short time.

A good potting compost is loam, sifted leaf mold, sand, and crushed stone, either sandstone or limestone. If sandstone is used it is wise to add lime to the soil in the form of crushed limestone rubble.

Another valuable ingredient for potting compost for alpines is crushed or broken flowerpot. A certain number of broken flowerpots always accumulate in the potting shed; these should be smashed up into coarse grit with a heavy hammer; such grit is extremely valuable in potting composts for alpine plants.

Provide ample drainage crocks and make sure that the pans are scrupulously clean when starting.

Watering is important; allowing the plants to become parched can soon prove fatal, but overwatering is also bad. One of the first signs of overwatering is when the leaves begin to turn yellow. The formation of Mosses and of Liverworts are also danger signals. Shading must be provided for the Saxifrages during the heat of summer, and at all times it is important to provide ample ventilation.

During the colder months the ideal to aim at is ample ventilation without direct drafts. In summer, as much ventilation as possible should be allowed. Saxifrages grown in the alpine house will be greatly helped by an occasional top-dressing of fine loam, sand and sifted leaf mold, well worked in between the leaf rosettes, and watered. When the plants have filled the pans, they should be shifted into larger ones, with perhaps a margin of room of from half an inch to an inch all around.

position. In full hot sun the red flowers fade quickly.

Saxifrages for the Scree or Moraine. Nearly all the Kabschia Saxifrages are best grown in a scree or moraine garden, or in a soil composed of loam, sand and leaf mold, to which has been added a liberal amount of crushed stone. The position should be open, and is best if it slopes west or northwest rather than directly south. Sharp drainage is absolutely essential, and many buried stones are a help, for the roots of these Saxifrages delight to go questing under the sides of a piece of buried porous rock.

As the plants grow large, they should be top-dressed with fine soil, which must be worked well down among the rosettes and stems. A mixture of fine loam, sifted leaf mold, sand and crushed rock may be used, and it is best applied in a dry state, both after flowering and in early autumn.

A few of the Kabschia Saxifrages are happiest when planted in a deep narrow crevice in a rock, or in a deep hole bored in tufa rock. When it is impossible to provide such crevices, the plants may be placed in the scree, tightly wedged between two medium-sized pieces of buried rock, which protrude just above the scree surface.

The propagation of Saxifrages is by seeds, cuttings and division. Such easily grown sorts as the Mossy Saxifrages, Saxifraga umbrosa variety primuloides, the stronger-growing Kabschias, such as Saxifraga apiculata, and many of the Silver Saxifrages can be increased by simply lifting the plants, pulling them to pieces, each division with some roots, and replanting where they are required. Choice varieties of Mossy Saxifrages may be reduced to single rosettes each one of which will soon root and make a young plant. This division is best done in spring or early autumn.

Mossy Saxifrages may be raised from seeds sown in pots or pans in a cold frame and kept cool and shaded, but they cannot be relied on to come true from seed, although many interesting and often beautiful forms and variations may be expected.

Taking Cuttings of Saxifrage. The Silver Saxifrages may be divided and replanted in spring or autumn, but many of the choicest sorts, such as S. cochlearis, S. lingulata, and S. Tumbling Waters, are best propagated by cuttings taken in spring, early summer, or autumn.

This is a simple process. Single leaf rosettes are removed from the parent plant with as much base stem as possible; a few of the lower leaves should be removed with a very sharp knife, and the rosettes are then dibbled in a pan of sand and kept in a close cold frame. They root readily, and in a few weeks they may be potted in small pots, where they are kept until large enough to plant out in the rock garden.

Saxifraga longifolia must be increased by seeds, as the plant, when true, never makes any offsets. Seeds may be sown in a pan of loam, leaf mold and sand in a cold frame; the seedlings are pricked off when large enough to handle, and grown in small pots until large enough to be planted out in the rock garden. Seed of Saxifraga longifolia, if obtained from wild plants in the Pyrenees, may usually be relied on to come quite true, but home-saved seed from plants which have been grown in the near neighborhood of other species of Saxifrage are very apt to turn out hybrids and not true S. longifolia.

Many of these hybrids, however, are extremely interesting and beautiful. Seedlings of S. longi-

folia which form several rosettes instead of one single rosette are not true to type.

Some of the choicer kinds of Kabschia Saxifrage are best propagated from cuttings—single leaf rosettes removed from the parent plant. These cuttings, which are extremely small, require delicate handling. A few of the lower leaves are removed with a razor-sharp knife, and then the rosette is dibbled in a pan of sand, which is kept in a close and shaded cold frame. When rooted, the little plants must be potted in small pots in a compost of loam, leaf mold, sand and grit, and grown with very great care.

The Kabschia Saxifrages are interesting to raise from seeds, which many of them set fairly freely, especially in the protection of the alpine house. They cannot always be relied upon to come quite true to their parents, and many cross-bred and hybrid forms are to be expected.

The Engleria Saxifrages are increased by leaf rosettes removed from the parent plant with as much basal stem as possible, and treating them like cuttings of silver or Kabschia Saxifrages. They may also be raised from seeds, and relied on to breed fairly true. Saxifraga Grisebachii and the lovely and superior Wisley Variety come quite true from seeds.

Saxifraga oppositifolia may be propagated by cuttings, short shoots removed when the plants are in growth after flowering, and rooted in pans of sand in a close and shaded cold frame. Or large established plants may be lifted and divided, and the self-rooted pieces replanted where they are to flower, or potted as required.

The oppositifolia Saxifrages benefit from periodical top-dressing, especially just after flowering. Dry, fine, gritty compost, loam, leaf mold, sand and crushed rock should be put all over the plant, worked in among the shoots, and then watered in with a fine spray. Such top-dressing keeps the plants healthy and vigorous, and prevents their going bare and patchy, and dying off in the center. Plants of S. oppositifolia, moreover, which have been well and frequently top-dressed, are easy to increase by simple division.

Kinds of Saxifrages

Saxifraga Ada is a Kabschia hybrid of neat

growth, with numerous pale pink flowers on stems only ½ in. tall, and it blooms in January and February. It is an excellent and free-flowering plant of great charm for the alpine house or the scree.

S. aizoides is a common plant in the European Alps, in boggy places and by streamsides. It is also found in arctic North America. It is an extremely handsome plant, forming strong mats of deep green foliage of rather mossy appearance, 3-4 in. high, covered in early summer with heads of starry, golden-yellow flowers. In the rock garden it is easily managed in well-drained, gritty loam in a position where it will not become parched in summer.

There are also two extremely handsome varieties in cultivation called aurantia and atrorubens, the former with beautiful orange-colored flowers, and the latter with flowers of a deep mahogany red. They are particularly desirable, not only for their rich coloring, but because they flower about midsummer, when alpine flowers are becoming scarce in the rock garden.

S. aizoides may be increased from seeds sown in a pan of loam, sand and leaf mold in a cold frame in spring, or by division of the roots after flowering. The named varieties may also be divided, or cuttings, made of single leaf rosettes, may be taken after flowering, and rooted in a pan of sand in a close and shaded cold frame.

S. Aizoon is the type of its group, the Euaizoonia or Silver Saxifrages. It is very widely distributed in the Alps, varies considerably, has hybridized freely with other kinds, and is a valuable rock-garden plant. In nature it is found usually on noncalcareous rock formations, but in the garden it seems to be indifferent to the presence or absence of lime.

The plant forms dense cushions of handsome rosettes of silver-edged leaves, the serrations or notches of the leaves pointing towards the tip of the leaf rather than to its base. It flowers in May, with sprays of showy white flowers, sometimes spotted on the petals with fine red dots, sometimes unspotted. There are pale pink and pale yellow varieties. The flower spikes vary from 2 or 3 in. to 9 or 12 in. high.

This plant is easily grown in well-drained loam, and is best displayed when placed in a

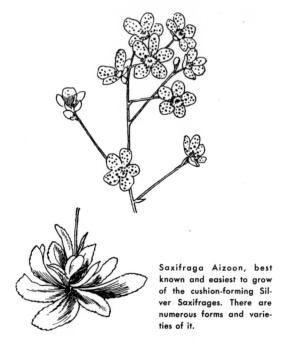

Saxifraga Aizoon, best known and easiest to grow of the cushion-forming Silver Saxifrages. There are numerous forms and varieties of it.

rather raised position among the larger rocks, from which its flower sprays may arch outwards in a semihorizontal direction. It is also admirable for planting in rock walls.

Saxifraga Aizoon may be propagated from seeds sown in spring in a pan of loam, leaf mold and sand in the cold frame, but the named varieties are best increased either by division of the roots, or by cuttings of single leaf rosettes.

The principal varieties or forms of Saxifraga Aizoon are as follows:

Balcana is small and neat, with light green, incurved leaves, and fine white flowers heavily dotted with red. The stems are dark red. Elongata has rather loose rosettes of longish leaves, and tall loose sprays of cream-white flowers on stems a foot or rather more tall. Flavescens is a name which has been given to various cream-white forms which are to be found in certain districts in the Alps. Hirsuta, a native of Corsica, is distinguished by being covered on its leaves and stems with short soft hairs, but is not of any great garden merit.

Intacta has large white flowers, usually spotted with red, on tall stems. Labradorica is a neat variety with white flowers on stems only a few inches high. Lagraveaba is a dwarf variety of great charm. The white flowers are on stems 3 or 4 in. high. It came from the Savoy Alps.

Lutea is a most beautiful variety with fine sprays of well-developed flowers of sulphur-yellow on stems some 9-12 in. tall. The foliage is a distinct pale green color, and the leaf rosettes somewhat lax.

Major, which has many synonyms, is a strong-growing form with handsome foliage, which colors well in winter; the rather large white flowers, speckled with red dots, are in a loose 18-in.-high spike. Notata is an attractive white-flowered variety with somewhat dwarf flower spikes. The leaf rosettes are distinctly incurved. Pectinata is a useful Silver Saxifrage with white flowers, but its chief beauty is in the leaves.

Punctata has white flowers densely marked with small red spots. The leaf rosettes are of good size, and the flower spikes handsome. Punctatissima is of neat, graceful habit, and the flowers are remarkable for the dense peppering of fine red spots which cover the petals so closely as to give a rosy flush. It grows only 3-4 in. high.

Rex has large leaf rosettes and spikes of large, cream-white flowers.

Rosea is one of the most distinct and beautiful of all; it was collected in the mountains of Bulgaria. It is a good grower, with handsome foliage which often becomes red in winter. The flower spikes, 12 in. or rather more high, bear graceful sprays of flowers of pale pink color. It may be classed with S. lutea among the hundred best alpines.

Rosularis is one of the best of the white-flowered sorts, with handsome incurved rosettes of blue-gray, silver-encrusted leaves, and fine flower sprays a foot or even more tall, the petals being slightly spotted with red.

S. ajugifolia is a rare dwarf mossy kind from Spain, small and prostrate. It is of very distinctive appearance and has heads of white flowers 2-3 in. high.

S. Andrewsii is said to be, and probably is, a hybrid between S. Aizoon and S. Geum hirsutum. The toothed leaves are handsome, and the pink flowers are borne in graceful 9-in. sprays.

S. androsacea is a high alpine which grows in rather damp cool places. It forms small rosettes of narrow leaves, and its flowers, in heads of two or three, on 1-in. stems, are snow-white, and of good size for so small a plant. Leaves and stems are downy. It is a plant of great charm.

S. apiculata is a hybrid between S. sancta and S. marginata Rocheliana. It is one of the most beautiful of all the early-flowering Kabschias, being easy to grow, and free-flowering. The plant is a rapid grower, soon forming fine, glossy, emerald cushions of smallish leaf rosettes. In late winter or earliest spring the plant produces innumerable flower heads, each about 2 in. high, and carrying a number of lovely primrose-yellow blossoms. Any light, well-drained soil in an open sunny position suits S. apiculata. It may be propagated by division in spring, or by cuttings made from single leaf rosettes after flowering.

S. apiculata alba is a beautiful variety with pure white flowers. It occurred as a "sport" among plants of the typical yellow S. apiculata.

S. aquatica is a large mossy kind from the Pyrenees, a handsome plant and very distinct, not difficult to grow. It forms strong clumps of leaf rosettes, each of which may be 9 in. or more across. The flower stems are 18 in. tall, and carry fine heads of big white flowers. The whole plant, stems and leaves, is covered with glandular hairs. Saxifraga aquatica requires a cool position, a soil rich in leaf mold, and abundant moisture at the root.

S. arachnoidea. The Cobweb Saxifrage is an extremely rare plant found only in a few spots in the Trentino. It inhabits the mouths of caves and hollows high up in the mountains, and is a strange frail annual or biennial. The stems and leaves are covered with long, shining, glandular hairs, and the flowers are of pale gold. Few living people have ever seen this incredibly rare plant.

S. arco-valleyi is of the Kabschia type. It is of neat dwarf habit, and its flowers, in earliest spring, are shell-pink and of faultless shape and form. This hybrid kind is a most desirable plant for the scree or for the alpine house.

S. aretioides is a choice Kabschia Saxifrage, a native of the Pyrenees and the mountains of northern Spain. It is a dwarf compact plant, with dark-green cushions of foliage, and bright yellow flower heads on stems 1 in. or 2 in. high. It is best grown in the scree, or it makes a good specimen in a pan in the alpine house.

The yellow-flowered Saxifraga apiculata is smothered with bloom in early spring.

S. aretioides is best increased by leaf rosettes rooted in a pan of coarse sand in a cold frame after the plant has flowered. It has produced a natural hybrid by becoming crossed with S. media; it is called S. luteo-purpurea.

S. aspera belongs to the Trachyphyllum group and forms mats of rather spinous mossy foliage, with loose heads of flowers on stems 3-4 in. high. The flowers, which are of good size, are pale butter-yellow, peppered with golden dots. This Saxifrage is, unfortunately, not very liberal in its show of flowers.

S. Bertolonii is an Engleria hybrid. It has handsome silvery foliage and attractive heads of pink flowers.

S. Biasolettii has very handsome rosettes of silver foliage and heads of crimson flowers in early spring. It is a cross between S. porophylla thessalica and S. Grisebachii.

S. biflora is near S. oppositifolia in general

appearance, and is found at great elevations in the European Alps, growing in damp moraines or screes. It is a straggling, prostrate plant, with small flattish leaves and flowers arranged in twos and threes, with rather small petals of a cold heather-purple or lilac. It is difficult to grow in the garden and scarcely worth the trouble it entails.

S. Bileckii is a choice and very charming hybrid Kabschia. It originated as a cross between S. Ferdinandi-Coburgii and S. tombeanensis, and resembles a neat dwarf S. tombeanensis, with pale yellow flowers on 1-in. stems. It is for the scree or the alpine house.

S. Borisii is a cross between S. Ferdinandi-Coburgii and S. marginata, with handsome blue-gray foliage and heads of sulphur-yellow flowers in early spring. It is a good scree or alpine-house plant.

S. Boryi is a distinct and attractive Kabschia for the scree or the alpine house. It has curious, smooth, rounded leaves, and heads of handsome white flowers in early spring.

S. Boydii is a beautiful Kabschia hybrid, derived from S. Burseriana and S. aretioides. A neat, slow-growing plant, it has tight rosettes of pointed leaves and heads of two or three flowers of a distinctive citron yellow on stems only an inch or so tall. The plant is not of robust constitution, but has very definite charm. It is best in the scree or in the alpine house.

S. Boydii alba. The plant known by this name is not a white form of the true S. Boydii, but a hybrid of entirely different parentage and distinct appearance. It forms rosettes of rather large, coarse, blue-green foliage of somewhat straggling habit. The white flowers are large and carried in heads on stems 3-4 in. tall. It should be grown in the scree or alpine house.

S. Brunoniana is an Asiatic kind of the Trachyphyllum group. It has small rosettes of pale green leaves, with bristly hairs, and multiplies exceedingly by sending out strawberry-like runners on pink, threadlike stems which root in all directions and themselves send out still more runners. The large yellow flowers on leafy stems are pretty in summer. This interesting plant should be given a sunny, well-drained slope in the rock garden and plenty of room in which to spread.

S. Burnatii is a singularly beautiful cross between S. Aizoon and S. cochlearis, and it combines the virtues of both parents. It has rosettes of blue-gray leaves heavily encrusted with silver, and the flower sprays, 4-5 in. high, are white. It is a good plant for rock ledges or pockets in the rock garden, or for the wall garden.

S. Burseriana is one of the most beautiful of all the Kabschia Saxifrages, and is the parent of many good hybrids. The plant forms rounded cushions of narrow, sharp-pointed leaves of a blue-gray color, arranged in neat rosettes, and

The exquisite Kabschia Saxifrage named Saxifraga Burseriana crenata, forming cushions of blue-gray leaves, is a gem for the alpine house.

the large, pure white flowers are carried singly on erect stems, usually red in color, and from 1-3 in. tall.

There are several distinct varieties of S. Burseriana in cultivation, the finest being Gloria, which has superbly formed flowers as large as a half dollar. Grandiflora and magna are also distinguished by their large, well-shaped flowers. Speciosa has narrow leaves and comes into flower later than the others, and crenata has very pretty flowers whose petals are crimped or crenated at the edge. S. Burseriana sulphurea is of hybrid origin, but has all the appearance of a true Burseriana, with flowers of a soft, delicate yellow color.

All the Burseriana varieties flower in earliest spring. They are best grown in a scree, or in rock crevices of light, rich, gritty soil. They are also

The White-flowered Saxifraga Burseriana.

admirable when displayed in the alpine house.

S. bursiculata is a hybrid between S. Burseriana and S. apiculata, with blue-green rosettes of rather broad leaves and heads of large, pure white flowers. It is easy to grow and of vigorous habit, and makes a fine specimen in the scree or in the alpine house.

S. caesia is a small Kabschia, common in the European Alps, growing either in scree or as a crevice plant, and usually on limestone formations. It is almost invariably found in positions facing away from the hottest midday sunshine. The plant has small rosettes of silver-encrusted leaves and produces numerous slightly branched heads or sprays of white blossoms on erect, slender stems 2-3 in. high. It is best on limestone scree, and it is excellent for planting in a pan in the alpine house. It flowers in May, later than most of the Kabschias.

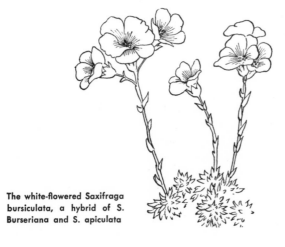

The white-flowered Saxifraga bursiculata, a hybrid of S. Burseriana and S. apiculata

S. caespitosa is a name much used in garden literature and often misapplied. The true plant is a small Mossy kind with dull white flowers, and is hardly worth cultivating.

S. Camposii is the correct name of the white Mossy Saxifrage often misnamed S. Wallacei. The true S. Camposii is a handsome Mossy kind with smooth, green, three-lobed leaves, and fine heads of white flowers, carried on stalks which are slightly winged.

S. canaliculata is a fine Mossy Saxifrage from the mountains of Calabria. The dark glossy green leaves are somewhat sticky and aromatic. The flowers are large and white.

S. cartilaginea belongs to the Euaizoon group, and is a native of the Caucasus. It is like S. Aizoon but with more pointed, triangular leaves. The flowers are pale pink, in sprays 6 or 8 in. tall. The plant is beautiful and easy to grow, but is somewhat rare in cultivation.

S. cernua has leaves that are thick, fleshy, green, and kidney-shaped. The flowers are white, and borne singly on stems some 3 in. high. This interesting plant is, however, often very shy of flowering, producing, instead, numerous little red bulbils on the stems, which fall and so reproduce the plant. It is an interesting curiosity for a cool, moist corner in the rock garden.

S. Cherry Trees. A rare and beautiful hybrid Kabschia of dense, very slow growth, and producing in great profusion, for so small a plant, large flowers of pale yellow on inch-high stems. The true plant is extremely rare, but most desirable for a choice spot in the scree, or for a pan in the alpine house. For many years a spurious S. Cherry Trees has been in commercial circulation. This latter is like a nonflowering or seldom-flowering S. Elizabethiae, a worthless plant.

S. chrysantha, a beautiful native of damp places at high elevations in the Rocky Mountains, is low, mat-forming and has golden flowers. It is difficult to cultivate.

S. Churchillii is a handsome hybrid between S. Aizoon and S. Hostii, and very free-flowering. It is a desirable plant for loamy soil.

S. Clarkei is a valuable Engleria hybrid. It has handsome silver rosettes, and heads of pretty pink flowers on 3-in. stems very early in spring. It should be grown in the scree or alpine house.

S. cochlearis belongs to the Euaizoon group, and is one of the most beautiful of all Saxifrages. It is a strictly cliff-dwelling plant, found in the districts of the Roja Valley, the Col De Tenda, and the Ligurian Apennines. The plant forms compact hummocks of silver leaf rosettes, and in May and June produces numerous sprays of pure white flowers on red stems 3-6 in. tall. The plant varies considerably in nature and two varieties have been named and distributed in cultivation—minor, with small compact rosettes, and major, of larger growth.

S. cochlearis in any of its forms is best planted in narrow rock crevices, with deep root runs, and a sunny exposure. There it will remain, increasing in size year after year, and producing its graceful plumes of flowers.

S. cortusaefolia belongs to the Diptera group, and enjoys loamy soil in a half-shaded position in the rock garden. It is also valuable as a pot plant in the alpine house. It grows indoors with sprays of starry-white flowers a foot or more high. See S. Fortunei.

S. corymbosa, a rare high Alpine, belongs to the Hirculus group; it is a dwarf plant with roundish leaves and yellow flowers. It requires a moist position.

S. Cotyledon is one of the most valuable of all Saxifrages; it belongs to the Euaizoon group and forms large glossy green rosettes, with only slight silvering at the edges of the leaves, and numerous side rosettes. In due course the rosettes reach flowering size, and in May or June produce superb arching sprays of white flowers 2 ft. or more tall. Each rosette dies after flowering, but meanwhile others are developing to replace it.

S. Cotyledon is of somewhat local occurrence and wide distribution in the Alps of Europe, and there are several distinct varieties in cultivation. In some the flowers are pure white throughout, and in others the petals are more or less freckled with fine red spots.

These are the chief varieties: pyramidalis, with pyramidal-shaped flower spikes; icelandica, supposed to come from the north of Norway, and said to produce very large rosettes and flower spikes, and caterhamensis, a hybrid or seedling form with flowers of great beauty that are heavily marked with red spots.

Saxifraga Cotyledon is a grand plant for planting in raised positions among the larger rocks, where its flower spikes may lean outwards in a semihorizontal direction. It will thrive in loamy soil, and although it grows exclusively on noncalcareous formations in nature, it prospers in acid or alkaline soil. Propagate by rooting single leaf rosettes in sand.

S. Cranbourne is a modern Kabschia hybrid and one of the finest yet raised. It forms close neat cushions of gray-green foliage and in earliest spring produces a multitude of large well-formed flowers of a lovely rose-pink, each carried erect upon a stem an inch or so high. It is a fine plant for the scree.

S. crustata, also known as S. cristata and S. incrustata, is a handsome Silver Saxifrage near S. Aizoon, but with longer, narrower leaves. The spikes of white flowers are 5-6 in. high. It is increased by rooting leaf rosettes in sand in a cold frame in early summer, or by division of the roots in spring.

S. cuneifolia is a woodland plant widely distributed in the Alps and a charming little plant for shady places in the rock garden. It is like a small S. umbrosa, with rosettes of dark green leaves, and sprays of white flowers on stems 3-4 in. high. It has numerous forms or varieties.

S. decipiens, as a true species, is now little known in gardens, but the name is attached to many seedling Mossy Saxifrages that have been derived from S. decipiens. Among these are bathoniensis, a fine free-growing sort with handsome red flowers; Rhei, of neat growth with pink flowers; Guildford Seedling, with bright red flowers and of compact habit; Fergusonii, with bright pink flowers; Diana, a lovely sort with large well-formed white flowers; Fairy, shell-pink; Glasnevin Beauty, white; and sanguinea superba with deep red flowers.

All these are showy plants for the rock garden, and are of the easiest possible cultivation in loamy soil in a half-shady position. It is a good plan to top-dress the clumps with a compost of loam, sand and leaf mold after flowering. They bloom in May and are easily increased by division of the roots in spring or early autumn.

S. Delight is a Kabschia hybrid Saxifrage which forms dense hummocks of deep green foliage and has bright pink blossoms of good form on short stems in earliest spring. It is a lovely plant for the scree or for the alpine house.

S. diapensioides is a choice rock-dwelling Kabschia of rather local occurrence in the Alps. In nature it is found on limestone cliffs, the plants packed into holes and cracks in the rock, where they form domed clumps of blue-green rosettes of minute leaves. In the garden it may be planted in narrow rock crevices, or in natural fissures in the rock; or it may be grown in the scree wedged tightly between two rocks.

S. diapensioides is a rare, choice, and lovely plant, very slow growing, and exacting in its wants. It must be grown in rock. But given that essential it is not difficult; when suited, it grows well and flowers profusely, and is one of the most desirable of its family.

S. Dr. Ramsey is a hybrid Silver Saxifrage of unknown parentage, and one of the most beautiful in this group. It forms shapely rosettes of blue-green leaves, heavily silvered and encrusted, and changing in winter to purple and red. The flower spike, which is slightly arched and about 9 in. high, is well furnished with round white flowers with a zone of heavy red spots. The plant is a good grower, flourishing in light loam; it is best placed in a raised position among the larger rocks. It is also a fine plant for the wall garden and for the alpine house.

S. Elizabethiae is one of the older Kabschia hybrids whose parentage is S. Burseriana and S. sancta. It is a strong-growing plant of excellent constitution, and very free-flowering. It forms cushions of rich green foliage, and produces in

The hybrid Silver Saxifrage, Esther.

earliest spring innumerable heads of primrose-yellow flowers on reddish stems, some 2 in. high.

S. Elizabethiae thrives in light, loamy soil in a well-drained position in the rock garden, and it is valuable on the wall garden. It is a good plan to top-dress the plant, soon after flowering, with a compost of fine loam, sifted leaf mold and sand. Propagation is most easily effected by division of the roots in spring after flowering; or cuttings of single shoots may be taken in early summer.

S. Esther is a hybrid Silver Saxifrage of exceptional charm and beauty. It forms strong cushions of foliage of special silvery brilliance, the leaves rather long and richly encrusted. The flowers are sulphur yellow, in graceful, arching sprays. One of the best of all the Silver Saxifrages and easily grown in loam, it should be planted on sunny ledges and in pockets in a raised position in the rock garden.

S. Faldonside is a Kabschia hybrid Saxifrage, and although one of the older ones, it is still the most beautiful yellow-flowered hybrid yet raised. It came from the same seed capsule as the rare and somewhat difficult S. Boydii, its parentage being S. Burseriana and S. aretioides, but it is a far better grower.

S. Faldonside forms close, neat cushions of rosettes of sharp-pointed, gray-green foliage and in earliest spring produces with great freedom large, round blossoms of soft yellow, on erect stems an inch or rather more in height. The form and outline of these flowers, with their full, overlapping, rounded petals with slightly crimped edges, is unsurpassed in the whole group. The buds before opening are of glossy, waxy texture, and their yellow is tinged with red. S. Faldonside does well in the scree, and it is also a superb plant for the alpine house.

S. Ferdinandi-Coburgii is a pretty Kabschia Saxifrage with branched sprays of yellow flowers in early spring and silvery leaf rosettes. It is free-flowering and of good constitution.

S. Forsteri is an interesting natural hybrid which occurs rarely in nature, where its two parents, S. caesia and S. mutata, grow in close proximity. In effect it is like S. caesia, with pale yellow flowers. It is best in a cool position in the scree, and may be increased by careful division in the spring, or cuttings of single leaf rosettes.

S. Fortunei belongs to the Diptera group and comes from Japan. It has a fleshy rhizome or root and is without runners. The stalked leaves are thick, broad, green above and bronze-red on their undersurfaces. The flowers are white, irregular in outline, with one or two of the petals conspicuously longer than the others, and are borne in loose panicles on 12-in. stems in October and November.

S. cortusaefolia variety Fortunei, which some botanists regard as a distinct species and call S. Fortunei is hardier than the typical S. cortusaefolia. The variety is a native of China and Japan and may be distinguished by the fact that the undersides of its leaves are gray-green in color and the flowers are somewhat smaller than those of S. cortusaefolia. The variety is not winter hardy in the vicinity of New York City but typical S. cortusaefolia lives satisfactorily as a hardy perennial there. Because of their late flowering, these very beautiful Saxifrages must be given a sheltered place in the rock garden. They appreciate light shade and woodsy soil. Propagation is by division in spring or by seeds sown in spring or fall.

S. Gem is a Kabschia hybrid with neat cushions of gray-green foliage and large, pale pink flowers on inch-tall stems in early spring. It is best in the scree or moraine.

S. geranioides is a handsome Mossy Saxifrage with rather large foliage and fine heads of pure white flowers on 6-8-in. stems. The plant has an aromatic fragrance. It is easy to grow in loamy soil, and is increased by division in spring or autumn. There is a variety called ladanifera, in which the leaves are coated with a kind of resinous exudation which gives a blue-gray appearance and enhances the aromatic fragrance of the plant.

S. Geum is akin to S. umbrosa. The leaves are distinctive, being roundish and borne at the end of long stalks. It is a useful plant for cool, damp corners of the rock garden. There are several interesting varieties in cultivation: crenata, with the edges of its leaves handsomely scalloped; dentata, with round leaves with sharply toothed edges; and hirsuta, very hairy. All are easily increased by division in spring or autumn.

Saxifraga geranioides is an easy kind to grow. Its flowers are white.

S. Godseffiana is a Kabschia hybrid between S. sancta and S. Burseriana speciosa. It is a free grower, forming cushions of rich green foliage covered in early spring with heads of primrose-yellow flowers on stems 1-2 in. tall. It enjoys a sunny position in the rock garden and gritty, well-drained loam.

S. granulata is the Meadow Saxifrage. It is plentiful in rather damp meadows in Europe. The wild form is very pretty and worth growing in the alpine lawn or in some less choice, sunny parts of the rock garden. It has broad, scalloped leaves and a 9-12-in. stem carrying a branched head of large, pure white flowers in May. The plant forms nutlike tubers at the root, by which means it is most easily propagated, although it may also be raised from seeds. There is a double-flowered variety called flore-pleno, which is decidedly handsome; this is increased solely by means of the root tubers. Loamy soil suits this plant. Soon after flowering, the plant disappears entirely, leaf and stem dying right away. A fresh crop of leaves will, however, appear in a few weeks.

S. Grisebachii is the most beautiful and important of all the Engleria group. It forms magnificent rosettes of heavily silvered leaves, and in early spring produces a flower spike, clothed with silver-edged, blue-green leaves and bright red, velvety furlike covering in the upper portion;

Saxifraga Grisebachii forms cushions of silvered leaf rosettes, from which rise stems covered with red glandular hairs. These hairs also cover the stem leaves and calyces of the small pink flowers.

the spike curls over at the top and bears numerous inconspicuous flowers half-hidden in the splendor of the red velvet.

S. Grisebachii is best grown in the scree and it makes a wonderful specimen in the alpine house. It may be raised from seeds, or single rosettes can be struck in sand in the cold frame in early summer.

There is a very superior form called Wisley Variety, with larger leaf rosettes and larger flower spikes more richly clothed in red velvet.

S. Haagii is a Kabschia hybrid of vigorous habit and very free-flowering. In this connection it might be classed with S. apiculata and S. Elizabethiae. In early spring it bears innumerable heads of golden-yellow flowers on stems 1-2 in. high. A truly valuable plant, it thrives in any light, well-drained loam in a sunny position in the rock garden.

S. Hirculus is a bog plant with rather large golden-yellow flowers on erect stems 3 or 4 in. tall. It is difficult to cultivate in the garden. There is a larger, more robust form, however, called major or grandiflora, which is easier of cultivation and, usually, densely red-hairy.

S. His Majesty is a Kabschia hybrid, with small, gray-green foliage, and extremely large white flowers with striking red centers, on stems an inch or so high. It blooms in the early spring, and is best grown in the scree or in the alpine house.

S. Hostii is a Silver Saxifrage, somewhat like a large S. Aizoon, with longer, less silvery leaves, and tall spikes of cream-white flowers, sometimes flecked with red spots. The flower spikes are rather wide at the summit. It is an easy plant, thriving in loamy soil, and is readily increased by division.

S. hypnoides is the type for the Dactyloides or Mossy group. It is a most variable plant. It forms wide mats of mosslike foliage, and in May produces countless graceful sprays of white flowers on wiry stems a few inches high. It is suitable for cool, rather shady corners of the rock garden. It is increased by division in spring or autumn.

There are many named varieties, such as densa, of wiry dwarf habit, and Kingii, also dwarf, the whole plant turning a fine red in winter.

S. Iris Prichard is one of the most distinct Kabschia hybrids. It is of neat, compact habit, forming close cushions of gray-green foliage, and, on inch-long stems in early spring, bears large, well-formed flowers of a curious and beautiful rose-apricot color. It is best in the scree or in the alpine house.

S. Irvingii is interesting as the first pink-flowered Kabschia Saxifraga that was raised. It still is one of the best of the hybrids.

S. Jenkinsae is a hybrid Kabschia, in appearance like an enlarged edition of S. Irvingii. It is of excellent constitution, and very free-flowering, and may be strongly recommended for the scree or for the alpine house.

S. juniperifolia is a rare Kabschia Saxifrage from the Caucasus, with dark green foliage, which smells strongly of juniper when bruised; in early spring it produces heads of rather inferior

Saxifraga lingulata lantoscana, a grand Saxifrage for a crevice in the rock garden, where it will produce its magnificent sprays of white flowers freely in early summer.

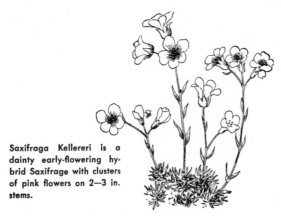

Saxifraga Kellereri is a dainty early-flowering hybrid Saxifrage with clusters of pink flowers on 2—3 in. stems.

yellow flowers in which the petals are extremely small, and the stamens conspicuous and protruding. It should be grown in the scree.

S. Kellereri is a hybrid Engleria. It is an attractive plant with pretty silvery leaf rosettes, and heads of pink flowers on 2-3-in. stems. It is one of the freest-flowering and quite the earliest of all the group. It should be given a sunny sheltered position in the scree, and it is admirable in the alpine house.

S. kestoniensis is a Kabschia hybrid of neat dwarf habit, and is very early-flowering. It produces its large solid white flowers on inch-high stems; it is excellent for the scree or the cold alpine house.

S. kewensis is an Engleria hybrid with handsome silvery rosettes and pretty heads of pink flowers on 3-in. stems in early spring. It does best in the scree or the alpine house.

S. Kotchyi is an easy, vigorous Kabschia, with heads of golden flowers in early spring. It flourishes in the scree, and equally well in the alpine house.

S. lilacina is a dwarf choice Kabschia from the Himalayas. It forms close flat mats of gray-green foliage, and in early spring come the rather large flowers on ½-in. high stems. They are of a curious and pleasing lilac color. The plant enjoys a cool half-shady position in the scree, and makes an admirable plant for growing in a flower pan in the alpine house. It is propagated from leaf rosettes rooted as cuttings in sand in a cold frame in early summer. S. lilacina has proved a valuable pollen parent in producing many of the fine pink hybrid Kabschia Saxifrages.

S. lingulata is one of the most beautiful and valuable of the Euaizoon group. It is variable, and several geographical forms have been distinguished and named. It is a cliff-haunting plant, growing on limestone formations in Italy, Spain, and Sicily. It forms handsome rosettes of long narrow leaves of a blue-gray color, margined with silver encrustations. The flowers are white and are carried in long plumelike sprays, which arch out gracefully from the plant as it hugs the side of the cliff. It flowers in May and June.

S. lingulata is very easy to manage, only needing well-drained loam, and preferring a raised position among the larger rocks, where its flower plumes may display themselves in a natural manner. It is also admirable in the wall garden.

S. lingulata has a number of varieties, the most important of which we shall now describe.

Australis, from southern Italy, has rather broad leaves, and the spikes are tall, the flowers sometimes slightly spotted with red, or of pure white, and the habit of the stems is somewhat stiff. Bellardii comes from near Tenda in the Maritime Alps, and is notable for its very long narrow leaves. The flower plumes are splendid, arched, and well furnished with white blossom. This is an easy and a superb plant for the rock garden.

Catalaunica comes from the cliffs of Montserrat, near Barcelona in Spain. It is a grand plant with rather broad leaves of iron blue, heavily encrusted with silver, and magnificent plumes of pure white flowers. Lantoscana is a distinct form from the neighborhood of St. Martin Vesubie in the Maritime Alps. The leaves are somewhat short, and spoon-shaped at their ends. The flower plumes, of purest white, arch gracefully and are extremely beautiful. There is a specially fine variety of it called superba.

S. longifolia is called the Queen of Saxifrages. It is a native of the Pyrenees and is a cliff dweller on limestone formations. It forms single rosettes, without offsets, of beautiful, heavily silvered leaves, and these grow larger and larger year by year until they measure about 1 ft. across, when the plant is a truly magnificent object. Eventually it reaches flowering size, and sends up a superb plumelike spike of white blossoms, sets seeds and dies. This monocarpic (once-flowering)

Saxifraga Cotyledon is one of the most beautiful of the Silver Saxifragas and one of the easiest to grow.

habit of the S. longifolia is the plant's one fault.

It may be increased by seeds alone, which should be sown in a pan as soon as ripe, and the young plants grown on and planted out when large enough. It is easily managed in loamy soil. The plant is best in a raised position among the larger rocks in the rock garden, from which its flower plume may eventually spray out sideways. It also makes a fine pot specimen; it should be repotted as necessary in larger pots; in this way large leaf rosettes will develop, to be followed by monster flower spikes.

S. longifolia has given many fine hybrids, among the best being Cecil Davies and Tumbling Waters. Seeds of S. longifolia saved from plants grown near other kinds of Saxifrage nearly always produce hybrid offspring, which vary enormously, and many interesting and beautiful forms will occur, most of them with the fortunate trait of producing offsets.

S. Macnabiana is a hybrid Silver Saxifrage of unknown parentage, though it is probable that S. Cotyledon is one of the parents. The true plant, which is rare, and of rather weakly constitution, makes large rosettes of broad green leaves, and bears 9-12-in. spikes of white flowers which are remarkable for the very heavy and handsome zone of red spots upon the petals. There are many spurious plants sold and grown as S. Macnabiana, but the true one is remarkably fine when well grown. Light loam and a raised, well-drained position suit the plant.

S. marginata is a fine Kabschia with blue-green foliage and heads of large, snow-white flowers on 2-3-in. stems in March. The constitution of the plant is vigorous. It does best in the scree or in the alpine house. Variety Rocheliana is dwarfer.

S. media is an Engleria, native to the Pyrenees, with blue-green, heavily silvered leaf rosettes and 3-4-in. flower spikes, covered with reddish velvet. The flowers are small, with pink petals. It does best in the scree.

S. moschata is a small, low-growing Mossy Saxifrage, with cream-white or pale pinkish flowers. It is a variable plant, and several named forms are in cultivation. These include atropurpurea, a good carpeter for cool positions in the rock garden; compacta, close and neat in habit; glandulosa, with velvety leaves; and laxa, of rambling habit and with whitish flowers. Many of these varieties are useful as quick ground cover in unimportant positions.

S. moschata variety Allionii is a comparatively unimportant, if interesting, minute Mossy Saxifrage, growing 1 in. or 2 in. high, and bearing white flowers.

S. Mrs. G. Prichard is a hybrid Kabschia with large, deep pink flowers; they are borne in profusion in early spring on inch-long stems. It thrives in the scree or alpine house.

S. mutata is an interesting alpine Saxifrage with rosettes of broad leaves somewhat like those of S. Cotyledon, though smaller, of a rich, somber green and without any silver encrustation. The flower stems, about a foot high, are somewhat sparsely furnished with starry flowers of a tawny-gold color. It is a plant for a cool corner in the rock garden, in loam and leafmold.

S. Myra is a beautiful dwarf hybrid Kabschia. The parentage is uncertain, but there is no

Saxifraga sarmentosa tricolor is tender and somewhat difficult to grow. Its leaves are handsomely colored with green, creamy white and deep rose pink.

doubt about its garden value. The habit is dwarf and compact, the foliage gray-green, and on inch-high stems are borne cherry-red flowers in earliest spring. It is happy in the scree or in the alpine house, flowering with the utmost profusion.

S. Obristii is a fine hybrid Kabschia, from S. marginata and S. Burseriana. It is a vigorous grower, having blue-green foliage and handsome heads of large white flowers on 3-in. stems in spring. It is best in the scree or in the alpine house.

S. oppositifolia belongs to the Porphyrion group and is widely distributed in many forms throughout the mountains of Europe, Asia and America. It is found on both calcareous and non-calcareous formations, and it grows both as a moraine and scree plant, and as a cliff dweller. In the rock garden it is of easy cultivation, delighting in the scree, and doing well in light, gritty loam. It is a good plan to top-dress the plant with a light, gritty loam compost after flowering.

All the forms of this Saxifrage can be propagated by simple division of the roots, or young shoots may be taken off after flowering and rooted as cuttings in sand in the cold frame. Seedlings may also be raised. The plants are of low prostrate habit, forming mats of dark green foliage and producing large, almost stemless flowers in various tones of lilac, heather-purple, crimson and pink in early summer. These are the best forms or varieties.

Alba is a white variety, but unfortunately it is somewhat poor and small-flowered, though extremely free-flowering. Latina is a beautiful form with rather silvery foliage and large, well-formed flowers of a particularly pleasing tone of pink.

Splendens is, perhaps, the finest form in cultivation, being of excellent constitution and having large, well-formed flowers of heather-purple. Wetterhorn Variety is of slender habit, with intensely brilliant flowers.

S. patens is an interesting and attractive natural hybrid which occurs occasionally between S. caesia and S. aizoides when these two widely separated species grow near one another. In effect it is like a rather green-leaved edition of S.

A floral drift in a rocky setting of the dwarf, carpet-forming, rose-purple Saxifraga oppositifolia.

caesia, with flowers of pale lemon yellow. It is best in a cool location in the scree.

S. Paulinae is a Kabschia hybrid Saxifrage of free growth and good constitution, but is sometimes not so free-flowering as one could wish. The foliage is a fine blue-green and the flowers, on 2-in. stems, are primrose-yellow. It is best in the scree, and is worth a place in the alpine house. It flowers in spring.

S. pectinata is a hybrid Silver Saxifrage of great value. Its parents are said to be S. Aizoon and S.

incrustata. The flowers are second rate, being of a poor tone of white, but the foliage is very fine indeed, being long, narrow, blue-green and richly silvered. It is easy to grow in light loam, and is increased by division of the roots, or by leaf rosettes rooted as cuttings.

S. pedatifida is a strong-growing, handsome Mossy Saxifrage, with fine heads of large white flowers. The rich green foliage makes particularly fine and fast-spreading cushions. It is increased by division.

S. peltata is now referred to Peltiphyllum, which see.

S. Petraschii is a hybrid Kabschia between S. marginata and S. tombeanensis, with heads of snow-white flowers in early spring. It is a plant for the scree or the alpine house.

S. porophylla is a choice Engleria, like a smaller and less brilliant S. Grisebachii. It is best in the scree or may be grown in the alpine house. It flowers in spring.

S. primulaize is an interesting hybrid between S. primuloides and S. aizoides. It forms mats of glossy green leaf rosettes and has loose, few-flowered sprays of starry flowers. Four color forms have been produced, pale pink, salmon, crimson and rose. It is an interesting and beautiful plant, best grown in loamy soil.

S. retusa is a charming Porphyrion Saxifrage of small, close-creeping habit, forming low dull green mats of minute foliage. It blooms in spring, sending up 1-in.-high stems, each bearing a head of several starlike blossoms of a brilliant ruby red. In nature S. retusa grows at great elevations; it is quite easy to grow in rock gardens, thriving in the scree or in gritty loam. It makes a beautiful specimen in the alpine house.

S. Riverslea is an extremely beautiful hybrid Kabschia Saxifrage, of neat, close growth, producing, in early spring, stems 1-2 in. tall, each carrying several flowers of rich plum-crimson. It is distinct and attractive. It does well in the scree, or in light, gritty loam, and is invaluable in the alpine house.

S. Salomonii is a Kabschia hybrid between S. Burseriana and S. marginata variety Rocheliana. It forms carpet mats of blue-green foliage. The large white flowers, four or five on 2-3 in. reddish stems, are beautiful, but the plant is unfortunately not always very free-flowering. It does well in the scree, or in light, gritty, well-drained soil and flowers in early spring.

S. sancta is a Kabschia Saxifrage from eastern Europe and Asia Minor. It is a good grower, soon forming cushions of rich, green foliage. The flowers, in early spring, are golden yellow, in heads of four or five on 2-3 in. reddish stems. The plant is often a shy flowerer. It is easy to grow in the scree, or in light soil in a sunny, well-drained position.

Saxifraga Macnabiana is one of the easiest of the Silver Saxifrages to grow. It is a hybrid.

S. sarmentosa, the Strawberry Geranium or Strawberry Begonia, is a popular tender kind that may be grown outdoors in mild climates and is much used as a house plant and for growing in greenhouses, where it thrives without trouble under benches and in other out-of-the-way corners. It is a trailing plant with runners, much like those of a Strawberry, and coarsely toothed, hairy leaves that are reddish beneath and marked with white veins on their upper surfaces. The branched flower stems, which are borne in summer, rise to a height of 18 in. or 2 ft., and bear numerous white flowers, each of

The Strawberry Geranium or Strawberry Begonia, Saxifraga sarmentosa, is a favorite window-garden plant.

which has two of its five petals conspicuously longer than the others.

The Strawberry Geranium grows without trouble in any ordinary soil and is propagated by separating the rooted runners. It needs light shade from strong summer sun. It is a good plant for pots and for hanging baskets.

A particularly lovely variety of the Strawberry Geranium is S. sarmentosa variety tricolor, which has its leaves handsomely marked with creamy white and rose-red variegations. This kind does not grow as freely as the plain type and is much more difficult to cultivate.

S. scardica is an extremely rare Kabschia from Olympus (Thessaly). Many spurious plants are grown as S. scardica, but the true kind is distinct and handsome, with large rosettes of triangular, sharp-pointed blue-green leaves, pitted at their edges with white encrustations. The flowers are large and white, in wide-spreading heads on pale green stems, 3-4 in. high. It is a plant for a position in the scree, or in the alpine house. The best means of propagation is by leaf-rosette cuttings rooted in sand in the cold frame in early summer.

S. Sibthorpii belongs to the Cymbalaria group, and is a pretty annual with smooth, fleshy, kidney-shaped leaves, and multitudes of bright, golden flowers, with pale yellow spots. It is a pretty plant for naturalizing in cool, shady places in the rock garden. Seeds may be sown where the plants are to flower.

S. squarrosa is the smallest of the Kabschias, and has the appearance of a small, compact S. caesia, with rather greener, less silvery foliage. It is delightfully free-flowering, with slender, erect-branched stems, 2-3 in. high, carrying heads of fine white flowers. It is abundant in the Dolomites, and eastward to the Carpathians. It is best in the scree or the alpine house and can be increased by careful division after flowering.

S. Stribrnyi is a fine Engleria Saxifrage with silvery leaf rosettes, and tallish branched flower sprays clothed in purplish-crimson velvet. It is best in the scree or the alpine house.

S. Sundermannii is a hybrid Kabschia of the same parentage as S. Obristii, S. Burseriana and S. marginata. It resembles the former more than the latter, and is an attractive, compact plant

Saxifraga tennesseensis is a native woodland plant of the southeastern United States. It bears pretty white flowers.

with silver foliage and heads of solid white flowers on 2-in. stems in spring. It is best in the scree or alpine house.

S. tenella belongs to the Trachyphyllum group, is a native of the Julian and Styrian European Alps, and is a charming, easily grown plant, making mats of mosslike appearance. The leaves are narrow and pointed. The white, starry flowers are on slender branched stems, 3-4 in. high. It is a delightful plant for cool, half-shady places in the rock garden.

S. tennesseensis, a native of the southeastern United States, is a delightful kind for growing in shaded places in light, woodland soil. It grows about 6-12 in. high and has white flowers each with a small yellow center.

S. tombeanensis, a native of South Tyrol, is one of the most beautiful of all the Kabschia group. It forms close, hard, compact domes of gray-green foliage; the leaves are narrow and blunt-ended. In spring, later than most Kabschias, it sends up numerous pale green flower stems, each carrying several large white blossoms.

The plant may be grown in the scree, preferably packed between two half-buried pieces of rock, or in a narrow rock crevice, with deep root run. In nature, it is almost exclusively a plant of the limestone cliffs. As a pot plant for the

Saxifrages and other alpine plants growing in a moraine.

alpine house it is first rate; here again it should be planted wedged tightly between two buried rocks. It may be increased by leaf-rosette cuttings rooted in a pan of sand in the cold frame in early summer.

S. Tumbling Waters is a seedling from Saxifraga longifolia. S. longifolia has been well named the Queen of Saxifrages, and Tumbling Waters might well be called the Emperor of the Saxifrages. It produces large starfish leaf rosettes, 12 or 18 in. across, of magnificent form and encrusted with silver. Unlike S. longifolia, Tumbling Waters produces numerous side growths, so that, when the main rosettes reach flowering size, and flower and die, the younger growths remain. The flower spikes are far larger and far more beautiful even than those of S. longifolia. They may reach a length of 3 ft. or more, and are covered from end to end with snow-white blossoms, of far greater purity than those of S. longifolia.

This glorious plant should be given a raised position in the rock garden, a deep crevice or pocket of loamy soil, from which the flower plumes may arch out sideways in the natural way that best suits them. Saxifraga Tumbling Waters is splendid as a pot plant in the alpine house.

S. turfosa is a beautiful Chinese member of the Hirculus group, of clump-forming habit, and with golden starlike flowers on 6-in. stems. It requires cool, rather moist, turfy or peaty loam.

S. tyrolensis is a natural hybrid between S. caesia and S. squarrosa. It is intermediate be-

tween the two parents in appearance, but is no improvement upon either. It is a native of the Tyrol, and occurs fairly frequently where the two parents are found growing together.

S. umbrosa is known in Great Britain as London Pride, St.-Patrick's-Cabbage, Prattling Parnell, Prince's-Feather, and no doubt has many other aliases. It does not thrive where hot summers prevail, but elsewhere is a fine garden plant. The rose-pink flowers are exquisitely spotted, the neat rosettes of stiff green leaves very attractive. London Pride is a lovely plant for the rock garden, easy to grow, exquisite in leaf and flower, and useful for cutting. It is simple to propagate by division of the roots in spring or autumn.

There are numerous forms and varieties of Saxifraga umbrosa in cultivation, notably: cuneata, very narrow leaves; Melvillei, rounded long-stalked leaves; Ogilvieana, handsome, deeply cut leaves, which color well in winter, and fine sprays of pink flowers on red stems; variegata, leaves variegated with white and pink, should be grown in poor soil; primuloides, a dwarf form, with neat, dark green foliage, and pink flowers on 6-8-in. stems; and Elliott's Variety, of dwarf, compact habit, with deep pink flowers on stem, 4-5 in. high.

S. valdensis is an extremely rare Kabschia, though it has all the appearance, superficially, of being a silvery Saxifrage. It is very much like a dwarfer S. cochlearis minor, and too often that good plant passes as S. valdensis. S. cochlearis minor has graceful 4-6-in. sprays of white, long-petaled flowers, on thin, smooth, wiry, reddish stems; those of S. valdensis are a dull white, in a rather dense head on short, thick, glandular stems.

Saxifraga valdensis is found as a cliff dweller in a few restricted areas in the Cottian Alps, where it forms fine dome-shaped cushions of hard, congested gray-green leaves. It may be grown in the scree, or in rock crevices, and is apparently indifferent as to the presence or absence of lime. As a pot plant in the alpine house it is particularly attractive, especially when, having matured and grown for two or three years, it assumes an air of immense antiquity. It is in no way difficult to grow, and may be increased by carefully dividing the plant, or by rooting leaf rosettes as cuttings.

SAXIFRAGE. Saxifraga, which see.

SAXIFRAGE, GOLDEN. Chrysosplenium, which see.

SCAB. See Pests and Diseases.

SCABIOSA—*Pincushion Flower, Sweet Scabious* (Scabio'sa). Hardy perennial, biennial and annual herbaceous plants, valuable for garden decoration and as cut flowers. They belong to the Teasel family, Dipsaceae.

These plants have terminal heads of pincushion-like flowers. There are upwards of forty kinds in cultivation, but only about half a dozen are popular garden plants. They are widely distributed in the various countries of Europe, and in Asia and Africa. The name Scabiosa is derived from *scabies,* itch, and refers to the plant's

Scabiosa caucasica Clive Greaves, rich mauve, a fine perennial plant and invaluable for cutting.

supposed properties of curing irritation of the skin.

The Caucasian Scabious, S. caucasica, is one of the finest border perennials, and the blooms are ideal for cutting. Unfortunately it is not hardy where severe winters occur, and cannot be relied upon to live outdoors at New York, but lives through satisfactorily if planted in a cold frame and protected over winter. It grows up to 30 in. in height, and has lance-shaped, deeply divided leaves; these and the stems are covered with fine hairs. The compact heads of mauve flowers are produced on long stout stems in summer. There are many varieties, some of the best of which are Diamond, dark blue; Isaac House, deep blue; Miss Willmott, white; Perfecta, pale blue; and, loveliest of all, Clive Greaves, rich mauve. In addition there are mixed hybrids which contain many charming shades of lavender-blue.

Well-Drained Soil Is Needed. These plants do best in deep rich well-drained soil. On heavy soils they are apt to die off in the winter, and for that reason they should be planted in spring. The soil should be made firm around the roots; they are best planted in groups of not less than three. The average distance apart for planting is 18 in. If the flowers are removed as they fade, a longer succession of blooms is maintained.

Propagation. The stock of plants can also be increased by dividing the plants in spring. The old clumps are lifted, separated into small sections, each consisting of two or three shoots, with roots attached, and planted where they are to flower. Old straggling plants can often be rejuvenated in this manner.

The rose- or lilac-colored Scabiosa Columbaria needs the same treatment as S. caucasica.

The Sweet Scabious. S. atropurpurea, an annual or biennial, is principally treated as a hardy annual. Of this there are many beautiful varieties, embracing a wide range of colors, including purplish-black, cherry-red, pink, salmon, salmon-rose, mauve and white. They grow from 18 in. to 2 ft. in height, and produce an abundance of flowers which are ideal for cutting, and last well in water.

Early summer flowers are obtained by sowing the seeds in a warm greenhouse in March. The

Flowers of the annual Sweet Scabious, lovely for garden display and cutting.

seeds are sown in a well-drained pan of light soil, which is moistened after sowing, and the pan is covered with a sheet of glass.

The seedlings, when large enough to handle, are transplanted, 2 in. apart, into flats, and, when well established, are gradually hardened off and planted out of doors in May. They require well-drained soil and a sunny position. The best effect is obtained by setting them in irregular groups; they should be planted 9 in. apart.

By sowing the seeds out of doors in April, and afterwards thinning out the seedlings to 9 in. apart, a show of blooms is obtained in the first year. Seeds may also be sown out of doors in September on light soil.

Sweet Scabious in Greenhouses. Sweet Scabious are very pretty when cultivated in cool greenhouses for blooming in late winter and spring; they may be grown in pots or planted in beds. For these purposes seeds should be sown from September to January, in pots or flats containing light, sandy soil. The seedlings are lifted and set 2 in. apart in flats or are potted individually in small pots. Later they are set in larger pots (those 6-7 in. in diameter are suitable for finals) containing rich, well-drained soil. The plants are grown in full sun in temperatures of 45-50 degrees at night and a few degrees higher by day. After the final pots are well filled with healthy roots the plants benefit from weekly applications of dilute liquid fertilizer.

For the Rock Garden. The dwarf tufted plant grown in rock gardens as S. pterocephala is now called Pterocephalus Parnassi, which see.

The Grass-leaved Scabious, S. graminifolia, grows 12 in. high, has narrow grasslike silvery leaves, and bears pale blue flowers. S. ochroleuca (Webbiana) is another dwarf kind with cream-yellow flowers borne on long stalks. These plants require a sunny position and light, well-drained soil, and should be planted in positions where water does not collect around them in winter. Planting is best done in March or April.

Propagation is carried out by lifting and carefully dividing the plants in spring. Seeds may also be sown in a well-drained pan of sandy soil in spring or early summer.

SCABIOUS. Scabiosa, which see.

SCABIOUS, SHEEP'S-BIT. See Jasione.

SCAFFOLD BRANCHES. See Pruning.

SCALDING. This term is used to describe the damage done to plants under glass when the sun shines on them, while the greenhouse is closed and the atmosphere inside is moist. The way to prevent damage is to ventilate the greenhouse a little, early in the morning, before bright sunshine has reached the roof; the moisture on the plants is thus evaporated and no harm is done. In warm weather it is a good plan to leave the top ventilators slightly open all night; this helps to keep the air of the greenhouse dry. See Sun Scald.

SCALE. See Pests and Diseases.

SCALLION. A young Onion that has not yet developed a bulb, although the base may be somewhat swollen. Scallions are pulled and eaten in salads and as greens. The term is also applied to young Leeks and Shallots.

SCANDENT. A term used in the description of shrubs and plants which are of climbing habit of growth.

SCAPE. A botanical term used in describing a leafless flower stem which arises near the base of the plant, as in many Orchids and bulbs.

SCAPHOSEPALUM (Scaphosep'alum). The Orchids grouped under this name are closely related to Masdevallia. They are found wild chiefly in Brazil. All are epiphytal (grow on trees),

without pseudobulbs; they are of tufted growth with evergreen leaves. The flowers are small. Summer and autumn are their chief flowering season. Scaphosepalum is derived from the Greek *skaphe,* a boat, and *sepalum,* a sepal, and refers to the shape of the sepals.

These Orchids are of easy management, requiring a greenhouse with a moist atmosphere and a cool temperature in summer. In winter the temperature should be as near 55 degrees as possible, and on cold nights it may be allowed to fall a few degrees lower. A suitable compost consists of cut osmunda fiber, Tree Fern fiber, Fir bark. or Redwood bark.

Drainage must be free, for the plants should be kept moist throughout the winter and require liberal supplies of water during summer. Shading is necessary in bright summer weather and the plants should be syringed freely then. Repotting is done in early spring; plants with a considerable number of leaves may then be divided if required.

The Chief Kinds. S. gibberosum has comparatively large flowers, cream-white shaded with green and spotted with purple. S. punctatum has pale flowers marked with purple-brown. Others sometimes grown are S. swertiifolium, S. anchoriferum and S. octhodes.

SCAPHYGLOTTIS VIOLACEA (Scaphy-glott'is). A curious epiphytal (tree-growing) Orchid which is found wild in Demerara, British Guiana. The slender, stemlike pseudobulb, a few inches high, bears two evergreen leaves. Between these, other ascending bulbs are produced, from the apex of which appear the small, bright, rose-colored flowers. These are often borne in pairs and open in winter and early spring. They are similar to small Dendrobium flowers in shape. The name Scaphyglottis is from the Greek *skaphe,* a skiff or boat, and *glottis,* a tongue, and refers to the fact that the lip is hollowed.

This Orchid may be grown in a moderately warm greenhouse with a moist atmosphere; a winter temperature of about 60 degrees is most suitable. The plants are grown in small pots or on a block of wood. The compost may be cut osmunda fiber, Tree Fern fiber, Fir bark or Redwood bark. It should be carefully packed around the roots.

SCARBOROUGH LILY. Vallota, which see.

SCARECROW. Various kinds of scarecrows are occasionally used in gardens to protect seeds and seedlings from damage by birds. Those simply made by placing an old coat on a stick or on crossed sticks, to spread the sleeves, are of little use, for birds soon become accustomed to them and take no notice of them. The scarecrow must be as lifelike as possible and have the appearance of a human being if it is to be effective, and should move in the wind. A scarecrow should be moved to a different location every few days. For other bird scares and methods of protecting plants from birds, see Birds Detrimental to Gardens.

SCARLET BUSH. See Hamelia.

SCARLET OAK. Quercus coccinea, which see.

SCARLET PIMPERNEL. Anagallis arvensis, which see.

SCARLET PLUME. Euphorbia fulgens, which see.

SCARLET RUNNER. The common name of a familiar climbing Bean. Its cultivation is dealt with under the heading of Bean, which see. See also Phaseolus.

SCARLET SAGE. See Salvia splendens.

SCARLET WINDFLOWER. See Anemone fulgens, the Scarlet Windflower of Greece.

SCELOCHILUS (Sceloch'ilus). South American epiphytal (tree-growing) evergreen Orchids; the pseudobulbs are very small. The slender spikes are produced from the base of the bulb. The flowers are about an inch across and usually appear in late summer and autumn. Only a few kinds are known. The name is from the Greek *skelos,* a leg, and *cheilos,* a lip, and refers to the shape of the labellum.

These Orchids need a greenhouse with tropical conditions in the summer, and a winter temperature of not less than 60 degrees. They may be grown on wooden blocks or placed in flower pans in a compost of three parts of osmunda fiber and two parts of sphagnum moss. Shading is necessary during the summer, but the plants should be exposed to full sun in winter. Water may be given freely during warm weather, but carefully in the winter. The plants should be examined in March, and repotted if necessary.

The principal kinds are S. Ottonis, with yellow flowers streaked with purple; S. variegatus, white, lined with purple; S. carinatus, with yellow sepals and white petals, and lip marked with purple; and S. saccatus, at one time called Comparettia saccata, with rose-tinted petals and lip.

SCENTED FLOWERS

Fragrant Flowers and Plants Provide Added Delight in the Garden

All the great civilizations of the world have valued the scents of plants very highly, and the offering up of perfumes in some form was an important feature in ancient religious rites. From the dawn of history in Mediterranean regions, the Sudan, etc., the most valued article of commerce, apart from gold, was frankincense, and more than one eminent authority has emphasized the interesting fact that it was probably due first to the jealousies surrounding the incense trade that Arabia for long remained an unknown land.

Scent, shade and water were features of the gardens of the ancient civilizations; Solomon's gardens were scented gardens, and "The Song of Songs" is full of the fragrance of plants so highly esteemed by the extravagant king. His descendant, Hezekiah, reckoned spices among the royal treasures and as such they were stored in a special house (see 2 Chronicles xxii: 27, and 2 Kings xx:13). In medieval times, references to gardens meant scented gardens. The same is true in the Orient today. The earliest medieval garden writer, Walafred Strabo (ninth century), esteemed above all Roses and Lilies and "the glow of their sweet scent."

Fragrant Trees and Shrubs. Among trees and shrubs, the most important and most commonly grown are those discussed below.

Buddleia globosa is a quick-growing shrub with orange-colored, ball-like inflorescences (flower clusters) in May and June, with a rich

[11–12a]
Salvia farinacea

·[11–12]
Sanchezia nobilis

[11–12c]
Sedum kamtschaticum

[11–12b]
Spanish Bluebell
(Scilla hispanica)

[11—13]

A Seaside Garden

honey scent. The Carolina Allspice (Calycanthus floridus), which blooms in summer, has reddish-brown flowers and aromatic leaves and bark. The Californian Allspice (Calycanthus occidentalis) has scented crimson flowers. The leaves and wood also are fragrant.

Chimonanthus praecox is a shrub that bears deliciously fragrant flowers.

Chimonanthus praecox is one of the most valuable of winter-flowering shrubs for regions where winters are moderately mild. The flowers, produced on its leafless branches from January to March, have a strong Honeysuckle scent.

Choisya ternata, the Mexican Orange Blossom, is an evergreen that is hardy in mild climates only. Its rich glistening leaves and fragrant clusters of flowers have made it a universal favorite.

Cistus ladaniferus, the Gum Cistus, attains over 5 ft. in height, and the white flowers in July and August are 4 in. across. Flowers and foliage are richly aromatic. C. cyprius, one of the most beautiful of the Rock Roses, has aromatic foliage and the young branches are covered with an aromatic gum. These are hardy only where severe winters are not experienced.

Clematis paniculata is a favorite garden plant. The flowers are almond-scented. Clerodendrum trichotomum, a shrub from the Far East, attains 8-10 ft. in height, and has deliciously scented white flowers.

Clethra alnifolia, the Sweet Pepper Bush, is a native American, summer-flowering shrub, with fragrant white flowers, and the leaves, when bruised, have a peculiar scent. Corylopsis pauciflora is a deciduous (leaf-losing) early spring-flowering shrub, with small catkins of fragrant yellow flowers, and C. spicata is even more striking, with scented flowers.

Nearly all the Daphnes are remarkably sweetly scented, the most popular being D. Mezereum, blooming in early spring, and D. Cneorum (April and May). Of the Heaths, Erica arborea, E. australis and E. Veitchii are the most attractively scented.

Hamamelis mollis and H. japonica have interesting and pleasing scents. Hyssop (Hyssopus officinalis) is strongly aromatic. The sweetly scented Jasmines are J. officinale, cultivated from time immemorial, and J. humile variety revolutum, a rarely grown yet valuable evergreen. J. nudiflorum, the hardy yellow Winter Jasmine, lacks perfume.

All the Lavenders have a strong, aromatic scent. Liriodendron tulipifera or Tulip Tree, flowering in early summer, is one of the finest hardy native trees; the yellowish-green flowers are fragrant.

Of the Honeysuckles, the most sweetly scented are Lonicera fragrantissima, flowering in late winter; the fragrant L. japonica, which blooms in summer; L. Periclymenum, the common Woodbine; the early and late Dutch Honeysuckles; and L. Standishii, blooming in winter.

Magnolias vary greatly in their scents. The most richly scented are M. grandiflora, M. obovata (hypoleuca), M. Sieboldii (parviflora), and M. Watsonii.

Mahonia (Berberis) aquifolium has deliciously scented flowers, produced in early spring, followed by an abundance of blue-black fruits. Mahonia Bealii has long racemes of yellow flowers in early spring; its scent is almost indistinguishable from that of the favorite Lily of the Valley.

Myrica Gale (Bog Myrtle) is a scented-leaved plant that likes a damp soil. Myrtus communis, the classical Myrtle, has been valued for its scent at least since Roman times. Eugenia apiculata (Myrtus Luma) has fragrant snow-white flowers.

Osmanthus ilicifolius (Aquifolium) and its varieties have sweetly scented white flowers in late summer and early autumn; a near relative,

Siphonosmanthus Delavayi, often called Osmanthus Delavayi, flowers in April and is very fragrant.

Of the Mock Oranges, Philadelphus coronarius has been cultivated and valued for its fragrance for centuries. P. grandiflorus has no fragrance. P. Virginal and other modern sorts have some scent.

Pieris floribunda, valuable for its early flowering, has curiously scented flowers in early spring.

Of the Rhododendrons, those with the most strongly scented flowers include R. azaleoides, R. canadense, R. decorum, R. Fortunei, R. luteum, R. Loderi and R. viscosum.

Among the Roses, many of the species or wild types are fragrant, and so are large numbers of the garden hybrids. See Rosa and Rose.

Rosemary (Rosmarinus officinalis) is one of the most beautiful aromatic shrubs, and has been grown in our gardens for centuries. Rubus odoratus, which flowers from June to September, is valuable for planting under trees; it has handsome leaves and scented, purple-red flowers.

Of the Salvias, S. officinalis or Sage has long been grown; there are several varieties, the most pleasing being the purple-leaved and the variegated. S. Sclarea is one of the most handsome of the Salvia family; it has a very strong but not very pleasing aromatic scent.

Sambucus canadensis, unlike the European Elder, has a delicious scent; it flowers in August.

Santolinas are pleasing and fragrant, notably S. Chamaecyparissus, when their foliage is bruised. Satureia montana, Winter Savory, is used as a seasoning herb; it is in full flower in August, a time when flowering shrubs are not plentiful.

Spartium junceum, Spanish Broom, has fragrant yellow flowers in summer and is very attractive to bees. Many of the Lilacs are richly scented and rank among the most valuable of garden shrubs.

Tilia europaea, the European Linden tree, has flowers with a peculiarly attractive scent. Ulex europaeus or Gorse has honey-scented flowers; in localities where it grows well it is particularly valuable on dry sandy soils and dry banks.

Of the Viburnums, one of the most richly scented is V. Carlesii, flowering in early spring.

The newer V. Burkwoodii is equally desirable. V. fragrans is one of the best winter or early spring-flowering shrubs; it has pinkish clusters of small, scented flowers. The cream-colored flowers of V. Lentago are very fragrant.

Vitex Agnus-castus is an old favorite. It blooms in August and September; the entire shrub is aromatic, and the flowers are fragrant. Of the Grapes, V. vulpina (cordifolia) has sweetly scented flowers, and the fruits of V. Labrusca have a curious musklike fragrance.

Of the Wisterias, the best scented are the common W. chinensis and its varieties.

Fragrant Herbaceous Plants and Annuals. Among herbaceous plants and annuals, the following are the most richly scented: Abronia; Alyssum (now called Lobularia) maritimum (Sweet Alyssum); Arabis albida; Asperula odorata (Woodruff); Satureia glabella (a small herbaceous plant with fragrant lilac flowers); Calendula officinalis (Pot Marigold); Cedronella; Centaurea moschata (Sweet Sultan); Coriandrum (Coriander). It is a curious fact that the seeds of Coriander become more fragrant with age.

Other fragrant plants are Cheiranthus (Wallflower); Border Carnation, Dianthus plumarius (Pink); Erysimum, the Alpine Wallflower; Geranium macrorrhizum, with exceptionally rich aromatic scent; Hesperis matronalis (Rocket); Hesperis tristis; Lathyrus odoratus (Sweet Pea), especially the old-fashioned or grandiflora varieties; Linnaea borealis, particularly sweetly scented in the evening. The semishrubby tree Lupine, Lupinus arboreus, and the hybrids are sweetly scented.

Matthiola bicornis (Night-scented Stock), Ten Week and other Stocks are all sweetly scented. All the Mints are pleasantly scented. Monarda didyma (Bee Balm) has fragrant leaves. Myrrhis odorata (Sweet Cicely) is an old favorite with scented, fernlike leaves. Nicotiana alata variety grandiflora (affinis) is the white annual Tobacco flower. Of the Oenotheras (Evening Primrose) O. biennis is one of the most exquisite of the evening scents. O. marginata and O. trichocalyx are also sweetly scented.

All the Marjorams (Origanum) are aromatic. Numerous varieties of the herbaceous Peony are sweetly scented. Of the Primula family, the following are scented: Auricula, Primrose, Polyanthus, Cowslip, P. Bulleyana, P. chionantha, P. Florindae, P. involucrata, P. nivalis and P. sikkimensis.

Reseda (Mignonette) has a peculiarly delightful, unusual scent. Both Romneya Coulteri and R. trichocalyx are scented. The garden varieties of Scabiosa have a honey-like scent. Tanacetum vulgare and its varieties have aromatic scents. Tropaeolum majus or Nasturtium has a strong scent. The Sweet Violet is exquisitely scented; so, too, are some varieties of the Pansy.

Bulbs with Fragrant Flowers. Among bulbous and related plants the following are the best scented: Anthericum Liliago, Paradisea Liliastrum, Convallaria majalis (Lily of the Valley), Crocus vernus and various other kinds of Crocus, Cyclamen europaeum, Gladiolus tristis and Hyacinth.

Of• the Irises, the following are scented: I. aphylla variety Swertii, I. flavissima (arenaria), I. germanica variety florentina, I. germanica, I. graminea, I. histrioides, I. reticulata, and I. unguicularis.

Among Lilies the following are scented: L. auratum, L. Brownii, L. candidum, L. leucanthum variety chloraster (centifolium), L. Duchartrei, L. giganteum, L. Hansonii, L. longiflorum, L. philippinense, L. regale. Of the Grape Hyacinths (Muscari), M. botryoides and M. moschatum are sweetly scented.

The following Narcissi are scented: N. Jonquilla and hybrids; most of the N. Leedsii hybrids; N. odorus Campanella; N. odorus rugulosus; N. poeticus recurvus, the Pheasant's-Eye Narcissus.

Of the Tulip species and varieties the best scented are, among the early singles, De Wet, Thomas Moore, and Prince of Austria. Of the May Tulips, Prince of Orange, Dom Pedro, Gesneriana rosea, and Gesneriana lutea are all very fragrant. T. patens (persica) is deliciously scented.

Among aquatics, Acorus Calamus (Sweet Flag) is so pleasantly scented that it was formerly used for strewing on floors. The flowers of Aponogeton (Water Hawthorn) have a very fragrant hawthorn-like scent. Many varieties of Nymphaea odorata (Water Lily) are scented.

SCHEFFLERA (Scheffler'a). Tropical and subtropical shrubs and small trees belonging to the Aralia family, Araliaceae. Some are grown outdoors in the warm parts of the United States and one, S. actinophylla, has, in recent years, become popular as a foliage plant for growing indoors in pots and tubs. The name commemorates J. C. Scheffler of Danzig.

Schefflera actinophylla forms a handsome and long-lasting decorative foliage plant when grown indoors in pots.

Schefflera actinophylla is a small evergreen tree that attains an ultimate height of 30 ft. and has large, handsome, digitate (fingered), deep green leaves on long stalks. It grows rapidly in any reasonably good soil and thrives in partial shade. It is a native of Australia.

When grown in pots or tubs, this tree should be watered moderately, not frequently enough to keep the soil constantly saturated nor yet so seldom that the earth ever becomes really dry to the extent that the foliage wilts. Plants that have filled their containers with roots benefit from receiving applications of dilute liquid fertilizer at weekly or biweekly intervals. Light shade from strong sun should be provided.

Scheffleras may be propagated easily from seeds and by means of cuttings and air layering. The last method is very useful for pot-grown specimens that have grown tall and leggy.

Schefflera digitata, a native of New Zealand, attains an ultimate height of about 25 ft. and has digitate leaves. S. venulosa, an Indian kind, is a shrub with leaves similar to, but smaller than, those of S. actinophylla.

SCHINUS—*California Pepper Tree, Peruvian Mastic Tree* (Schi'nus). Tender trees which are found wild chiefly in tropical America. They belong to the family Anacardiaceae, and the name, derived from *schinos*, mastic, refers to the resinous juice which exudes from the trees. This juice is more freely exuded after a shower of rain and the air in the vicinity of the trees is then highly perfumed.

In California S. Molle (California Pepper Tree) is one of the most popular trees for planting on lawns and to form avenues. To ensure fruiting it is necessary to plant staminate (male) and pistillate (female) trees in proximity. The females only bear fruits, of course. One staminate tree will fertilize several pistillate trees planted nearby.

Schinus Molle is evergreen, about 20 ft. tall, broad-headed and of graceful habit. It has attractive fernlike foliage. Its flowers, creamy white, are borne in large terminal panicles; its fruits are rose-red. It is a native of the American tropics.

The Brazilian Pepper Tree or Christmasberry Tree is Schinus terebinthifolius, a native of Brazil. This evergreen kind has coarser foliage than S. Molle and its flowers are in tighter clusters. It grows to a height of about 20 ft. This is the Schinus most popular for planting in Florida, where it succeeds better than does S. Molle. The fruits are bright red.

Another kind is S. dependens (Duvaua dependens), an evergreen tree growing 15 ft. in height; its twigs are terminated by spines. The leaves are 1 in. in length, obovate (egg-shaped, with the widest part at the top), and the flowers are greenish-yellow; the small purple berries which succeed the flowers are a conspicuous feature. This kind is a native of western South America.

These trees are easily propagated by seeds and grow well in sunny places in a variety of soils.

SCHISANDRA (Schisand'ra). A group of leaf-losing and evergreen shrubs, with long twining branches densely clothed with leaves, and more or less aromatic. The sepals and petals of the flowers are similarly colored, and male and female organs are in different flowers; sometimes whole plants bear male flowers, and others female. Some kinds have attractive fruits.

Most of these shrubs are natives of Asia, but one is found in North America. Schisandra belongs to the Magnolia family, Magnoliaceae, though some botanists place it in Schisandraceae. The name is taken from the Greek *schisio*, cleaving, and *andros*, male, and alludes to the cleft anthers.

Propagation can be carried out by means of short cuttings of half-ripe wood inserted in a warm frame in July; or branches may be layered in the open ground in early spring.

Seeds should be sown in well-drained pots of sandy soil in a warm greenhouse. After sowing, the pots are covered with a piece of glass. When watering is necessary it should be done by immersing the pots to the rims in a vessel of water. As soon as the seedlings are large enough to be handled conveniently they are potted separately in small pots.

Suitable for Training over Trellis. The various kinds thrive in deep, loamy soil; they should be planted in positions where the long branches can arrange themselves naturally over a support. The foot of a bush, trellis, rough pole, building or wall is a suitable position. Pruning to keep the plants within bounds is carried out as soon as the flowers fade, but it is a mistake to prune too much; the plants should be left to grow as a natural tangle of branches.

Chinese Kinds. Schisandra Henryi was introduced from western China in 1900. Its leaves, which fall in autumn, are 3-4 in. long, and almost as wide, thick in texture with a shining surface. The white flowers are half an inch across and the female flowers are followed by red, pulpy fruits that are eaten in China. Closely allied kinds are S. glaucescens and S. pubescens from central China.

A Vigorous Climbing Shrub. S. chinensis is a vigorous climber, 25-30 ft. high, with leaves 2-4 in. long, pale rose-colored flowers in April and May, and bright red fruits. In order to have fruits, it is necessary that male and female plants be grown together. It is a native of both China and Japan, and has been grown in occidental gardens since 1860. It is hardy toward the North.

Other kinds are S. repanda (nigra), with white flowers and black fruits, a native of Japan and Korea; and S. coccinea, which occurs as a native from South Carolina to Florida but is not hardy in the North.

SCHISMATOGLOTTIS (Schismatoglott'is). Tropical, perennial herbaceous plants which are cultivated for their ornamental foliage. They are found wild in Malaya, Borneo, New Guinea, and Sumatra, and belong to the Arum family, Araceae.

Schismatoglottis neo-guineensis, a fine foliage plant that is suitable for growing in greenhouses and as a house plant.

Ornamental-leaved Hothouse Plants. These plants have small, green or yellowish, arum-like flowers which are inconspicuous and the spathes quickly fall. Because of the way in which the tongue-like spathes split off, they have been given the name Schismatoglottis, from *schismatos,* splitting, and *glottis,* tongue.

These plants have slender rhizomes. The heart-shaped or oblong leaves vary in length from 10-16 in., and are either green or striped with silvery gray, yellow or purple.

To cultivate the plants successfully, a greenhouse in which a minimum winter temperature of 55 degrees can be maintained is necessary, or they may be grown as house plants. When they are grown in a greenhouse, a semishaded position is required and a humid atmosphere should be maintained at all times of the year.

In March the plants are turned out of their pots, the crocks and loose soil are removed from the roots, and, if the roots are crowded, the plants are set in slightly larger pots, which must be well drained. The best potting compost consists of one part of loam and two parts of leaf mold or peat moss with enough sand added to make the mixture porous. After potting, it is necessary to exercise great care in watering, the best system being to allow the soil to become moderately dry before moistening it, then to soak it thoroughly, then to allow it to become nearly dry again before the next watering, and so on until the roots have permeated the new soil.

When the pots are well filled with roots, the soil must be kept moist, and weak liquid fertilizer applied once a week during the summer. From September to March it is sufficient to water only when the compost becomes nearly dry. A light syringing twice a day in summer, and once a day in winter, is beneficial, as it freshens and cleanses the foliage. The stock of plants is easily increased by division of the rhizomes at potting time, in March, and by cuttings.

The Chief Kinds. There are upwards of seventy kinds of Schismatoglottis but very few are in cultivation. S. asperata, a native of Borneo, has dark green ovate or obovate leaves that have minute white spots on their upper surfaces. S. asperata variety albo-maculata (crispata) has similar leaves, with a central stripe of silvery gray; and S. Lavallei (concinna) has oblong or lanceolate leaves, 16 in. in length, blotched with silvery white. There are two varieties of S. Lavallei—purpurea, having purple blotches on the underside of the leaves and silvery gray blotches above, and immaculata, with purple leafstalks and leaves which are purple beneath and blotched with gray above.

S. neo-guineensis has heart-shaped leaves blotched yellowish-green; S. ornata has pointed heart-shaped leaves, dark green in color and with slender stalks; S. pulchra (S. decora) has oblong green leaves, heavily blotched with silvery white. S. Ruttenii is a low-growing kind with corrugated, satiny green leaves.

SCHIVERECKIA (Schivereck'ia). Low perennials belonging to the Mustard family, Cruciferae, and related to Alyssum. They are hardy and are adapted for cultivation in rock gardens.

Schivereckia Bornmuelleri is an easy plant to grow in the rock garden. It thrives best in full sun where the soil is very well drained.

The name honors Professor S. B. Schivereck, of Lemberg.

Culture. These plants thrive in full sun and in any gritty, well-drained soil. For the best results the soil should not be very rich. They are easily raised from seeds sown in spring and from cuttings taken shortly after blooming. Division of the plants immediately after they are through blooming or in early fall affords another simple means of increase.

The best-known kind is S. Bornmuelleri, which forms a spreading specimen 2-4 in. tall with its leaves in rosettes. In spring it is covered with white flowers. It is a native of Asia Minor.

S. podolica hails from southeastern Europe and Asia Minor and is generally similar to S. Bornmuelleri but is usually taller.

SCHIZAEA PUSILLA—*Curly Grass Fern* (Schizae'a). An interesting native North American Fern that looks much more like a small, fine grass than a Fern. It occurs in coastal regions from Newfoundland to New Jersey. It belongs to the family Schizaeaceae, the Schizaea Fern family. The name is derived from *schizo,* to split, and refers to the divided fronds.

Schizaea pusilla is occasionally cultivated by fanciers of Ferns and by wild-flower enthusiasts. It is difficult to establish and not easy to keep. For its satisfactory growth it needs a strongly acid, moist medium. Sphagnum moss or acid sand are most commonly used. It is propagated by spores.

Other species of Schizaea occur, mostly in the tropics, but these are not generally known in cultivation.

SCHIZANTHUS—*Butterfly Flower* (Schizanth'us). Annual plants, which grow wild in Chile and are in the Nightshade family, Solanaceae. The name Schizanthus is derived from *schizo,* to cut, and *anthos,* a flower, and refers to the deeply cut or fringed petals of the flower.

Few, if any, of the original species or wild types are now grown in gardens; they have been superseded by the numerous beautifully colored forms or varieties which have been raised by crossbreeding between them, and by selection. The plants vary in height from 12-18 in. out of doors, and grow taller under glass. Where summers are not excessively hot, they are suitable for planting out of doors in a sheltered sunny place, but are even of greater value for flowering under glass in late spring and early summer. Well-grown plants in pots are magnificent specimens and become smothered in bloom.

The way to grow the finest plants of Schizanthus is to sow seeds during the first or second week in September, in a flat or flower pan of finely sifted soil. The soil is moistened through a watering can having a "rose" or fine spray nozzle on the spout, and the seeds are sown thinly and covered with a mere sprinkling of the sifted compost of loam, leaf mold and sand.

The flat of seeds is placed in a greenhouse or cold frame, and a piece of glass is put on top. The frame must be kept close and shaded until the seedlings appear, and the soil is moistened by using a fine spray. As soon as the seedlings are large enough to be handled with safety—that is to say, when they are about 1½ in. high—they are transferred separately to flowerpots 2½ in. in diameter, filled with a soil compost similar to that used for the seeds. They are returned to the frame, which is kept close for a few days. Subsequently the frame must be ventilated freely in mild weather.

Watering needs to be done with care or the seedlings may damp off. The soil should not be watered until it is moderately dry; the pots are then filled to the rim, and no more water is given until the soil again approaches dryness. The plants are kept in the frame until cold weather sets in; they ought then to be moved to a greenhouse that is slightly heated.

The secret of success with these plants is to keep them as cool as possible during the winter months, and near the glass roof, so that they will not become "drawn" (attenuated). They must make sturdy growth if they are to develop into really fine plants. A temperature of 45 degrees at night is high enough, and the thermometer may fall to 40 degrees without harm being done. The greenhouse should be ventilated freely in mild weather.

When the plants are well rooted in the small pots, they should be repotted in pots 5 in. in diameter, and transferred to larger ones as growth necessitates. The best soil compost for this potting consists of two parts of loam (pieces of old turf) and one part of leaf mold, and a scattering of sand.

If the plants are treated in the way advised, they will be ready for the final potting, in 7- or 8-in. pots, in February. During the winter months they need comparatively little water; the soil should not be watered until it is moderately dry.

Pinching or Stopping. When the plants are well rooted in 2½-in. pots, the tops are pinched off and a week or ten days later repotting is carried out; it is a mistake to stop the plants and repot them at the same time. Repotting should not be done until they have started to make fresh growth. When well rooted in 5-in. pots, the plants must again be stopped by pinching off the ends of the shoots which developed as a result of the previous stopping. In this way well-branched plants are obtained.

At the final potting, the compost should consist of two parts of loam (this to be of coarse texture and fertile, not fine soil) one part of leaf mold and decayed manure, and a scattering of sand. The plants will come into bloom in April and May and, if the treatment has been correct, they will be laden with flowers almost from tip to base.

The chief details to observe are to keep the plants cool, to stop the shoots to ensure well-branched plants, and to water carefully—especially while the seedlings are small, and during the winter months. The plants are useless after the flowers are over.

Sowing Seeds in Spring. To provide plants for the decoration of the greenhouse or conservatory during the summer, and for planting out of doors in the summer flower beds, seeds are sown under glass in a slightly heated greenhouse early in March.

If the plants are to be grown under glass, the seedlings are treated in the way already advised, except that 5-in. or 6-in. pots will be large enough; the plants will not be so large as those from an autumn sowing.

If they are to be set out of doors late in May or early June, the seedlings should be placed about 3 in. apart, in flats 4 in. deep, filled with the compost already recommended. From the flats they will be transferred to the flower beds. The plants need to be supported by sticks or thin bamboo canes to keep them upright.

The chief kinds are S. Grahamii, lilac-rose; S. retusus, deep rose; and S. pinnatus, lilac. The chief hybrid strains or types are hybridus grandiflorus and wisetonensis. The varieties comprised in these types exhibit a wide range of color, through pink, crimson, mauve, violet, salmon, yellow, and apricot. The pansy-flowered Schizanthus are particularly handsome; they have unusually large blooms of rich coloring. Mention must also be made of the dwarf strains, of compact habit, which will appeal to owners of small greenhouses.

SCHIZOBASOPSIS VOLUBILIS (Schizobasop'sis). Also known as Bowiea volubilis, this curious South African plant has a large, greenish bulb from the top of which it produces annual, much-branched, twining green stems that are slender and leafless. The stems perform the functions of leaves and bear the small, greenish flowers.

Schizobasopsis belongs in the Lily family, Liliaceae. The name is derived from the Greek and means like Schizobasis. Schizobasis is a genus of African plants of no horticultural importance.

This peculiar plant is of interest as a curiosity. It may be grown out of doors in mild, dry climates, such as that of southern California, and also as a greenhouse and window plant. Its culture presents no difficulties.

The soil in which it is planted should be very

Bulbs and young foliage of the curious South African Schizobasopsis volubilis.

porous and well drained. When preparing a mixture to be used for potting, it is well to add a generous amount of finely broken brick as well as coarse sand to the soil mixture.

Potting or planting should be done, when necessary, in fall just as the first signs of new growth begin. Plants will remain in the same containers for several years without needing potting. When potting or planting, the bulbs should be placed so that they are mostly above ground; only a little of their bases should be below soil level.

From the time when new growth starts until the stems begin to die down after flowering, the soil should be watered often enough to keep it always reasonably moist. When the stems begin to turn yellow naturally, watering should be reduced, and when they have died down completely all moisture should be withheld and the soil kept quite dry until the beginning of the next growing season.

A sunny position in a cool greenhouse or in a window in a cool room is suitable for this plant. Increase is easily secured by natural offsets of the bulbs, which are produced freely. Stakes, strings or other supports around which the stems may twine are necessary.

SCHIZOCENTRON (Schizocen'tron). A genus consisting of one species, Schizocentron elegans, more familiarly known as Heeria elegans. It is a tender herbaceous plant from Mexico, of creeping habit, the stems rooting at the nodes and forming a dense mat. The reddish stems are furnished with small, ovate leaves, and the short side shoots are terminated by deep purple flowers about an inch across.

It is a charming little pot plant for the front of the warm greenhouse benches, thriving in a compost of loam, peat and a little sand, and easily increased by detaching and potting the rooted portions. Schizocentron belongs to the family Melastomaceae; and the name, from *schizo*, to cut, and *kentron*, spur, refers to the shape of the flowers.

SCHIZOCODON — *Mirror-of-the-Mountain* (Schizoco'don). A genus of one species and one or two varieties, belonging to the family Diapensiaceae and, by some botanists, included in the genus Shortia. The name Schizocodon is from *schizo*, to cut, and *kodon*, a bell, from the shape of the flowers.

A Lovely Woodland Plant. Schizocodon soldanelloides, or Mirror-of-the-Mountain, as the Japanese call it, is a Japanese woodland plant of quite unusual beauty. It has rounded leathery leaves, not unlike those of a Shortia, carried on wiry stems, 4 or 5 in. high; the flower stems bear four to six large bell-shaped flowers, rosy-pink and deeply fringed like those of a Soldanella, in early spring. The flowers are of exquisite beauty and rather waxy texture.

The dainty fringed flowers of Schizocodon soldanelloides, a charming little woodland plant.

A Difficult Plant to Establish. It is a difficult plant to establish in the garden, and well-rooted specimens suitable for planting are not easy to come by. It should be given a shady position in the woodland or in the shelter of shrubs such as Rhododendron, and a soil consisting of well-decayed leaf mold or peat, mixed with sand and lumps of broken sandstone or millstone grit rock. The roots are extremely sensitive to exposure to the air, which causes them to dry out and perish very quickly. The plant is an inveterate lime hater, and it is only worth while attempting its cultivation where the soil is acid.

For a Cool Greenhouse. It may be grown with care in a flower pan in the alpine house, in a compost similar to that described, and should be watered only with soft or rain water. Old, well-established plants may be divided with care, but such plants are seldom to be found, and when found are far better left alone. The plant can be increased with difficulty and much care from seeds sown in a pan of peaty soil, leaf mold and sand in a shaded cold frame.

The variety magnus (macrophyllus) seems to be a stouter plant and somewhat easier to manage. It has flower stems 5 or 6 in. high of beautiful pink-fringed bells, veined with deeper pink, carried four or five on an erect wiry stem. It requires the same woodland treatment as the type, and makes a lovely plant for the alpine house.

The variety ilicifolia is distinguished by having smaller leaves with larger and fewer teeth on their margins than the type. It responds to the same care and has the same uses.

SCHIZOPETALON WALKERI (Schizopet'-alon). A hardy annual, found wild in Chile, which belongs to the Mustard family, Cruciferae; it is grown for the sake of its white flowers, which are fragrant towards the evening. It reaches a height of 12-15 in., and has deeply cleft or fringed petals. The name is from *schizo,* to cut, and *petalon,* a petal, and refers to the deeply cut or fringed petals.

Schizopetalon is raised from seeds sown out of doors in the position where the plants are to bloom, but they should not be sown before danger from frost has passed, as they are not very hardy. The flowers open from July onwards.

Fragrant in the Evening. This plant thrives best in light or well-drained soil, and must be grown in a sunny place in the garden. It is an excellent plant to sow in a border beneath the house windows, where its evening fragrance is delightful. The seeds are scattered thinly in groups, and covered with about $\frac{1}{4}$ in. of soil; the seedlings are thinned out gradually until eventually they are 4-5 in. apart.

In cold districts the seedlings may be raised in a cold frame or greenhouse late in March or early in April, and planted out of doors in May.

In cool greenhouses this pretty annual may be grown in pots from seeds sown in September to produce flowers in late winter and early spring. An ordinary, well-drained, fertile soil, full sunlight and a night temperature of 45-50 degrees provide satisfactory conditions.

SCHIZOPHRAGMA (Schizophrag'ma). A small genus of leaf-losing, climbing or scandent shrubs, which cling to their supports by aerial roots in the same way as Ivy, and, like Ivy, alter their habit of growth when they have reached the top of their support. They then bear short, rootless branches and it is from these, and from branches thrust out from the front of the supporting branches, that flowers are produced.

Self-clinging Climbing Shrubs. These shrubs are closely allied to the Hydrangea and, like the Hydrangea, produce numerous sexual flowers

An unusual hardy climbing vine that attaches itself to masonry and flowers freely in summer is the Japanese Schizophragma hydrangeoides.

which are not very attractive, intermixed with showy sterile flowers made up of bracts only. However, there is a difference between the sterile flowers of the two genera, for, in Hydrangea, the sterile flowers are made up of four bracts each, whereas in Schizophragma each sterile flower has one bract.

Schizophragma belongs to the Saxifrage family, Saxifragaceae. The name is from the Greek, *schizo,* to cut, and *phragma,* a wall, and refers to the opening of the carpels of the fruit.

Propagation. The Schizophragmas are increased by means of short cuttings of side shoots made with a slight heel of old wood, inserted in a bed of sand in a greenhouse or cold frame in July. The climbing shoots with aerial roots do not make good cuttings, but they may be layered in spring and removed as separate plants in fall.

The young plants should be planted in moist, loamy soil at the foot of a tree or wall and allowed to grow with little or no pruning. Plants from pots may be set out any time from spring through early fall; when transplanting from the open ground has to be carried out, it may be done in early spring.

S. hydrangeoides may grow 30-40 ft. high in suitable conditions and is hardy in the North. It is a native of Japan and is rare in cultivation in North America, the plant often grown under that name being Hydrangea petiolaris. S. hydrangeoides and H. petiolaris are very similar in habits of growth, and in their broadly ovate leaves, which are 4-6 in. long, $2\frac{1}{2}$-4 in. wide, and toothed at their margins. The inflorescences are also somewhat alike, with cream-colored flowers, but the difference between the two can be seen in the single bract of each sterile flower of the Schizophragma as contrasted with the 4 bracts that each sterile Hydrangea flower has. In S. hydrangeoides the bract is heart-shaped and 1-$1\frac{1}{2}$ in. long.

S. integrifolium was introduced from central China in 1901. It differed from S. hydrangeoides in the shape of the leaves, which are ovate with a heart-shaped or rounded base, 3-7 in. long and $1\frac{1}{2}$-$4\frac{1}{2}$ in. wide at the base. The margins of the leaves are not toothed. The sterile flowers are few in number, but conspicuous. They are white

or cream colored, lance-shaped, $3\frac{1}{2}$ in. long and $1\frac{3}{4}$ in. wide at the base. S. integrifolia is not hardy in the North.

SCHIZOSTYLIS COCCINEA—*Kaffir Lily* (Schizos'tylis). A fall- or winter-flowering bulb plant which was introduced into cultivation in 1864. It is hardy only in milder districts and is greatly valued for its late flowering, coming into bloom in November and December.

Schizostylis belongs to the Iris family, Iridaceae. The name is derived from *schizo,* to cut, and *stylos,* a style, and refers to the fact that the styles (anther stalks) are divided.

This plant has rhizomes (underground stems), sword-shaped leaves like the Gladiolus, 2 ft. in length, and bears one-sided spikes of bright red flowers, each $2\frac{1}{2}$ in. in diameter. It does best when planted where the flowers are sheltered from cold winds, and where the early morning sun cannot shine on them. There are a bright pink variety called Mrs. Hegarty, and another named Viscountess Byng, with pale pink flowers.

For a Sunny, Sheltered Place. The best position is in a flower bed at the foot of a sunny wall. Good drainage must be provided and the best soil is loam. Clayey soil should be excavated and

Schizostylis coccinea, the Kaffir Lily.

replaced by suitable soil, and very light soils need a liberal amount of compost or leaf mold added.

Planting is done in spring, when small clumps, each consisting of two or three shoots, are set 6 in. apart. During dry weather the soil must be kept moist, and occasional applications of weak liquid fertilizer are beneficial in summer. In severe winter weather the soil should be covered with salt hay, dry leaves or ashes.

The plants should not be disturbed for three or four years or until they become overcrowded and blooming deteriorates. They are then lifted in spring, divided, and the strongest shoots replanted in freshly prepared ground.

The less vigorous pieces may be planted in a reserve bed to increase the stock of plants.

In Cold Frames. In climates not more severe than that of southern New York, Schizostylis can be grown very satisfactorily in cold frames. The frames should be sufficiently deep or should be built up at their sides and the glass sash be appropriately raised as the height of the plants increases towards flowering time.

During the summer there is no need for the sash to be in place, but as soon as danger of frost comes in fall the plants should be covered every night. After flowering (the flowers are fine for cutting) the stems are cut down and, after the ground is frozen, a heavy layer of leaves or salt hay is placed over the soil and the sash put in place. On all mild winter days the frames are ventilated freely.

Each spring the rhizomes (roots) are dug up, separated and replanted, the soil being first deeply dug and enriched with organic material and bone meal.

An alternative method is to lift the rhizomes after flowering and plant them closely together in slightly moist sand or peat moss and keep them over winter in a cellar or similar place where the temperature is about 35-40 degrees.

As a Pot Plant. The Kaffir Lily is a very valuable pot plant for a cool greenhouse. Five strong shoots are potted in a 5-in. pot in spring; a compost of equal parts of loam and leaf mold, lightened with sand, is used. The pots are placed in a cold frame until May, when they are plunged in ashes out of doors until November. They are then taken into the greenhouse, where the blooms will expand. After flowering, they are returned to the cold frame and repotted in fresh compost in spring.

SCHLIMMIA (Schlim'mia). A small group of Orchids found wild in Central America and Brazil. All are epiphytal (grow on other plants) and have short or comparatively short pseudobulbs, each of which bears a single evergreen leaf. The flowers are of curious shape, and fragrant. The upper sepal is erect or arched, the lower sepals are partially inflated and joined to form a helmet, almost hiding the lip and narrow petals. Late autumn and winter are the usual flowering periods. The name Schlimmia commemorates a plant collector named Schlimm.

Schlimmias require a greenhouse in which the winter temperature does not fall below 60 degrees, and a tropical atmosphere in summer. Water must be given very carefully in winter, but freely in summer. Shading is necessary in summer, but full exposure to light in autumn is equally important.

These Orchids should be grown in baskets rather than pots. They may be planted in osmunda fiber, Tree Fern fiber, in Fir bark or in Redwood bark. The compost should be replenished when necessary, without disturbing the plants. Complete repotting should be done in spring as growth appears, if really needful.

The two chief kinds are S. jasminodora, which has erect spikes of white fragrant flowers, and S. trifida, with drooping inflorescences of white, purple-spotted, inverted flowers, the lip being marked with orange.

SCHLUMBERGERA (Schlumberger'a; Schlumberg'era). A group of Brazilian Cacti, one variety of which, S. Gaertneri, is commonly cultivated under the name of Easter Cactus. The name honors Frederick Schlumberg, an amateur student of botany. These plants belong to the Cactus family, Cactaceae, and in general appearance resemble Zygocactus (Christmas Cactus) but differ in having regular or nearly regular flowers that have much shorter tubes than those of Zygocactus.

In gardens both Schlumbergera and Zygocactus are often misnamed Epiphyllum. Both are epiphytes (in nature they grow, like many

The Easter Cactus, Schlumberg-era Gaertneri, closely resembles the Christmas Cactus but blooms later. It requires the same culture.

Orchids, on other plants, but without taking nourishment from the plants on which they grow). Schlumbergera requires the same culture as Zygocactus, which see.

The commonest kind is S. Gaertneri, the Easter Cactus, which is of more or less upright or spreading growth with pendant, green, flattened branches which are often mistaken by amateurs for leaves. The flowers are showy, red or purple-red and are usually at the tips of the branches. They are borne in late winter or early spring.

Other kinds are S. Bridgesii and S. Russelliana. Both have red-purple flowers.

SCHOLAR TREE, CHINESE. See Sophora japonica.

SCHOMBURGKIA (Schomburgk'ia). These Orchids are closely allied to Laelia, one kind, in fact, being still commonly known as Laelia superbiens. All are strong-growing epiphytal Orchids found wild from Jamaica to Brazil; the large pseudobulb has two evergreen leaves and the flower stem in some kinds is several feet long. The flowers are arranged in loose clusters. The flowering seasons are winter and early spring. The name commemorates Sir Robert Schomburgk, a South American traveler.

Schomburgkias are not difficult to grow in a greenhouse with a warm, moist atmosphere in summer, and a winter temperature of about 60 degrees; it should never fall below 55 degrees.

Usually they are grown with Cattleyas. In autumn the plants should be exposed to as much light as possible. In winter little if any water need be given, although abundance is required in summer. The plants flower better when the growths are allowed to project beyond the pot rim, and they should therefore not be repotted frequently.

When repotting is necessary, it is done after flowering, when the fresh growths appear, in osmunda fiber, Tree Fern fiber, Fir bark or Redwood bark. The plants must be potted firmly and given plenty of drainage. The compost needs to be replenished from time to time, and should be examined every spring.

The Principal Kinds. The flower stems of S. superbiens, better known as Laelia superbiens, may reach a length of 9 ft. and bear twenty large flowers of deep-rose coloring. The flowers of this kind are more like those of Laelia than others. S. undulata has purplish-brown flowers with rose and purple lip. S. Lyonsii has whitish flowers marked with purple; and S. crispa is brown shaded with yellow.

The hollow-bulbed plants at one time included under Schomburgkia are now grown under the name of Myrmecophila.

SCIADOPITYS VERTICILLATA—*Umbrella or Parasol Pine* (Sciadop'itys). A very curious evergreen tree found in forests in restricted areas in Japan, where the best trees grow in sheltered places among rocks. The finest trees range from 70-120 ft. high, and the trunk is up to 10 ft. in girth. They are usually gaunt trees from which the gray or grayish-brown bark strips off naturally, revealing reddish-brown bark beneath. Under cultivation in North America, the Umbrella Pine is seen as a small, pyramidal tree or bush, densely branched from the ground line upwards, the plants having a definite tendency to produce rival leaders. It is hardy in southern New England.

Two Kinds of Leaves. This tree has two kinds of leaves—one kind is difficult to find for they are small, brown, and scalelike, about ¼ in. long. The other type, though leaves to all intents and purposes, are often regarded as leaflike shoots or cladodes which function as leaves. They are stiff and leathery, 2-5 in. long, dark-green

The Umbrella Pine, Sciadopitys verticillata, is a distinctive and handsome evergreen that is a native of Japan. It thrives in non-alkaline soil and in sheltered locations.

and glossy above, paler beneath, with two grayish bands. They are arranged in whorls after the manner of the ribs in an umbrella or parasol, hence the common names.

Male and female flowers are on the same trees, the male flowers being yellow, in dense clusters from near the tips of the shoots. The female flowers are also borne from the ends of the shoots. They are first seen as small, rounded, greenish or brown-tinged bodies, and they develop into cones 2½-4 in. long and 1½-2. in. broad, ripening at the end of the second season.

Sciadopitys belongs to the Pine family, Pinaceae, and the name is derived from the Greek *skias,* a parasol, or sunshade, and *pitys,* a Fir tree.

Propagation and Cultivation. This very interesting and attractive conifer should be increased by means of seeds sown in a frame or greenhouse in autumn or spring. The young plants should be planted in soil free from lime and be placed in their permanent positions when 12-18 in. high. Growth may be slow for some years and some trees may never grow very freely. When purchasing this conifer, choose specimens with definite leading shoots.

Needs a Sheltered Place and Lime-free Soil. In selecting a site, choose a place sheltered from cold winds where the ground is permanently moist without being water-logged. This conifer thrives in loamy soil to which peat has been added, also in sandy peat. Regular pruning is unnecessary, but rival leaders may have to be removed now and then. Once a tree seems to be well established it should not be moved, even though the owner may find what he thinks to be a more favorable position, for it is one of those trees that may thrive without trouble in one part of a garden and fail if moved to another part.

The variety pendula has drooping branches, and in variegata some of the leaves are yellow. Neither of these varieties is any improvement on the typical kind.

SCILLA—*Squill* (Scil'la). A large group of hardy and greenhouse bulbs, some of which are among our most charming spring-flowering plants. They belong to the Lily family, Liliaceae, and are found wild in the Mediterranean district, other parts of Europe and in North Africa and Asia Minor. The word Scilla is an old Greek name.

All the hardy kinds are of easy cultivation in ordinary garden soil, though they thrive best in sandy, loamy ground; they are invaluable for planting in the rock garden, the wild and woodland garden, and in grass. The Spanish Bluebell is one of the best of all hardy bulbs for planting under the shade of trees, where, in the month of May, it provides delightful color. The English Bluebell is daintier and thrives in similar places.

Planting. The best time to plant the bulbs of Scilla is in late summer or early autumn, as soon as they can be purchased from the bulb dealer. It is necessary to plant the bulbs of the small kinds in early September to ensure a good display of bloom the following year; the earlier in autumn they are put in, the finer will be the first year's flowering. They may, however, be planted in October, or even in November if necessary.

Bulbs of the small kinds are set in holes 2-3 in. deep; those of the larger kinds in holes 5 or 6 in. deep.

For the Rock Garden and Planting in Grass. The chief small kinds, which grow only 4-6 in. high and bloom in late winter and early spring, are S. bifolia and its white variety alba; S. sibirica and its varieties alba, white; atrocaerulea, deep blue; and taurica, light blue. These make charming early groups of color in the rock garden and look well in grass; they may be planted near the edge of the lawn, in the shrubbery, or in grass beneath leaf-losing trees. It is a good plan to scatter the bulbs by hand, and to plant them where they fall; groups of natural appearance are thus ensured. They may be left undisturbed for years, and will eventually yield a beautiful display of bloom every spring.

If it becomes necessary to lift and replant them, the work should be done as soon as the leaves have died down; if it is deferred until the leaves have disappeared, it will be a difficult matter to find the bulbs.

The Siberian Squill. Of the spring-flowering Squills, Scilla sibirica is most popular, and indispensable, for it blooms freely in March or April, bearing vivid blue flowers in loose sprays on 6-in. stalks. We have already mentioned that there are a lovely white variety, alba, and a more vigorous, larger-flowered kind, atrocaerulea; this last is

The Siberia Squill, Scilla sibirica, is excellent for growing in pots or bowls of soil to bloom early.

aptly called Spring Beauty. The Siberian Squill is ideal for planting in the rock garden among carpeting plants, or in sunny borders where it can be left undisturbed, the bulbs being set 2 in. deep and 4 in. apart.

Scilla bifolia is another early spring beauty, with rich blue flowers. Variety alba has ivory-white flowers, and those of rosea are soft pink.

Scilla Tubergeniana, with flowers of porcelain-blue with darker stripes, rivals the two foregoing in beauty, and, like them, is invaluable for garden display, and for growing in pots for early flowering.

The English Bluebell. Of the larger Squills, one of the best known is the English Bluebell (Scilla nonscripta). This is a familiar plant in woods in many parts of Great Britain; in May it carpets the ground with exquisite coloring just as the trees are bursting into fresh leaf, providing one of the most enchanting pictures the countryside has to show. In the garden, English Bluebells should be restricted to the less formal places, among trees and shrubs, or in the wild or woodland garden; they flourish in shady places. The large leaves die down slowly and, if the bulbs are set in prominent places in the garden, the fading leaves are rather an eyesore. The bulbs should be planted in holes 6 in.

The dainty rich blue flowers of the Siberian Squill, Scilla sibirica, one of the most welcome of early spring bulbs.

deep and about 4 in. apart, in early fall.

There are varieties of this Bluebell with white and rose-colored flowers.

The Spanish Bluebell or Spanish Squill, Scilla hispanica (S. campanulata), is very handsome; the flowers are of various colors, and are on strong, erect spikes, 12-15 in. high. This kind flourishes under the same conditions as the English Bluebell, and looks particularly well if planted among hardy Ferns. The plants come into bloom just as the Fern fronds are unfurling, and, as the latter make progress, they hide the fading leaves of the Squills. There are many named varieties of the Spanish Squill—for example, Azalea, deep pink; Heavenly Blue, porcelain-blue; King of the Blues, sky blue; Mount Everest, white; Myosotis, Cambridge Blue; Peach Bloom, pink; Perle Brilliant, light blue; Queen of the Blues, and Queen of the Pinks. In many parts of North America the Spanish Bluebell multiplies much faster than the English Bluebell.

For summer bloom Scilla chinensis, the Chinese Squill, is very worth while. It flowers in August and early September, attains a height of 6-12 in. and has pretty spikes of lilac-pink flowers. It thrives without difficulty in any well-drained soil in a sunny location.

Scilla chinensis increases rapidly by means of self-sown seeds. In gardens it is sometimes misnamed Scilla japonica.

Blooms in Autumn. Scilla autumnalis is an autumn-flowering plant which bears purplish-blue flowers in late summer or early autumn—August–September; it grows about 6 in. high, and is chiefly suitable for planting in the rock garden. The bulbs are planted in spring.

Other notable kinds are Scilla italica, the Italian Squill, 6 in., lavender-blue; S. pratensis, 6 in., lavender-blue; and S. verna, 4 in., light blue. These all bloom in spring.

Cultivation in Pots in a Greenhouse. All the low-growing, hardy spring-flowering kinds are

Scilla pratensis.

Spanish Bluebell, Scilla campnulata.

suitable for planting in the rock garden, and for cultivation in pots in a cool greenhouse. For the latter purpose the bulbs are potted in September in sandy, loamy soil; they should be placed out of doors under sand or ashes for 6 or 8 weeks, so that they may become well rooted before top growth begins. They are then placed in the greenhouse, where they will come into bloom in advance of those grown out of doors.

Another excellent kind for greenhouse and window garden—and for planting outdoors in a sunny border in mild climates—is S. peruviana, the Cuban Lily. It should be noted that Cuban Lily is a somewhat misleading name. The plant is a native of the Mediterranean region.

The bulbs of this Scilla are quite large and, when planted outdoors, should be set at a depth of 6 in. or so, but, when grown in pots, the tips of the bulbs may be permitted to just show above the soil surface.

Pot them in well-drained 4-5-in. pots, singly, or several together in larger, deep pans. The soil should be fertile. Repotting will be necessary every 3-4 years only; in intermediate years top-dress with rich soil at the beginning of each growing season. Water and feed them freely when in active growth, but keep them quite dry when dormant.

A greenhouse or sunroom with a night temperature of 40-50 degrees and a day temperature about 10 degrees higher is satisfactory. These bulbs need full sunlight while growing.

S. peruviana starts into growth in fall. It grows about 12 in. high and bears its fine, heavy

spikes of lilac-blue flowers in late winter or spring. The flowers of S. peruviana alba are similar but white.

S. violacea, native of South Africa, has olive-green leaves marked with silver variegation. The leaves are wine-red beneath, the flowers are green and blue. They appear in winter. This kind is suitable for greenhouse cultivation.

SCINDAPSUS—*Ivy Arum* (Scindap'sus; Scin'dapsus). A small group of tropical climbing plants with large, bright green or variegated leaves, and arum-like flowers with greenish spathes. Scindapsus is an old Greek name for an ivylike plant. These plants belong to the Arum family, the Araceae.

Climbing Plants. These plants are useful for draping pillars, walls, or the roof of the greenhouse and for cultivating in pots as foliage plants for house decoration. When grown in a greenhouse, they require a minimum winter temperature of 55 degrees, and the atmosphere should be kept moist at all times.

When grown as pot plants, they need supports to which to cling; sticks wrapped around with moss, or pieces of rough bark, are satisfactory.

The best potting compost consists of equal parts of loam and peat with sufficient sand to make it porous and a few small pieces of charcoal to keep it "sweet." Repotting of young plants is done in March, but when they are well

The Ivy Arum, Scindapsus aureus, is attractive when grown as a house plant.

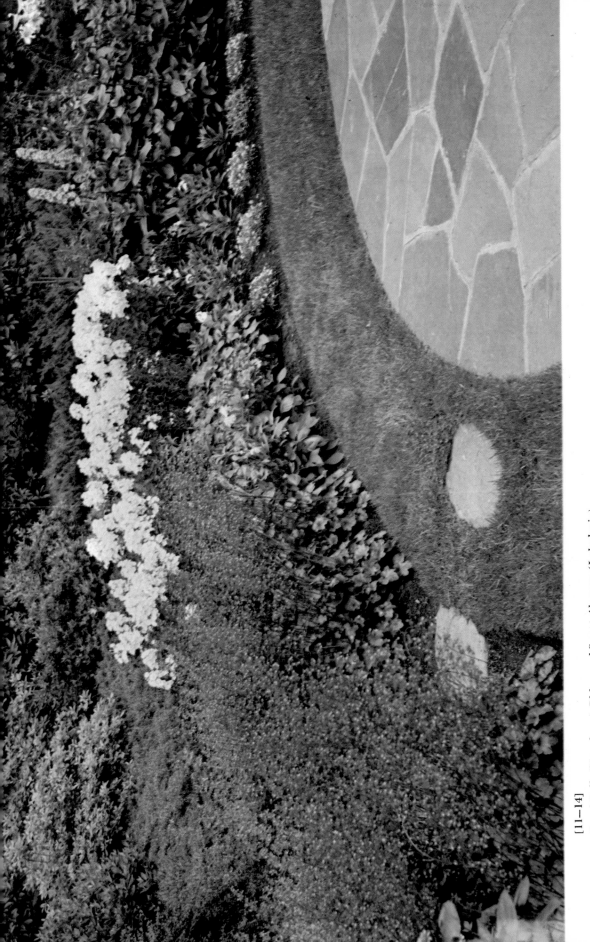

[11–14]

Coral Bells (Heuchera), Phlox and Sweet Alyssum (Lobularia)
in a garden near the sea

[11—15]
Cosmos

[11—15a]
Peony

[11—15b]
Petunias, Verbenas and Nicotiana

[11—15c]
American Holly
(Ilex opaca)

established in 5- or 6-in. pots, they may be planted out in a prepared bed of soil in the hothouse. The bed is prepared by taking out a hole 2 ft. in diameter and 2 ft. 6 in. in depth. A layer of broken bricks or stones is placed in the bottom, and these are covered with rough fibrous material from the compost. The remainder of the space is filled with the prepared compost and the plant set in position. Wire or a trellis is fixed in readiness, to which the long shoots can be tied.

Water is applied moderately to the soil after potting or planting, but when the plants are established the soil is kept moist at all seasons, although much less watering is required in winter when growth is not active.

Propagation. Young plants are easily obtained by taking cuttings; the tips of the shoots are taken off, about 6 in. in length, and inserted in well-drained pots of sandy soil. They are set in a propagating case, with bottom heat, to form roots, and then potted in separate pots.

The chief kinds cultivated are S. aureus, a tall climber with ovate green leaves that are blotched with pale yellow, and its varieties: Wilcoxii, with more clearly defined variegations, and Marble Queen, with white variegations. Another popular kind is S. pictus variety argyraeus, which has heart-shaped green leaves spotted and blotched with silvery white.

SCION. A gardening term which describes the shoot used in grafting; the stock is the rooted plant or tree, and the scion is the shoot which is grafted on it. The spelling is sometimes Cion.

SCIRPUS—*Club Grass, Bulrush* (Scir'pus). A large group of hardy perennial plants, few of which have any decorative value. The most popular kind is S. cernuus, an evergreen, grasslike plant with slender drooping stems. It is principally used as an edging to the greenhouse benches. This plant is commonly known in gardens as Isolepis gracilis.

The flowers of Scirpus are inconspicuous. They are grasslike and are formed in compact tufts near the tips of the stems, hence the common name Club Grass. This plant belongs to the Cyperus family, Cyperaceae, and the name Scirpus is an old Latin name for the Rush.

The Club Grass, Scirpus cernuus (Isolepis gracilis), is an evergreen Grass, native to the

Scirpus cernuus (often called Isolepis gracilis), a graceful little plant with drooping, grasslike stems, often used as an edging to the greenhouse staging.

tropics, and useful for greenhouse cultivation under moist conditions. This dainty little plant has slender, cylindrical drooping stems, 18 in. in length, bearing small, light green, grasslike flower heads at their tips. The plants are grown in 5-in. pots.

This plant requires a minimum winter temperature of 45 degrees and a compost of equal parts of loam and leaf mold. The plants are divided into small pieces in March and potted separately in 3-in. pots and, later on, in 5-in. pots. They are carefully watered until established, but afterwards the soil is kept moist at all seasons of the year.

The Common Rush, S. lacustris, which is a weed in ponds and rivers of Europe, has slender, round, green, leafless stems 2-6 ft. in height. It is sometimes planted in clumps on the margins of ponds, but S. Tabernaemontani zebrinus (often regarded as a variety of S. lacustris) is much more decorative, as its stems are transversely banded with green and white. It is a native of Japan, hardy, and thrives in shallow water. S. Holoschoenus, a native of Asia, grows 3 ft. in height; its variety, variegatus, has green and white stems.

Suitable for the Margin of a Pool. The cultural requirements of these plants are very simple; all that is necessary is to push the roots into the mud at the margin of the pond or lake, when they quickly become established and need no further attention.

Propagation is by division of the clumps at

the planting time, between September and April.

The stems of the European Rush, S. lacustris, are cut and dried and used for making beehives, mats, chair bottoms, ornamental baskets, etc.

SCLEROCACTUS (Sclerocac'tus). A genus of two spiny plants that are natives of the south-western United States. They belong to the Cactus family, Cactaceae. The name is derived from *scleros,* hard or cruel, and Cactus.

Sclerocactus closely resembles Ferocactus and Echinocactus and requires the same culture as the latter. See Echinocactus and Cacti.

The two kinds are S. polyancistrus and S. Whipplei. The former attains a maximum height of 15-16 in. and has rose-magenta or yellow flowers that may be 3½ in. long. It grows naturally in California, Nevada, western Arizona and southern Utah. S. Whipplei grows to a maximum height of about 6 in., has purplish or lavender flowers, about 1½ in. long, and occurs natively on high mesas in Colorado, Utah, and northern Arizona.

SCLEROTIA. The name given to the resting bodies of many fungi. They are black or brown in color, and their size ranges from that of a pin's head to that of a pea or bean. They can withstand very unfavorable conditions; many chemicals, toxic to other plant parts, will not kill them. They contain no spores, usually germinating directly when moisture and other conditions become favorable. As a rule, they can live in a dormant condition for at least a year, and very often longer.

Fungi that cause some plant diseases, such as crown rot of Delphinium and other plants, form sclerotia. Some very large sclerotia are found in tropical countries and are eaten by natives, the best example being Polyporus Mylittae, the Blackfellows' Bread of Australia.

SCOLOPENDRIUM. Phyllitis, which see.

SCOLYMUS—*Spanish Oyster Plant, Golden Thistle* (Scoly'mus). Rather uncommon hardy herbaceous plants of thistle-like appearance. The flowers are not very showy, and the plants are therefore chiefly grown in botanical collections. The three principal kinds in cultivation are S. hispanicus and S. maculatus, from southern Europe, and S. grandiflorus, from northern Africa. Scolymus belongs to the Daisy family, Compositae, and is closely related to Cichorium (Chicory). The name is an ancient Greek one.

The Spanish Oyster Plant, S. hispanicus, is grown as a vegetable. The plants average 3 ft. in height, have large, thistle-like, deeply divided, prickly edged leaves, and bear solitary heads of yellow, thistle-like flowers, with strap-shaped florets. They are cultivated for their long, thick taproots, which are cooked and eaten like Salsify; their flavor is similar to that of Salsify, but milder; the plants are not grown to the same extent as Salsify, owing to the discomfort in working among and handling the prickly leaves.

S. hispanicus is a biennial, and is raised by sowing seeds in drills ½ in. deep out of doors, in April. The seedlings are afterwards thinned out to 12 in. apart, and are left to develop until the roots are large enough for use. A sunny location and a dry, light, rich soil are required.

Ornamental Foliage Plant. S. maculatus, an annual with ornamental leaves, is sometimes grown for the value of its light green, thistle-like leaves, which are heavily spotted and veined with white; they are very ornamental and show with fine effect among herbaceous border plants.

On light, well-drained, warm soil, self-sown seedlings appear every year, and it is only necessary to lift them when large enough, and plant them where they are wanted.

On colder soils it is necessary to sow the seeds each year, in April. They are scattered broadcast in the location in which the plants are to grow, and raked in, the seedlings being thinned out to one foot apart.

The Perennial Kind. The perennial kind, S. grandiflorus, is a suitable plant for light soil. It forms a dense clump, with stems 3 ft. in length, which bear, at their tips, yellow, thistle-like flowers in May. Plants are raised from seeds sown in a drill ½ in. deep, out of doors, in April, the seedlings being thinned to one foot apart and transplanted to their permanent positions in the autumn.

SCORPION IRIS. See Iris alata.

SCORPION SENNA. Coronilla Emerus, which see.

SCORZONERA—*Viper's Grass* (Scorzon'era). Hardy herbaceous perennial plants which belong to the Daisy family, Compositae; they are found

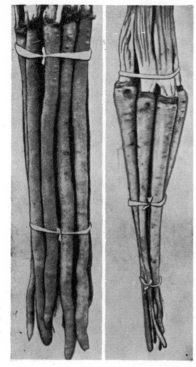

Two of the less common but worthwhile root vegetables, Scorzonera *(left)* and Salsify.

well developed they are thinned out gradually, until eventually they are left about 6 in. from each other.

Scorzonera suffers little, if at all, from pests and diseases and the only attention needed during the summer months is to hoe the soil between the rows occasionally to keep down weeds and to encourage free growth of the plants.

In autumn, when the leaves have changed color, the roots may be lifted and stored in sifted soil or sand in a cool, frostproof cellar, or they may be left in the ground to be dug as required during the autumn and winter months.

SCOTCH BROOM. Cytisus scoparius, which see.

SCOTCH HEATHER. Calluna vulgaris, which see.

SCOTCH KALE. A type of Kale which has curled leaves. See Kale.

SCOTCH LABURNUM. Laburnum alpinum, which see.

SCOTCH ROSE. Rosa spinosissima, which see.

SCOTCH THISTLE. See Onopordum.

SCOTS PINE. Pinus sylvestris, which see.

SCREE. The scree or moraine, and the alpine plants suitable for cultivation there, are dealt with under the heading of Moraine.

SCREW PINE. Pandanus, which see.

SCROPHULARIA—*Figwort* (Scrophular′ia). A group of annual and perennial herbaceous plants and subshrubs of minor horticultural importance. They belong in the Figwort family, Scrophulariaceae. The name is derived from *scrophula* and refers to the virtues these plants were supposed to possess as preventives or cures of the disease of that same name.

Scrophularias are mostly waterside or wet-ground plants. Most kinds have a fetid odor which they emit when bruised. They occur as natives in various parts of the Northern Hemisphere including Canada and the United States.

Hardy kinds sometimes grown in gardens are S. chrysantha, a native of the Caucasus that has yellow flowers and that grows 6-18 in. tall, and S. nodosa variegata. The latter is a handsome foliage plant with green leaves beautifully marked with creamy white. S. nodosa variegata is a variety of an Asiatic and European species.

wild in southern and eastern Europe and in northern Africa chiefly. The name is said to be derived from an old French word, *scorzon,* meaning serpent, because the roots of one kind were used in the treatment of snake bites.

A Root Vegetable. The only kind worth consideration here is Scorzonera hispanica, which is cultivated as a vegetable for the sake of its long, narrow roots, which are dark, almost black without, and white within. They are in season in late autumn and in winter.

These plants are easily grown. The site chosen for Scorzonera should be an open sunny one, and the soil must be crumbly—free from lumps and fresh manure. As with other root crops, it is usual to cultivate Scorzonera on land which was deeply cultivated and manured for another crop the previous summer, such as Pea, Bean, Onion or Leek.

When to Sow. As soon as the soil is dry enough to be broken down finely, in early spring, drills are drawn 12 in. apart; they should be rather less than 1 in. in depth. The seeds are scattered thinly along the drill, and are covered by raking the soil very lightly. When the seedlings are

Scrophularia nodosa variegata.

It forms a bold plant that will grow 2-3 ft. tall.

Scrophularia nodosa variegata is readily propagated by cuttings. In mild climates its foliage remains attractive all winter. Increase of S. chrysantha may be effected by seeds and by division.

Both kinds grow in any ordinary soil that is not excessively dry; both may be planted in spring or early fall.

SCUM ON PONDS. The surface scum on ponds of fresh water consists of masses of minute Algae (see Algae), which are green or brown in color. They grow most rapidly in warm weather.

To get rid of the scum copper sulphate is dissolved in the water. This chemical is used at the rate of 2 oz. in 10,000 gallons of water. Used at this strength it will not usually harm the fish (except trout) or living plants, but it is not wise to employ this remedy if the pond contains expensive fish. To estimate the number of gallons of water, multiply the average length of the pond in feet by the width; the result, when multiplied by the depth, will give the number of cubic feet. Multiply the number of cubic feet by 7½ to find the number of gallons.

The safest method of applying this chemical is to enclose it in a piece of fine burlap or cheesecloth. It is then attached to the end of a pole and dragged through the water until thoroughly dissolved.

Another method is to dissolve the copper sulphate in water, using a glass or earthenware vessel (not metal), and spray it on the surface.

Most of the scum can be removed from small pools by a mechanical method. A large loop of wire, over which a piece of cheesecloth is stretched, is fixed to the end of a pole, and the scum is skimmed off. Duckweed, which is not killed by copper sulphate, can also be removed by this method.

SCUTELLARIA — *Skullcap, Helmetflower* (Scutellar'ia). Although this is an extensive group of plants, comparatively few kinds are cultivated. Those which are met with are free-flowering and easy to grow. Representatives of this genus, or group, of which there are about one hundred and eighty species or wild types, are found in nearly all parts of the world, especially in temperate regions. A few are wild in Canada and the United States, and others are from Europe, Asia, Mexico and elsewhere.

Flowers of Scutellaria, the Skullcap or Helmetflower, of which there are several hardy and tender kinds worthy of cultivation.

In general appearance these plants are all much alike. They have stiff, four-angled stems, opposite, ovate leaves with serrate edges, and terminal spikes of tubular, two-lipped, blue, violet, scarlet or yellow flowers. The flowers are succeeded by cap-shaped seed pods; hence the common names Skullcap or Helmetflower. The name Scutellaria is derived from *scutella*, a little shield, and refers to the shape of the calyx. Scutellaria belongs to the Mint family, Labiatae.

For the Greenhouse. The principal greenhouse kinds are S. coccinea and S. Mociniana. Both grow about 2 ft. in height, the former having scarlet flowers and the latter scarlet and yellow. They bloom in midsummer. Although these plants are perennial and may be grown to form large specimens in time, the best results are to be obtained by raising fresh plants annually.

Propagated by Cuttings in Spring. Young shoots, 2 in. in length, are taken off, trimmed and inserted in sand or vermiculite. They are kept in a close, warm propagating case until rooted and then potted separately in 3-in. pots, using a compost of two parts of loam, one part of leaf mold or peat moss and a little sand.

As soon as the plants are well rooted the tips of the shoots are pinched out, and when side shoots commence to develop the plants are shifted into 5-in. pots. For this potting, a richer compost is necessary; it should consist of two parts of fibrous loam broken into small pieces, one part of leaf mold or peat moss, and a little well-decayed manure and sand. The compost is made firm with a potting stick; when the plants are established, the tips of the side shoots are pinched off.

After each repotting, and until they are established in the 5-in. pots, watering must be done moderately; afterwards the soil is kept moist, and when flower buds are forming a weekly application of liquid fertilizer should be given. A close, moist atmosphere is necessary while the plants are young and until they are established in 5-in. pots. Afterwards they should be hardened off by ventilating the greenhouse freely and exposing them to full sunlight to ripen the shoots for flower production.

After flowering, less watering is necessary, and the compost is kept on the dry side until February. The shoots are then pruned back to within 2 in. of the base and frequently syringed to make them break into growth. They are then potted in larger pots, or the side shoots are taken off as cuttings. The minimum winter temperature for these plants is 50 degrees.

Summer-flowering Rock-Garden Plants. S. alpina is a prostrate plant with stems 9 in. in length, small ovate leaves and long spikes of purple flowers in summer. It is a variable plant. Purple and white or yellowish flowers are often produced by seedlings. S. indica japonica is a creeping kind which bears spikes of purple and white flowers 6 in. high, June–July.

These plants are of easy cultivation. They succeed in well-drained garden soil. A sunny position is needed, and planting may be done in fall or early spring. After flowering, the stems are cut down to within 1 in. of the soil. A mulch of rich soil is given in early spring.

Dwarf Border Plants. For planting near the front of the herbaceous border several kinds are useful for providing color in late summer. S. lateriflora grows 18 in. in height, has ovate leaves 3 in. in length, and slender spikes of pale blue flowers. S. baicalensis is about 12 in. in height, and has bright blue flowers, and S. altissima is intermediate in height, with cream-yellow flowers.

These plants do best in moist, rich soil, but they are not fastidious, and will grow in ordinary soil which has been deeply dug. A sunny position is necessary.

Planting may be done in fall or spring when the soil is in a workable condition. These plants do not spread very rapidly, and may therefore be left undisturbed for many years.

Propagation by Seeds. Seeds of the hardy kinds are sown in pans of sandy soil in spring; they are set in a cold frame. When the seedlings are large enough to move, they are transplanted 2 in. apart in flats of soil, and planted in their permanent positions in autumn or spring.

Additional plants may also be obtained by lifting and dividing the old specimens in spring.

SCUTICARIA (Scuticar'ia). Only two species of this curious but handsome Orchid are met with in cultivation. Both are epiphytes (grow on other plants) with pseudobulbs which are little more than the thickened bases of the evergreen leaves. The leaves are set closely together on a

Scutellaria.

woody rhizome. S. Hadwenii from Brazil has erect leaves; those of S. Steelei from British Guiana are pendulous and sometimes 4 ft. long. In both kinds the flowers are produced on short stems from the base of the growths, and are about 3 in. across, fleshy, with spreading sepals and petals and a large three-lobed lip. Both usually bloom in summer. The name Scuticaria is from *scutica,* a whip, and alludes to the shape of the leaves.

Scuticaria Steelei will succeed in a flower pan which should be suspended in a tilted position, but is more easily grown on a flat piece of wood or a raft in a greenhouse with a tropical temperature in the summer. Liberal waterings are then required, and the syringe may be freely used. Shading should never be heavy and must be removed early in autumn. The temperature in winter should be 60-65 degrees at night, but little watering is required at that season.

Scuticaria Hadwenii requires similar treatment, but is not affected by a slightly lower temperature and can be grown in a pan or pot, although a wooden block may be used. The potting compost for both kinds is osmunda fiber, Tree Fern fiber, Fir bark or Redwood bark. Potting is done early in spring.

S. Hadwenii has yellow flowers shaded with green and blotched and marked with rich brown. There is a variety of it named Dodgsonii, sometimes classed as a separate species, in which the flowers are brownish, with yellow, red and white markings. S. Steelei, at one time called Maxillaria Steelei, has slightly larger, fragrant flowers, primrose-yellow, with mahogany markings.

SCYTHE. The scythe consists of a curved steel knife or blade and a snead, snath or wooden handle. The snead has two small handles whereby it is held fast and used with a swinging motion. The blade is passed over the ground an inch or so above it and, as it passes, it cuts the grass or hay. The blade is fixed firmly to the snead by means of one or two wedges. Experience is required to "set" a blade in a manner to suit the person who is using it, and for the purpose for which the scythe is to be used.

A scythe is kept sharp by frequent whetting or sharpening with a scythestone. The blade should have a very sharp edge so that it will cut the grass without tearing up the plants. A scythestone is a piece of hard sandstone about a foot long and rather more than an inch in cross section; it is drawn down the blade in a semicircular motion. The newer stones are made of Carborundum.

SEA BUCKTHORN. Hippophaë, which see.

SEA CAMPION. Silene maritima, which see.

SEA DAHLIA. Coreopsis maritima, which see.

SEAFORTHIA. Palms, natives of Queensland, now included in the genus Ptychosperma, which see.

SEA GRAPE. Coccolobis uvifera, which see.

SEA HEATH. See Frankenia.

SEA HOLLY. See Eryngium.

SEA KALE. A hardy vegetable (Crambe maritima) which is wild in maritime districts in Europe; it is grown for the sake of its blanched shoots in winter and spring. The roots are lifted in autumn and forced into growth in a dark, warm place for the earliest supplies; the roots out of doors may also be forced, to supply successional produce, by covering the dormant roots with boxes or large pots and surrounding these with fresh manure in early spring.

This vegetable needs deeply dug and rich soil to ensure well-developed roots which will provide

Sea Kale that has been forced in the open ground without disturbing the roots.

satisfactory produce when forced. It should be grown in a sunny part of the garden. There are two methods of propagation: by root cuttings and by seeds. The former will provide roots fit for lifting and forcing at the end of the summer; the roots of seedlings will not be large enough for use until the end of the second year.

Seeds are sown out of doors in spring in deeply dug soil, enriched with manure; drills rather less than 1 in. deep are drawn 12 in. apart. The seeds are scattered thinly in the drills and are covered by raking the soil level. The seedlings must be thinned out gradually until they are about 6 in. apart. During the summer the only attention needed is to cultivate the soil frequently to keep down weeds and promote satisfactory growth.

The Sea Kale plants are not disturbed until early the following spring, when they are lifted and replanted 2½ ft. apart on a fresh site which has been prepared in the way already described. Steps must be taken to prevent the plants from producing flowering stems, and this is done by cutting off the crown or top of each root.

The roots are set so that their tops are an inch or so below the surface of the ground. They need no further attention throughout the summer other than restricting the shoots to one on each plant and hoeing between the rows, which is necessary to promote the growth of first-class roots and to keep the ground clean.

In autumn, the roots will be large enough to be lifted for forcing, if they are required for the purpose.

Propagation by Root Cuttings. Once the garden contains a stock of Sea Kale plants the usual method of propagation is by means of root cuttings or pieces of root. The cuttings are made from the smaller pieces taken off the main roots when the latter are lifted for forcing in autumn. If no forcing is done, root cuttings are taken in late fall.

It is necessary to be able to distinguish the top of the root from the bottom, and to enable this to be done at a glance it is usual to cut one end straight across and the other in a slanting direction. Usually the top is cut straight across and the bottom with a slanting cut.

The root cuttings are stored for the winter in a heap of soil or sand out of doors, care being taken that they are well covered. There they remain until planting time in early spring.

Planting the Root Cuttings. As soon as the ground is workable in spring the root cuttings are set out in deep, rich soil, 15-18 in. apart, in rows 2 ft. from each other. The cuttings, which are 5 or 6 in. long, are placed at such a depth that the tops are 1 in. below the soil.

The routine cultivation during the summer months consists of hoeing and feeding with liquid fertilizer when the plants are in full growth. Care must be taken to limit each plant to one strong shoot; all others should be removed while they are small.

Forcing under Cover. If the roots are required for forcing in a warm, dark cellar or other suitable place, they should be lifted and planted 2 in. apart in deep boxes of soil. If set in a temperature of 45-50 degrees, fresh growth will soon begin. The soil must be kept moist and the roots dark.

The boxes of roots may be placed beneath the benches in a greenhouse (temperature 45-50 degrees), providing light is excluded by hanging mats or sacking along the edge of the benches. Or the roots may be placed in a greenhouse, shed, or cellar, each pot being covered with another one inverted. The young shoots are ready to be cut when about 6 in. long.

Forcing Out of Doors. Sea Kale roots are easily forced out of doors without being disturbed. The quickest way is to place boxes or large flowerpots over the roots in late winter and to surround these with fresh stable manure which gives off considerable warmth and thus starts the roots into growth.

Later supplies are provided by covering the boxes or pots with mounds of sifted ashes; as soon as the tips of the shoots show through the top of the heap of ashes they are ready to be cut.

Roots which have been lifted and forced in warmth are useless and should be destroyed. Before they are placed under cover, however, the smaller pieces should be taken off as root cuttings, and treated in the way already described to provide plants the following year. Sea Kale roots which are forced into growth out of doors without being disturbed will continue profitable for several years.

The ground in which this vegetable is grown should be top-dressed with manure every spring.

SEA KALE, ORNAMENTAL. See Crambe.

SEA LAVENDER. See Limonium.

SEA OATS. Uniola paniculata, which see.

SEA ONION. Urginea maritima, which see.

SEA PINK. See Armeria.

SEA POPPY. See Glaucium.

SEASIDE GARDENS. Although almost all the shrubs and plants commonly grown in inland gardens will thrive in gardens near the sea if adequate shelter from strong winds is provided, certain kinds do remarkably well there. Shelter is essential. This is often provided by walls, fences or hurdles as a first line of defense against fierce winds.

Certain kinds of trees and shrubs also make

Shelter is all-important in gardens near the sea. In this garden the windbreaks consist of fences with glass panels between the uprights.

effective windbreaks. Among the hardiest and best of these are Japanese Black Pine (Pinus Thunbergii), which thrives in practically pure sand and stands exposure extraordinarily well; Dragon Spruce (Picea asperata), Arborvitae (Thuya), Privet (Ligustrum), Beach Plum (Prunus maritima), Tamarisk (Tamarix) and Rugosa Rose (Rosa rugosa).

The kinds mentioned above will grow in the most exposed locations. Where conditions are somewhat less severe the choice of hardy trees and shrubs that may be used is wider. Among the best are Jack Pine (Pinus Banksiana), Pitch Pine (Pinus rigida), Norway Spruce (Picea Abies), Red Maple (Acer rubrum), Sycamore Maple (Acer Pseudo-Platanus), Black Oak (Quercus velutina), London Plane (Platanus acerifolia), Honey Locust (Gleditsia triacanthos), Birches, Junipers and Poplars, Rose-of-Sharon (Hibiscus syriacus), Inkberry (Ilex glabra), American Holly (Ilex opaca), Hydrangeas, Sweet Pepperbush (Clethra alnifolia), Scotch Broom (Cytisus scoparius), Russian Olive (Elaeagnus angustifolia), Sea Buckthorn (Hippophaë rhamnoides), Bayberry (Myrica pensylvanica and M. cerifera, the latter also called Wax Myrtle, and Rosa multiflora and other shrub Roses.

Good vines and trailers include Virginia Creeper (Parthenocissus quinquefolia), Hall's Honeysuckle (Lonicera japonica Halliana), Climbing Hydrangea (Hydrangea petiolaris) and Memorial Rose (Rosa Wichuraiana).

In mild climates kinds that can be used in addition to a suitable selection of those mentioned above include the Japanese Euonymus japonicus and its varieties, Escallonia macrantha, Olearia Haastii, the Monterey Cypress (Cupressus macrocarpa), Pittosporum Tobira, Coconut Palm (Cocos nucifera), Sea Grape (Coccolobis uvifera), Palmetto (Sabal), Trifoliate Orange (Poncirus trifoliata), Rock Rose (Cistus), Rosemary (Rosmarinus), Lemon Verbena (Lippia), Hebe, Australian Pine (Casuarina), Atriplex Breweri, Lavatera assurgentiflora and Cajeput Tree (Melaleuca Leucadendra).

Herbaceous perennials and low subshrubby plants that are particularly satisfactory in seaside gardens include Thrift (Armeria), Dusty Miller

Cold-frame sash stood on edge serve as windbreaks in this seaside garden.

(Artemisia Stelleriana), other kinds of Artemisia, Yucca, Rock Cress (Arabis), Coreopsis, Iris, Evergreen Candytuft (Iberis sempervirens), Loosestrife (Lythrum), Basket of Gold (Alyssum saxatile), Butterfly Weed (Asclepias tuberosa), Hollyhock, Day Lily (Hemerocallis), Columbine (Aquilegia), Pinks (Dianthus), Rose Mallow (Hibiscus), Sea Holly (Eryngium maritimum), Fleabane (Erigeron), Globe Thistle (Echinops), Coral-Bells (Heuchera), Blanketflower (Gaillardia), Anchusa, Veronica, Lavender Cotton (Santolina Chamaecyparissus), Leopard's-Bane (Doronicum), Sun Rose (Helianthemum), Nepeta Mussinii, Baby's-Breath, Peonies, Chrysanthemums, Sandwort (Arenaria), and Sea Lavender (Limonium).

Annuals that grow well under seaside conditions are Ageratum, Calendula, California Poppy, Coreopsis, Candytuft, Cornflower, Cosmos, Gaillardia, Globe Amaranth, Ice Plant (Cryophytum or Mesembryanthemum crystallinum), Larkspur, Marigold, Petunia, Phlox,

Hydrangea macrophylla is a fine shrub for planting near the sea.

Poppy, Pinks, Sand Verbena (Abronia), Snap-dragon (Antirrhinum), Salvia, Love-in-a-mist, Mignonette, Strawflower (Helichrysum), Portu-laca, Spiderflower (Cleome), Sweet Alyssum (Lobularia), Verbena, Scabious, Zinnia, Snow-on-the-Mountain (Euphorbia marginata), Nas-turtium (Tropaeolum).

In addition, Geranium (Pelargonium), Lan-tana, Mesembryanthemum, Sweet William, Pansy, Dahlia and Gladiolus are satisfactory.

Special conditions that most commonly affect plants grown near the sea are intense light, lack of good topsoil, and exposure to strong winds and salt spray.

Very few plants indeed will withstand expo-sure to salt spray. A few suitable for windbreaks near the shore are available, but most flower garden and vegetable garden plants must receive shelter from this.

Wind is a limiting factor when gardening near the sea. Quite apart from the damage it does by breaking plants, it harms them by causing them to lose moisture from their tissues faster than normal and perhaps faster than the roots can replace it. In general, exposure to more or less continuous wind has a stunting effect even on those plants that withstand it. Only drought-re-sistant plants will ordinarily grow in exposed places near the sea.

Brilliant sunshine with a great deal of light reflected from water, sand and other surfaces characterizes coastal regions; therefore, most of the plants used in gardens should be of sun-loving types.

Soils vary greatly in different localities near the sea. Where they are reasonably deep, and of a good loamy character, their treatment is similar to that in inland areas. But in many places they are so sandy that it is very desirable to mix with them some heavier (more clayey) loam if this is procurable and to dig in liberal quantities of humus-forming organic materials, peat moss, humus, compost, leaf mold, manure, cover crops and the like.

A mulch of dark-colored material such as peat moss cuts down the light and heat reflected from light-colored soils (so often found near the sea) and benefits the plants by keeping the roots cooler and moister.

Staking and tying early in the life of plants and periodically through their growth before they are broken and damaged by wind and storm is one of the secrets of having a good garden by the sea. Another important point to which attention must be given is watering. This will usually need to be done more frequently than in inland gardens. It is well to remember, too, that more frequent fertilizing is needed on sandy soils than on those of a heavier character.

SEASIDE TOADFLAX. Linaria maritima, which see.

SEATS, GARDEN. Attractive seats, appropri-ately located, add much to the charm of a gar-den. They invite both owners and visitors to pause and enjoy beauty; they provide places to laze away an idle hour, to read, converse and engage in other pastimes. In summer, seats in shade are much appreciated; at other seasons those located where the benefit of the sun is had are usually more desirable. Seats may be used with good effects as focal points at the ends of views or vistas; they can be decorative as well as useful.

Garden seats may be made of wood, metal, stone, concrete and other materials. In past cen-turies seats of turf were much used but these are rarely made today. Many excellent types of seats are obtainable from commercial sources but good ones are fairly costly and frail ones and those of poor design should not be purchased. The home handyman will have little difficulty in constructing attractive garden seats of various

A rustic garden seat.

A bench-type garden seat.

This garden seat is made of concrete.

types. The accompanying drawings show a seat which has been designed for ease of construction. All difficult joints have been eliminated, the only ones used being lapped joints, which are quite easy to cut, and require only a saw, hammer, and chisel.

The seat is rather lower than the usual type, so that cushions can be used to soften its hard-ness and yet leave a comfortable height for the legs; the length is 6 ft. It is suitable for most purposes. It can be made shorter if desired, or even adapted as a single seat, thinner wood then being used.

The first step is to cut all pieces to the requisite size before assembling, care being taken to en-sure that the ends are square. Fig. A shows how

A well-placed garden seat may be used as a focal point in the garden scene.

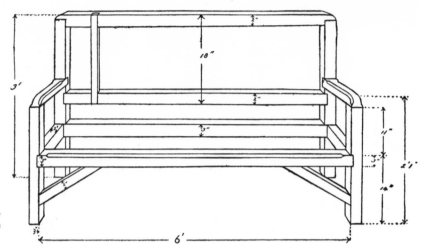

The garden seat of which constructional details are given in the accompanying notes.

the two back pieces are cut to receive the rails; and the beginner should beware of making two pieces for one end. Fig. B shows the cuts in the top rail for the back slats, and the lower rail is similarly treated, these cuts being ½ in. deep. All others are 1 in. deep, and make a good strong joint.

Nearly all the dimensions can be seen on the general front view, from which the seat slats, and all except one of the back slats, have been omitted for the sake of clarity. The front and back legs, the three back rails, and the front rail are cut from wood 3 in. square. The side rails supporting the seat slabs are cut from wood 3 in. by 2 in., and the arms and diagonal struts at the front are the same.

The front rail and the two lower back rails are 6 ft. 2 in. long, and the top back rail is 6 ft. 6

in. long, the ends being cut as in Fig. C. The arms are 19 in. long, and the short side rails are 17 in. long. (The odd inches are to allow for the fitting into the joints.)

The slats for the seat, made of 1-in. wood, are 6 ft. 6 in. long and 3 in. wide. They are spaced ½ in. apart and are simply nailed on to the end rails. One slat, 6 ft. long, is fixed along the front rail between the front legs. The edges of all of them should be beveled, as should those of the arm, and if a small plane is not available the work can be done with a coarse wood file.

The back slats are ½ in. thick, 2 in. wide, and are spaced 3 in. apart, while the length is 18 in.

When all the pieces have been cut to shape the back can then be assembled. The legs are joined by means of the three rails, carpenters' glue and cut nails being used for the joints, the

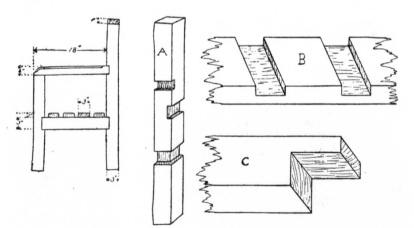

(Above) Side elevation of the garden seat. (Right) Diagrams showing how the joints are made.

heads being driven below the surface. The back slats are then fixed. Next the front is put together in the same way, and when both are set, the back and front are joined by means of the side rails and arms and the long slats are fixed.

When the whole is set the joins should be smoothed with sandpaper, and the surface rubbed down for painting, the nail holes being filled in with plastic wood or putty. A coat of priming, followed by two coats of good white paint, completes the work, which will last a lifetime if kept painted when necessary.

It is essential, however, not to be sparing with the paint, as it is false economy to try to save expense by neglecting outside woodwork. For a plain wood seat, Oak, Cypress or Redwood is used and this only requires oiling or treating with a wood preservative.

SEAWEED. Seaweeds of many different kinds are thrown up on the coast during the storms of winter. They may be collected and used as fertilizer. By far the greater proportion of the seaweeds consist of kinds of Laminaria and Fucus, known popularly as Tangle, Kelp, Oarweed, Wrack, Bladder Wrack, Sea Lettuce, and Grass Wrack.

Most of these weeds contain about the same percentage of nitrogen as farm manure. The decomposition of seaweed is much faster than that of manure, so that some of the nitrogen becomes available speedily and the rest of it follows later. An average sample of seaweed contains about 75 per cent water; the remainder is composed of solid organic matter, rich in potash and containing other plant foods, salt, etc.

Seaweed is especially rich in potash, and, as potash is a most important fertilizer, seaweed is valuable. It is deficient in phosphates. It does not contain fibrous material, such as is present in littery farm manure; hence it does not add so much to the store of humus in the soil. It has a great advantage, nevertheless, in that it contains no weeds, seeds of weeds, or the spores of disease.

Seaweed is best dug into the land as soon as it is secured; it is not a good plan to let it remain long in a heap. The better plan is to mix it with manure, litter, or lawn mowings, so that the rich plant foods formed from the seaweed may be retained. Such mixtures make valuable fertilizer which may be used for general garden purposes.

Seaweed may be used in gardens at the same rate as farm manure; it is spread over the ground and dug in at the earliest opportunity. It is particularly good for light and sandy land, and is beneficial to Potato, Beet, Carrot, Tomato, Onion, Asparagus, Cabbage, Pea, Bean, fruits, Roses and border flowers.

Seaweed is sometimes dried; the high proportion of water in fresh seaweed makes it uneconomical for transportation. The dried material contains as much as 75 per cent organic matter. Whereas the wet seaweed may contain 5 or 6 per cent potash, and $1\frac{1}{4}$ per cent nitrogen, the dried weed or kelp contains three times these amounts.

In certain parts of the world the seaweeds are collected, dried in summer and burned to a fine ash; the ash is used for the recovery of potash, iodine and certain other chemicals that are found in these plants. The amount of potash in the ash is very high; it may be as much as 28 per cent. It is one of the finest forms of potash for gardening purposes, and may be used at the rate of $\frac{1}{4}$ lb. per square yard, a few days before any crop is sown or planted.

SECALE—_Rye_ (Seca'le). A well-known cereal that belongs in the Grass family, Gramineae. Secale was the Roman name for Rye.

Rye is an annual Grass. Its chief horticultural use is as a cover crop and green manure. Its special value for these purposes lies in the fact that even in cold climates it may be sown in late summer and fall to provide a quick green cover. The crop may be dug or plowed under in the late fall or early in the following spring. In decaying, its tops and roots add substantially to the humus content of the soil. A crop of Rye sown in late summer also "ties up" for the winter, in unleachable form, soluble fertilizer elements that might otherwise be lost from the soil during winter. As the Rye decays in spring these are slowly made available again.

Rye is also excellent for preventing erosion of slopes of bare soil during the winter. The type of Rye normally used for garden purposes is called Winter Rye. It may be sown at a rate of 2-3 ounces to each 100 sq. ft. The seeds are then simply raked into the surface.

SECHIUM EDULE—*Chayote, Christophine* (Se'chium). A tropical American tender vine of the Gourd family, Cucurbitaceae. The name is derived from the vine's West Indian name, Chacha.

The Chayote is a tall vine that runs along the ground or climbs by tendrils. It is grown in warm countries, including the warmest parts of the United States, for its edible fruits and roots. The flowers are unisexual and a planting should consist of more than one plant to ensure fruiting.

Any reasonably fertile soil is suitable for the cultivation of this plant. The entire ripe fruits are planted in spring in the positions where the plants are to grow, the fruits being set with the broad end of each sloping downwards and the opposite end exposed slightly at ground level.

Trellis or other suitable support should be provided and the plants may be spaced 9-12 ft. apart.

Particularly good varieties of Chayote may be increased by means of cuttings taken from the crowns of old plants near soil level. In regions where the roots are not exposed to frost the plant is a perennial.

SECONDARY SHOOT. A term used by gardeners to indicate the small growths which develop as a result of pruning the side shoots on the main branches of Apple, Pear and other fruit trees; they are also known as sublaterals.

SEDGE. Carex, which see.

SEDUM: THE STONECROPS

Plants for Rock Gardens, Walls, Borders, Windows and Greenhouses

Sedum (Se'dum). A very large group of hardy and tender succulent plants, both annual and perennial. Only one of the annual sorts, Sedum caeruleum, is of any considerable garden value.

The name Sedum is from *sedo,* to sit, and refers to the manner in which the plants fix themselves to walls and rocks. Sedum belongs to the Orpine family, the Crassulaceae.

It is unfortunate that the Stonecrops are in a confused state as regards naming. This is no doubt partly due to the remarkable freedom with which Sedums propagate themselves. The smallest scrap will root itself where it falls, and so start a fresh plant. Even single leaves of certain kinds are capable of taking root where they fall, and becoming plants.

There are about three hundred distinct species of Sedum known to botanists, but comparatively few of these are, or have been, in cultivation. Again, of the great number of sorts actually in cultivation, many are only of interest to botanists and have no horticultural importance. For practical garden purposes the great number of known Stonecrops may be reduced to about thirty or forty. Among these are plants of first-class importance.

The Sedums are widely distributed in the Northern Hemisphere, especially in temperate countries. When they occur near the Equator they are usually found at high altitudes. A few are found in the far North, Iceland, Arctic Siberia, Alaska, and Greenland. Some grow wild in the Philippines and others near the Equator on the mountains of central Africa. In North America, Stonecrops are abundant and they are found as far south as Bolivia. Mexico has an exceedingly rich Sedum flora, with many striking and widely varied forms. None of the Mexican Sedums, unfortunately, is hardy in cold climates.

Good Plants for Poor Soil. The hardy rock-garden Sedums are extremely easy to grow. In the majority of cases they are best suited when given light, poor, well-drained soil and a fully sunny position. Sedum pulchellum is an exception to this rule, and enjoys richer, moister soil. Their propagation is of the easiest possible description. Clumps may be taken up, divided and replanted at almost any time of year; single shoots will root if merely stuck into the soil, and even single leaves may be used as cuttings to produce new plants.

Many of the Sedums have extremely beautiful and interesting leaves, and some kinds take on brilliant coloring during autumn and winter.

Low-growing Sedums are excellent for planting in crevices between flagstones in locations where they receive full sun.

The leaves color particularly well when the plants are more or less starved, as on the top of an old wall, or when given the poor, well-drained soil that suits them.

A Novel Way to Grow Stonecrops. A novel feature can be made by selecting a good-sized pocket or earth terrace and devoting it to a clump of mixed Sedums. In doing this it is important first to see that the pocket is well drained, and that the soil is light and rather poor. The location should be the hottest that can be found. The soil may be mounded up into a sort of low cushion, and planted closely, all over, with as many different sorts of Stonecrop of the smaller kinds as are available. They should be mixed, for the more varied they are the better. They will soon join up into one great patch of variegated color, an opalescent blending of reds and greens and purples, most fascinating and beautiful to behold.

Any of the following sorts may be used on such a mixed Sedum patch: acre, album, dasyphyllum, hispanicum, lydium, oreganum, reflexum, rupestre, sexangulare, and spathulifolium.

Apart from such specialized use as that just described, Sedums are invaluable for furnishing all sorts of out-of-the-way sunny corners and crevices in the rock garden. Sedum spathulifolium and its lovely purple variety, purpureum, are extremely decorative when planted in mass to join up and form rounded hummocks of fine gray-green or gray-purple foliage.

Plants for the Wall Garden. Seldom are Stonecrops so happy or so appropriately placed as when naturalized on an old wall. Many of them live happily in crumbling mortar between the bricks or stone. Some will actually establish themselves in patches of moss; they give a brilliant touch of color with their flowers or autumn-tinted leaves.

Stonecrops May Flourish on Roofs. Sedums, too, can be charming when established on an old and mossy tiled roof. The golden-flowered Sedum acre is often seen on roofs in Europe, but others may well be introduced, such as lydium, album, dasyphyllum, rupestre, and sexangulare; here, too, the blue-flowered Sedum caeruleum may be established by broadcasting its seeds on the moss in spring.

For Crevices in Paved Paths. All the smaller Stonecrops make charming plants for the crevices in paved paths. For this purpose Sedum acre in its various forms, album, dasyphyllum, hispanicum, lydium, and sexangulare are first-rate. They are extremely easy to establish and, once planted, will look after themselves indefinitely. These are also most attractive for planting in an informal way along the sides of the rock-garden paths. They will flourish planted in the gravel or stone chips of the path, and give an excellent effect if tucked in at the bases of the rocks to spread outwards as far as passing traffic allows.

A Good Window Plant. Sedum Sieboldii, a Japanese kind, is not grown nearly as much as its beauty deserves. It is absolutely hardy and can be used with exceedingly good effect in the rock garden, or as a neat flower border edging. Unfortunately slugs are fond of this lovely Sedum. Apart from Sedum Sieboldii the only other Stonecrops that find a place in the flower border are S. spurium and S. spectabile.

As a Flower-Border Edging. Sedum spurium, especially in its dark-flowered variety called splendens, may be used in the front of the flower border to form an edging or a section of a mixed edging along with Pink, Aubrieta, and

Alyssum. It is a handsome plant when in flower.

Sedum spectabile, the Japanese Stonecrop, is a true herbaceous plant, and is very well worth a place in the flower border for the sake of its great heads of blossom, which are like pink or crimson Cauliflowers. It is worth growing, moreover, for the sake of the butterflies which crowd to it. A good clump of Sedum spectabile in full flower, in September, crowded with a dozen or two brilliant butterflies, is a grand sight and no uncommon one.

Apart from the hardy perennial Sedums and the pretty annual Sedum caeruleum, there are two brilliant hardy biennial sorts, S. pilosum and S. sempervivoides, which are easily raised from seeds and are worth a place in the rock garden or in the alpine house. A description of the principal hardy Sedums follows. For the best and fullest account of all the Sedums in cultivation the reader should consult Lloyd Praeger's Monograph, which was published in the *Journal of the Royal Horticultural Society*, May, 1921. This has since been published separately. This valuable work is very full and complete, but is beyond the practical needs of the ordinary gardener.

Sedum acre is an Old World plant, common in many places, especially near the sea. It is the Wall Pepper, or yellow Stonecrop of European

In this city garden Sedum acre forms a perfect substitute for a lawn on a sunny slope.

cottage roofs and is well worth growing, being one of the showiest of the whole family. It is wild in Europe, Asia Minor, northern Asia and northern Africa. The fleshy, flattish, triangular green leaves are broad at the base, and the spreading heads of golden flowers in June, on 2-3-in. stems, are extremely beautiful. The name acre, meaning biting, refers to its acrid flavor, and in days gone by the plant was used medicinally as an emetic and cathartic.

There are several distinct varieties of Sedum acre. Majus, more commonly known in gardens as Maweanus, is rather larger in all its parts, the foliage is a paler green and the flowers larger and paler. Aureus is a pretty sort, probably of garden origin: the tips of the shoots are a bright golden color, making an attractive show when the plant is not in flower. It is a good edging plant which might with great advantage be used more frequently on the margins of narrow sunny borders, especially where the soil is poor.

Elegans resembles the last-named, except that the variegation of the shoot tips is silver instead of gold. Though pretty, it is not so desirable as aureus nor is it quite so hardy. Minimus is a dwarf variety only about ½ in. high; it is a neat, compact and attractive plant, and is especially desirable for the small rock garden, or for growing in the miniature sink or trough garden.

S. Aizoon is a very old garden plant, with distinct, perennial, carrot-like roots, erect stems a foot or more tall, unbranched and with broad fleshy toothed leaves. The flower head, 2 or 3 in. across, is yellow or orange. It is definitely a hardy herbaceous perennial, the stems dying to the ground in winter. It is a native of Siberia, Mongolia, Manchuria, China and Japan. It was introduced into European gardens as long ago as 1753.

S. album is one of the commonest of all Stonecrops in the garden, and has been misnamed more than most. It is wild on the continent of Europe, in Siberia, western Asia and northern Africa. It is of semicreeping habit, forming large mats. The flowers are white, sometimes fading to pink, and are in flattish panicles 1-2 in. across. It is a variable plant, and several distinct varieties or forms have been named and are worth garden room; nearly all are linked together

A popular Stonecrop for rock and wall gardens, the purple-leaved Sedum album murale.

by a numerous series of intermediate varieties.

The two best varieties are chloroticum, a very distinct and most attractive garden plant with vivid green leaves and stems, and a mass of snow-white flowers; and murale, which has purple foliage and pinkish flowers. This is of considerable garden value, and is widely grown in rock and wall gardens.

S. Anacampseros is a very distinct Stonecrop with trailing stems, clothed with thick, rounded leaves, and roundish heads of dull purplish flowers. It flowers in July and August, and is common in southern Europe. It may be increased by division, or by pulling off nonflowering shoots and inserting them as cuttings anywhere at any time.

S. bithynicum. See S. hispanicum, below.

S. caeruleum is the only annual Stonecrop worth garden room, and the only one, too, with blue flowers. It is an extremely pretty plant, a rather frail, much-branched annual 3-9 in. tall, carrying a cloud of starry, light blue flowers in July and August. Grown as it should be, in rather light, poor soil and in full sun, the whole plant,

The charming blue annual Sedum caeruleum.

stems and leaves, becomes bright red, a most striking contrast to the blue flowers. The plant is hardy, and seeds may be sown thinly, in spring, where the plants are to flower in summer. In some gardens the plant sows itself. It is delightful in the rock garden and wall garden. It is a native of southern Europe, northern Africa, Corsica and Malta.

S. dasyphyllum is a charming little Stonecrop, forming small compact masses of roundish leaves, an inch or so high, and bearing heads of pinkish flowers in June. The leaves are gray-green. It is delightful in the rock garden, never becoming a nuisance but fitting itself into all sorts of odd corners and crevices and looking almost prettier when not in flower than when flowering. It is also one of the best of all the Stonecrops for the wall garden. It propagates itself with the utmost freedom, small portions becoming detached, taking root, and rapidly forming fresh clumps. It is hardy, and is widely distributed on the continent of Europe except in the north, and extends to northern Africa. It is naturalized on old walls in Britain, but is not a native.

S. Ewersii is a distinct and pretty Stonecrop from the Himalayas, with trailing stems clothed with opposite pairs of stem-clasping leaves, and dense roundish heads of purplish-pink flowers in August and September. It is an easy plant to grow in any sunny position. There is a smaller variety, called homophyllum, which is only 2 or 3 in. high.

S. glaucum. See S. hispanicum, below.

S. hispanicum, in its typical wild form, is a small glaucous annual with pinkish-white flowers. This is unimportant as a garden plant. There is, however, a perennial form, Sedum hispanicum bithynicum, sometimes listed as S. glaucum, and sometimes S. lydium glaucum, and also known as S. hispanicum minus. It is the neat little gray-leaved Stonecrop which has been much used for carpet bedding, and is useful and charming in the rock garden, the wall garden, and in the crevices of flagged paths.

S. kamtschaticum is a first-rate rock-garden plant, with erect or ascending stems 3-4 in. tall, broad dark green leaves, and broad heads of orange flowers. It forms a thick woody rootstock from which the leafy stems arise in spring. It flowers from July to September, and is a native of northeastern Asia. There is a handsome form with variegated foliage in cultivation, the leaves having a broad marginal band of white.

S. lydium, from Asia Minor, is a charming little plant for the rock garden, wall garden or for pavement crevices. It forms neat masses of erect evergreen shoots, an inch or two tall, densely clothed with narrow leaves. It is green, though when grown as it should be, in sunshine, it becomes tinged with red, and sometimes the whole plant is brilliant. The white flowers are in flat heads. For S. lydium glaucum see S. hispanicum.

S. Middendorffianum. An attractive Stonecrop, with yellow flower heads, in general appearance rather like Sedum kamtschaticum, but with narrower leaves, usually more definitely tooth-edged. It grows 5 or 6 in. tall, flowers in July and August, and is a native of eastern Siberia and northern Manchuria. It is not so common in gardens as its merits deserve.

S. multiceps is an interesting little Stonecrop of subshrubby habit, growing 4 or 5 in. high. The lower portion of the stem becomes bare of leaves. The flowers, which are not very abundant, appear in July. It is a native of Algeria.

S. Nevii is an attractive and distinct little Stonecrop growing in the mountains of eastern North America. It forms rosettes of pale green leaves and bears heads of white flowers in June. It prefers light shade.

S. oreganum is a distinct and very attractive

The pink-flowered Sedum pilosum.

Stonecrop from western North America. It grows 3-4 in. high and has spatula-shaped leaves, which are green, tinged with red. The flowers are yellow. In a hot position the leaves turn red.

S. pilosum is an extremely pretty biennial Stonecrop from the Caucasus and Asia Minor. In general appearance it much resembles a Sempervivum or Houseleek, especially during its first year. In its second year it sends up heads of rose-pink flowers which almost suggest a Crassula. The plant sets abundant seeds and is quite hardy. It is charming in the rock garden, where it delights in sunny crevices. It is fine, too, in the alpine house.

S. populifolium, from Siberia, is a quaint little subshrubby Stonecrop, 6-18 in. tall, with little woody trunks and branches, deeply toothed or lobed leaves, and, in August, heads of white flowers. It is an old garden favorite, having been introduced in 1780 into European gardens. The

Pale yellow-flowered Sedum pruinosum.

flowers have a pleasing scent of Hawthorn, an unusual trait in the family.

S. pruinosum is an evergreen kind about 6 in. high which has white waxy stems and leaves and pale yellow flowers. It is a native of California very closely related to S. spathulifolium.

S. pulchellum, a native of eastern North America, is one of the best of all Stonecrops. Of tufted habit and with fresh green foliage, it has charming heads of bright pink flowers on erect stems 5-6 in. tall. It flowers abundantly from June till August, and often later still. The plant is unique in preferring or even requiring, a damp soil.

S. reflexum is one of the commonest of the European Stonecrops and very variable. It has a creeping stem and heads of yellow flowers. It flowers in July. There is a curious fasciated form of Sedum reflexum called cristatum, in which the stems are flattened out into a monstrous green cockscomb, often several inches wide. It is an old curiosity of cultivation.

S. Rosea, also known as Sedum Rhodiola, is our native Roseroot, so called because its roots, especially when dried, smell of rose water. It is a very variable plant, with a woody rootstock, from which grow the thick, erect, leafy stems bearing heads of greenish-yellow or reddish-purple flowers. Its height is about 18 in. Its range is wide, from Nova Zembla and Greenland to the Pyrenees, Japan and New Mexico. There are numerous forms and varieties.

S. rupestre is a common Stonecrop, native to western Europe, from Spain to Germany. It is naturalized in some parts of North America. It is a creeping plant, similar to S. reflexum, and is somewhat variable. A useful rock and wall plant, it bears heads of yellow flowers on stems 5-9 in. high.

S. sarmentosum is a trailing evergreen kind that grows with great ease and may become a nuisance if admitted to choice locations in the garden. Its leaves are broad, lance-shaped, about 1 in. long, and are arranged in threes. The bright yellow flowers are produced in early summer. This kind, which is a native of eastern Asia, is naturalized locally in North America.

S. sempervivoides is also known as Sedum Sempervivum from the resemblance of its leaf rosette to a Houseleek or Sempervivum. It is closely allied to S. pilosum and comes from the Caucasus. It is a biennial, forming the first year from seed a fleshy rosette of handsome leaves marked with dark red. The second year, in June or July, the plant flowers a head of intensely brilliant scarlet blossoms of great magnificence, after which the plant dies. Seeds are produced abundantly and fresh plants are easily raised.

This is a most attractive plant for sunny, well-drained ledges and nooks in the rock garden, or for the alpine house.

S. sexangulare is not unlike S. acre in general appearance, but the arrangement of the leaves is different, the general habit is neater and more compact, and the golden-yellow flowers are of a richer tone. It is one of the best of Stonecrops, for the rock garden, the wall garden, and for the crevices of paved walks. It is found over a wide area in Europe. It flowers in July.

S. Sieboldii is a beautiful Japanese Stonecrop introduced into Europe in 1836. It has arching stems, 6-9 in. long, with roundish, glaucous leaves arranged in threes. The rosy-purple flower heads are produced in September and October. It is quite hardy, though often grown as a greenhouse or a window plant.

This is one of the prettiest of all Stonecrops. It is a first-rate rock-garden plant and makes a neat edging. The variety medio-variegatis is a variegated variety with a large golden splash in the center of each leaf. It is a popular pot plant and is less hardy than the green-leaved form.

S. spathulifolium, a native of western North America, Vancouver Island, etc., is one of the most distinct and beautiful of all the Stonecrops. It forms close cushions of thick, fleshy gray-green leaves. In May or June it produces heads of golden flowers on 4-5-in. stems. It is an easy plant to grow, and is most decorative for filling hot rock ledges in the rock garden. Sedum spathulifolium purpureum has larger leaves of purple color, with a heavy gray waxy coating. It is even finer than the type, and is looked upon by many good gardeners as the finest of all the Stonecrops; although it flowers shyly, it probably is the best. The variety majus has rosettes and leaves twice the normal size, but less glaucous.

S. spectabile is an herbaceous perennial, with thick fleshy roots, erect, thick stems, 18-24 in. tall, and fine heads of purplish-pink flowers, 1 ft. or more across. There is a finer variety called atropurpureum with darker, richer-colored flow-

Sedum Sieboldii growing in an earthenware jar.

Sedum spectabile, a Japanese Stonecrop, with bluish foliage and pink flowers, a first-class perennial plant.

ers. It is a grand plant for the front of the flower border, flowering in August and September. It is native of Japan. It is a great attraction to butterflies, which crowd on the wide flower heads to gather nectar.

S. spurium is a common plant, growing almost

anywhere. It has creeping stems, broad leaves and heads of pink flowers on stems 4 or 5 in. tall, in July and August. It is a native of the Caucasus and Transcaucasia.

The best variety is one with flowers of a strong, rich crimson, called splendens.

S. stoloniferum is a creeping, nearly evergreen kind that grows about 6 in. high and has pink flowers in early summer.

S. Telephium attains a height of 1½-2 ft. and has greenish-white or purplish flowers in late summer. This kind is known by the common names of Orpine and Live-forever, and is a strong-growing perennial suited for planting in sunny borders.

S. ternatum is an evergreen that grows 6 in tall and has white flowers in late spring; its leaves are in threes.

Tender Kinds

In addition to the very large number of hardy Sedums there are a number of tender kinds. These will not withstand the winters outdoors in cold regions but are grown in the open in places where low rainfall and mild winters prevail, such as the southwestern United States, and also as greenhouse and window-garden plants.

The tender Sedums thrive in loose, porous soil that is well drained and in full sun. They are very easily propagated by stem cuttings and leaf cuttings. Specimens grown in pans, pots and baskets normally require transferring to larger containers or dividing and repotting every two or three years only. In the intervening years an annual top-dressing given in spring or early summer, just as new growth begins, is all that is necessary. After the flowers have finished the plants should be rested for a few weeks by keeping them drier and cooler than normal. Just before new growth begins they may be trimmed lightly to shape them.

Pot-grown Sedums need watering moderately from the time when new growth begins until they are through flowering, more sparsely at other times. Specimens that have filled their pots with healthy roots benefit from an occasional application of dilute liquid fertilizer.

S. Adolphii is a bushy kind with light green

foliage tinged red sometimes. Its flowering stems, which arise from the base of the plant, terminate in flattish heads, 2-3 inches wide, of white flowers. It is a native of Mexico and blooms in March and April.

S. bellum is a Mexican kind that is very attractive for growing in pans or pots. It is a glaucous plant with flower stems about 4 in. long,

Sedum bellum is an attractive kind for growing in window gardens and—in warm, dry climates—for planting outdoors.

each terminated by a head of pure white flowers which have conspicuous pink anthers. The flowers are numerous.

S. compressum, a native of Mexico, has glaucous, gray-green spoon-shaped leaves that are about 1½ in. long by ½ in. wide and are

Sedum compressum is a winter- or early spring-flowering kind that is well adapted for growing in pots or pans as well as for planting outdoors in climates such as that of southern California.

Sedum Nussbaumerianum bears heads of creamy-white fragrant flowers and has thick fleshy leaves.

arranged in loose rosettes. The bright golden-yellow flowers are profusely borne along the spreading inflorescence branches. It normally blooms in winter or early spring.

S. cupressoides is a native of Mexico that is 4-6 in. tall and has much-branched, decumbent stems. Its leaves are arranged very closely together. The yellow flowers are borne in summer.

S. dendroideum, a Mexican native, attains a height of about 2 ft. and has spoon-shaped leaves, flattened on one side and rounded on the other, crowded towards the ends of its branches. The flowers are bright yellow; they appear in late spring or early summer.

Sedum Palmeri has bright yellow flowers and bluish foliage. It is a winter-flowering kind.

S. Nussbaumerianum somewhat resembles S. Adolphii and is sometimes misidentified as that species. It forms a vigorous plant with rather lax older stems and younger ones that are more or less erect. The leaves are thick, fleshy and glossy, often tinged with red. The creamy white, slightly fragrant flowers are in hemispherical heads that measure about 3 in. in diameter. The flowers are borne in winter.

S. Palmeri, a native of Mexico, rather resembles S. compressum. It has glaucous, spoon-shaped leaves in rosettes and bright golden-yellow flowers. It blooms in winter and grows 5-7 in. tall.

SEED. The ovules of flowering plants (except those of gymnosperms such as Pines) are contained within an ovary. Fertilization is effected by pollen grains, which, when they come into contact with the stigma, germinate and send down long tubes through the style into the ovary. These pollen tubes contain nuclei which fuse with the nuclei of the ovules and fertilization is effected. The ovules then develop into perfect seeds capable of producing new individual plants.

Structure of Seeds. A seed consists of a seed coat or testa, two seed leaves or cotyledons (in the case of dicotyledons), or one seed leaf in monocotyledons, and the embryo plant. The embryo consists of a primary root or radicle and a primary shoot or plumule. At the end or one side of the seed coat is a scar (hilum) which indicates where the seed was attached to the pod. Near the hilum is a microscopic hole, the micropyle. This is where the pollen tube entered to fertilize the ovule, and through which the root emerges when germination commences.

When saving seeds it must be remembered that many hybrids which had been obtained by intercrossing one kind with another do not breed true to type, so that it is necessary to increase them by vegetative means—that is, cuttings or division. Most of the original species or wild types of plants breed true, however, provided the flowers are prevented from being cross-pollinated. To do this the flowers are enclosed in muslin bags, and artificially pollinated with pollen from flowers of the same plant or the same species of plant. Unless the flowers are protected in this way, there is no guarantee that the flowers will not become cross-fertilized by insects or wind.

As soon as the seeds are ripe they should be gathered and, kinds not harmed by drying, spread out to dry in a well-ventilated room. In the case of soft berried fruits, the seeds are first squeezed out of the pulp; the larger seeds are rubbed in a handful of sand before spreading them out to dry. When they are quite dry the seeds are packeted and stored in a dry, cool, frost-proof place.

Except with rare plants or especially good strains, it is not worth the trouble of saving seeds, as they can be purchased so cheaply.

Stratifying Seeds. The best way to deal with dryish berries such as Berberis, Cotoneaster, etc., is to place them between layers of nearly dry sand in a box, which is then stored in a dry, cool place. By March the berries will be dry, and, when rubbed with the sand through the hands, the seeds will separate quite readily, the seeds and sand being then sown. Details of instructions on seed sowing are given under the heading of Propagation.

Some few seeds, notably those of many water plants and bog plants, as well as those of many plants belonging in the Arum family (Araceae) and some others, are killed if they are permitted to dry. These should be stored in moist moss or, in some cases, in water.

Yet other seeds, such as those of Maples and Oaks, do not retain their power of germination for long and should be sown soon after they are ripe.

The Vitality of Seeds. The length of time that seeds will retain their vitality depends a good deal on how they are stored, as well as on the texture of their seed coats. Some seeds, such as those of Willow, only retain their power of germination a few days, whereas others, such as Cassia, have been known to germinate after being kept dry for over 80 years. Seeds of the Coconut, Rubber and many Palms are very short-lived. The fables about the Mummy Wheat, which is supposed to germinate after lying in the Egyptian tombs for centuries, are well known. Such stories have no basis in fact.

Investigations on stored herbarium seeds were made in Paris by Becquerel. Some seeds were 135 years old. Four kinds of Leguminosae, and one each of Malvaceae, Labiatae, and Nymphaeaceae germinated after being stored for 50 years, and Cassia germinated after 87 years. Altogether 500 kinds of seeds were tested, and 50 kinds gave a percentage of germination after 25 years of storage as herbarium specimens.

Generally speaking, oily seeds quickly lose their vitality, whereas those with hard seed coats, especially the members of the Leguminosae (Pea family), are the longest-lived.

The majority of seeds, especially of annuals, biennials, herbaceous perennials, alpine plants and vegetables, will germinate as soon as they are ripe if placed under suitable conditions. Others, especially those of forest trees and shrubs, will not germinate until the following spring or summer; examples are the Fir, Pine, Beech and Ash. In many cases this is due to the immaturity of the embryos, which do not become fully developed until some time after the seeds have apparently ripened.

How Long Seeds Remain Sound When Stored. *Flowers:* Ageratum, Alyssum, Anchusa, Antirrhinum, Aster, Aubrieta, Begonia, Coleus, Coreopsis, Cyclamen, Gaillardia, Lilium, Nicotiana, Scabious, Schizanthus, Sweet William, Viola and Wallflower, 2 years.

Aquilegia, Chrysanthemum, Clarkia, Nasturtium, Papaver, 3 years; Delphinium and Sunflower, 4 years; Lupine, 5 years; Sweet Pea, 10 years.

Trees and Shrubs: Willow, a few days; Hazel, Beech, Fir, 1 year; Hornbeam, Linden, Elder, Sycamore, Mountain Ash, 2 years; White Pine, Robinia, Scots Pine, Holly, 3 years.

Cereals: Wheat, 15-16 years; Barley, 8-10 years; Oats, 5-9 years; Maize, 4-5 years.

Vegetables: Asparagus, 4-8 years; Beans, Broad, 3-4 years; Beans, String, 2-3 years; Beans, Runner, 3-4 years; Beet, 3-4 years; Brassicas, 3-4 years; Carrots, 4-9 years; Celery, 8-10 years; Cucumber, 5-10 years; Leek, 3-7 years; Lettuce, 5-9 years; Melon, 5-9 years; Mustard, 4-8 years; Onion, 2-4 years; Parsley, 2-6 years; Parsnip, 2-4 years; Pea, 2-7 years; Pumpkin, 6-8 years; Radish, 3-9 years; Spinach, 5-7 years; Turnip, 3-9 years; Squash, 4-5 years.

Testing Seeds. Seeds of doubtful germinating

power should be tested before sowing, or much time may be wasted by having to purchase fresh seed and make a second sowing. The best way to do this is to take 100 representative seeds, large and small, and place them on flannel or blotting paper which should be laid on a plate or dish and kept moist in a warm greenhouse with a minimum temperature of 50-60 degrees.

SEED FLATS are extensively used in gardens and nurseries for raising plants from seeds, and for growing the seedlings until they are large enough to pot separately, or plant out of doors. Seed flats are used in preference to flowerpots

A seed flat containing young plants.

for raising large quantities of seedlings, especially of bedding plants such as Petunias, Verbenas and Begonias. They are sometimes called boxes.

Suitable flats can be purchased, but they are easily made at home. The sizes may vary according to the available material, but a useful size for general use is 15 in. long, 9 in. wide, and 3 or 4 in. deep. Flats of this size are easy to handle and they can accommodate four dozen bedding plants when these are set 1½ in. apart.

The important point to remember in making flats is to provide for the exit of surplus water. The bottom should be nailed on in pieces, with ½-in. gaps between the boards. If this is not done, drainage holes should be bored. They should be ½ in. in diameter and 6-8 in. apart.

Seed flats can be made to last for two or three

seasons if they are thoroughly dried after use, treated with a nonharmful wood preservative, and stored in a dry shed until required again. A water-resistant wood such as cypress is the best kind to use for making seed flats. See Flats.

SEED SOWING. See Propagation.

SELAGINELLA (Selaginel'la). The Selaginellas, which are nearly related to the Ferns, but closely resemble Mosses in general appearance, are very elegant foliage plants. They are used for a variety of purposes, such as for decorating terrariums, for edging the greenhouse benches, carpeting the ground under the benches, furnishing hanging baskets, and draping pillars. Many are trailers; a few are climbers.

These plants do not flower, but are reproduced sexually by spores. Two kinds of spores are produced, male and female. They are borne in spikelike cones at the apices of the branches, the male spores at the top and the female spores below. When the ripe spores are shed they give rise to two kinds of prothallia, male and female, and when the female prothallus becomes fertilized by the male, a young Selaginella plant is formed. As the two kinds of spores do not always ripen together on the same cone, it is best to obtain the spores from more than one cone, to ensure the chance of two types of spores developing in close proximity.

The most distinctive feature of the Selaginellas is found in the small scalelike leaves which are set close together all along the stems; in most cases they are sessile (without stalks), and set

Selaginella Kraussiana is a creeping plant that makes a dense low ground cover of fernlike foliage.

parallel to the stems (not at right angles as in the majority of plants), so that the branches and leaves are in one flat plane, as if they had been pressed between two boards. Generally, they are of a light green color, but in some kinds, especially S. uncinata, are bluish and in others, such as S. Willdenovii, they have a blue or bronze sheen.

The Selaginellas number some 700 species, inhabiting all parts of the world. The majority are found wild in tropical America and Asia, but a few come from Japan, China, North America, Australia and South Africa. Selaginella belongs to the Lycopodium family, Lycopodiaceae. The name is a diminutive of Selago, a related plant.

Summer and Winter Treatment. Although these plants vary much in habit of growth, they all flourish under the same treatment, except that some are hothouse and others are cool greenhouse plants. A rich, porous soil compost is necessary. The best mixture consists of loam, one part, leaf mold, two parts, sand, one part, and a small quantity of lump charcoal. Wide pans are the best receptacles in which to grow them—shallow pans for the creeping and tufted kinds, and deeper ones for the robust kinds and for climbers.

Selaginellas are raised from cuttings, and produce roots with remarkable freedom. The pans are well drained and filled with the compost recommended above, and the tips of shoots are inserted. It is then only necessary to moisten them daily with a light spray and they quickly take root.

During the summer months, they require an abundance of water, both in the soil and the atmosphere, but during the winter slightly drier conditions must be maintained. They should at all times be shaded from direct sunlight.

Edging Plants for the Greenhouse Bench. S. Kraussiana is an ideal plant for edging the greenhouse benches, which it quickly covers with its slender, trailing, mosslike shoots. There are two methods of growing the plants for this purpose. They may either be grown in small pots or planted directly into gritty soil spread on the benches. The advantage of growing them in pots is that they can be moved about from place to place if desired.

For this purpose a sufficient number of 4-in. pots are crocked by having an inch of drainage material placed in their bottoms and are filled with compost. To produce an unbroken edging of greenery there should be enough pots to stand so close together that they nearly touch each other. Tips of shoots, 1 in. in length, are then dibbled an inch apart all over the surface of the soil. The compost is kept moist and the trailing stems quickly cover the pots and hang downwards over the edge of the bench.

When the bench is made of slabs of slate, concrete, tiles or galvanized iron, a layer of compost, 3 in. wide and 1 in. thick, may be spread along the edge of it. The shoots are dibbled into this, and by keeping the soil moist a continuous band of verdant foliage is eventually formed.

For Hanging Baskets. The following kinds are useful for furnishing hanging baskets: S. Kraussiana, S. uncinata, and S. denticulata. They make long trailing shoots which hang down over the sides of the baskets and transform them into masses of beautiful greenery.

The baskets are lined with moss and filled with the prepared compost. Pieces of shoots are dibbled in and treated as advised for plants in pans; attention must be paid to the watering, as the soil dries out more rapidly in suspended brackets.

For Covering Pillars in the Greenhouse. The best kind for draping a pillar is S. canaliculata, which has stems over 6 ft. in length. This is planted in a large flower pan or a prepared bed of soil at the base of the pillar, and, as the shoots develop, they are tied to the support.

To Plant Under the Greenhouse Benches. If it is desired to cover the soil beneath the benches, S. Kraussiana is the best to use. Prepared compost to the depth of a few inches is spread out and the shoots are set into it. No further attention is needed beyond a daily damping with a fine spray.

Resurrection Plant is the common name of S. lepidophylla, a native of desert and semidesert regions from Texas to South America. It is so called because of its habit of curling into a tight ball and turning brown when dry, and opening out flat and becoming green again when moisture is available to it, without suffering any harm. S. lepidophylla forms a rosette 6-8 in. across.

Another plant sometimes called Resurrection Plant, and for the same reason, is Anastatica hierochuntica. A native of Asia Minor, it belongs in the Mustard family of plants. It is also known as Rose of Jericho. See Anastatica.

The chief kinds for the hothouse are S. Martensii, 12 in., erect; S. uncinata, trailing, blue foliage; S. Braunii, 18 in., erect; S. delicatissima, tufted, 3 in.; S. canaliculata, trailing, 6 ft.

For the Cool Greenhouse. S. Kraussiana, trailing; S. caulescens, erect, 9 in.; S. apus, tufted, dwarf; S. Douglasii, trailing; S. helvetica, trailing.

SELECTIVE WEED KILLERS. These are synthetic hormone and other preparations, available in several proprietary brands, which are lethal to broad-leaved plants but do not harm narrow-leaved grasses, and are therefore more valuable for the destruction of weeds on lawns. For further details, see Lawns, and also Weeds.

SELENICEREUS—*Queen of the Night* (Selenice'reus). A genus of night-flowering Cacti for the warm greenhouse and for growing outdoors in tropical and subtropical areas. They have slender, ribbed, climbing stems, furnished with small spines, which can be trained up supports and along greenhouse rafters. They are quick-growing, the stems producing aerial roots in some species, and all bear large, white flowers, which in some kinds are strongly scented. The name is from *Selene,* the moon, and refers to the night-flowering habit.

Queen of the Night. Loveliest of them all is Selenicereus grandiflorus, from Jamaica and Cuba, with very large, strongly scented flowers. Other notable kinds are S. Boeckmannii, a native of Mexico and the West Indies; S. coniflorus and S. pteranthus, both from Mexico; and S. spinulosus, from Mexico and Texas.

SELENIPEDIUM (Seleniped'ium). The Orchids usually known under the names of Selenipedium are correctly called Phragmipedium and are usually grown under the name Cypripedium, which see.

SELF-COLORED. A term used in reference to plants with flowers wholly of one color.

SELF-FERTILE. A term used to indicate those varieties of plants which are able to set seeds when their blossoms are not cross-fertilized by pollen from the flowers of other varieties of the same kind. The term is commonly used in reference to fruit trees.

SELFHEAL. Prunella, which see.

SELF-STERILE. A term used to indicate those plants, the flowers of which are not fertilized by their own pollen, and do not bear seeds unless they are planted in the vicinity of other varieties of the same kind so that their blossoms shall be cross-fertilized. The term is often used in reference to fruit trees.

SEMIARUNDINARIA (Semiarundinar'ia). A group of erect Bamboos that differs from Arundinaria in technical characters only. They belong in the botanical family Gramineae, the Grass family. The name is derived from *semi,* half, and Arundinaria, an allied genus of plants.

Semiarundinaria fastuosa is a native of Japan that grows 15-40 ft. tall and has hollow stems that are usually marked with purplish-brown. Its leaves are up to 7 in. long by 1 in. wide and are glossy green above and bluish beneath. The plant retains its stems and foliage throughout the

One of the loveliest of all Cacti is the white, strongly scented, large-flowered, night-blooming Selenicereus grandiflorus, the Queen of the Night.

year. It is hardy as far north as Washington, D.C. This Bamboo requires the same culture, and is propagated in the same ways, as Arundinaria, which see.

SEMPERVIVUM or HOUSELEEK
An Easy-to-grow Group of Hardy Succulents

Sempervivum (Sempervi'vum). The Sempervivums or Houseleeks are hardy and tender succulent plants belonging to the Crassula family, Crassulaceae. The name Sempervivum is the old Latin name used by Pliny; it is derived from *semper,* forever, and *vivo,* to live, and alludes to the tenacity to life of these plants.

The Sempervivums are natives of the mountains of central and southern Europe, Asia Minor, northern Africa and the western Himalayas.

Hardy and Tender Kinds. The plants grown in gardens as Sempervivums may be roughly divided into two classes: (1) the hardy European Sempervivums proper, and (2) the tender kinds,

A group of Houseleeks or Sempervivums on a dry, sunny bank in the rock garden.

which have been subdivided into Aichryson, Aeonium, Greenovia, and Monanthes. The latter are natives of the Islands of Madeira, the Azores, the Cape Verde Islands and the African mainland. See Aichryson, Aeonium, Greenovia and Monanthes.

The Sempervivums are difficult and bewildering to identify. The actual species or wild types vary widely under normal conditions; besides this, individuals will show marked variation under different cultural conditions. Further, they hybridize endlessly, intercrossing with their own parents both in nature and in the garden. Their fecundity is only exceeded by their promiscuity. The result is that nurserymen, amateur gardens, and botanic gardens have distributed Sempervivums under a great number of "specific" names, the vast majority of which are entirely unauthentic.

There are indeed a few definite species, and a few well-marked varieties and hybrids of those species, which it is possible, with care, to identify, but after that the wise gardener will pick the sorts that he likes and use them in his garden for what they are, and not for what they are called.

The serious student of this interesting group of plants cannot do better than consult the monograph of Sempervivum by Dr. R. Lloyd Praeger, published by the Royal Horticultural Society in 1932.

Sempervivums are found mostly in the Alps. They extend westward to the Pyrenees and eastward as far as the Caucasus. A few grow wild in the Balkans and fewer still in Turkey and Asia Minor. One species only, Sempervivum atlanticum, is found on the African side of the Mediterranean. Sempervivums have been found in the Alps growing at an altitude of 11,000 ft., and they descend as low as 3,000 ft. or rather less. At the lower elevations they are usually found as saxatile or rock-haunting plants, no doubt to avoid the competition of strong-growing plants that are found in deep soil. At the higher altitudes they are often in the stunted herbage that grows there.

The Hardy Houseleeks Are Extremely Easy to Cultivate. These plants thrive in any light, well-drained loam, and should always be given a well-drained, sunny location. They may also be planted on the tops of old walls, where they will flourish indefinitely with a minimum of soil.

Sempervivums are admirable plants for the dry wall garden and should, of course, be put on the sunny side, where they will remain from year to year, increasing slowly in size, and giving a venerable and picturesque air to the wall that no other plant can impart.

Houseleeks on Tiled Roofs. The sight of a great clump of Houseleek on an old tiled roof is familiar in many European country districts; there is an old superstition that a Houseleek on the roof keeps away lightning and averts fire. It is from this planting of Sempervivum tectorum upon roofs that the plant has gained its common name, Houseleek, and also its Latin specific name, tectorum.

In the rock garden the Sempervivums are extremely valuable and ornamental plants. They may be planted in any sunny position; a few plants, or even single rosettes, put out in a group will soon grow together and form a solid clump which will remain a perennial ornament for an almost indefinite period of time. They look best when established on narrow terrace rock formations and horizontal crevices. They may also be grown on the flat top surfaces of the larger rocks.

All that is necessary is to put a shovelful or two of loam on the rock, and then plant it with one or more Sempervivum plants. It is a wise precaution to protect the plants with a wire netting covering until they are well established. If this is not done the plants are very likely to be scratched out by birds in their search for grubs and insects. Once the Houseleeks have joined up into a solid mass they will be fairly safe from the bird menace.

Houseleeks in Barrels and Vases. Sempervivums make delightful specimens for planting in strawberry barrels and pots and in stone vases. A stone vase containing a good specimen Houseleek, especially if it be one of the more ornamental sorts such as S. arachnoideum, the Cobweb Houseleek, or the handsome Sempervivum ornatum of gardens, is a very attractive object. It improves in appearance from year to year, and has the advantage of needing little attention in the matters of weeding and watering.

In planting, it is important to mound up the soil before putting in the plants. A well-mounded specimen is far more handsome and more effective than a flat one.

Easy to Propagate. Single rosettes may be pulled from a parent plant, and merely stuck in the ground; they will form roots in a very short time. Seeds may be sown in a pan of light sandy soil in a cold frame, and usually germinate readily. Early summer and spring are the best times for sowing. Houseleeks may also be propagated by leaf cuttings, in spring.

A charming way of growing Houseleeks is as a mixed collection in a miniature rock garden, in a stone or earthenware vessel or deep tray. Very thorough drainage must, of course, be provided, and the container should be filled with a mound of light, gritty loam. A few pieces of rock of appropriate size should be well embedded in the soil, to form a simple rock garden rising at its highest point 1 ft. or 18 in. above the general level.

Many Sempervivums do very well in towns, and a Sempervivum garden can be strongly recommended for the smallest town gardens, provided they are sunny, or even for roof gardens or sunny balconies.

Some of the principal kinds are:

Sempervivum Allionii has small, roundish rosettes of pale green color, the small leaves being covered with glandular velvetlike hair. The leaves are incurved, and sometimes red-tipped. The flowers are greenish-white. This plant is a native of the southern Alps.

S. arachnoideum, the Cobweb Houseleek, is by far the most attractive of all. The leaf ros-

ettes, which vary considerably in size, are comparatively small, being seldom more than 1 in. or 1¼ in. in diameter. In some varieties they are extremely small. The leaves vary in color from deep red to pale green or dark green, or they may be red and green. The plant, however, is always easy to distinguish by the curious and beautiful system of white, cobweblike threads which stretch from tip to tip of the pointed leaves. In some forms this spider's web is extremely dense, almost hiding the leaves beneath a white silken canopy. In others, it is much less prominent, and in winter it often disappears almost entirely.

Apart from the beauty of the cobwebbed leaf rosettes, the flowers of S. arachnoideum are far more attractive than those of any other Houseleek. They are carried in a head on a stem usually 3-4 in. high and are bright cherry red or pink.

S. arenarium. One of the smallest Houseleeks, this kind has green rosettes, the leaves often tinged with red. It is a native of the eastern Alps, Salzburg, Tyrol, and Carinthia.

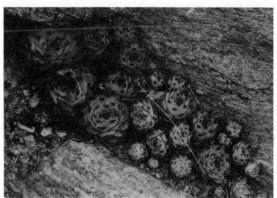

The leaf tips of Sempervivum calcareum are clearly tipped with red-brown.

S. atlanticum is interesting as being the only Sempervivum that is a native of Africa. It is very near S. tectorum, but is of no great horticultural value. It is found in Morocco.

S. calcareum. This native of France is a very attractive kind. It forms many rosettes each measuring to 2 in. across. The leaves are glaucous and are prominently tipped with red-brown. The flowers are pale red.

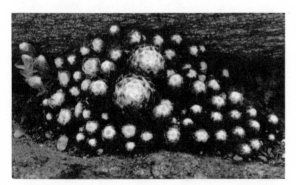

The dainty Cobweb Houseleek, Sempervivum arachnoideum.

S. ciliosum. This is a very distinct Houseleek and a most beautiful one; moreover, it is easy to distinguish from all others. The leaf rosettes are globular, and gray with long translucent hairs. The flowers are yellow. It is a native of Bulgaria.

S. dolomiticum is an interesting little Houseleek of very local occurrence in the Alps, and is extremely rare in cultivation. It resembles a small, dense S. montanum, with more acute leaves, the hairs at the edges and tips being longer than those on the general surface. The flowers are very distinct, having short, broad, rose-pink petals, as opposed to the long, narrow, bluish-purple petals of S. montanum. The plant is a native of the eastern Alps on limestone formations.

S. erythraeum is distinct on account of the soft grayish-purple color of its leaves, which are covered with fine white hairs on a purplish ground. The rosettes are small, neat, flattish and open. The short broad leaves are without purple-brown tips. The branched inflorescence is purplish and covered with white hairs and the flowers are purplish-red. It is found in Bulgaria.

S. Funckii is a hybrid or crossbred Houseleek. Its numerous leaf rosettes are dense, medium-sized, green and covered with soft, glandular hair. Its parentage is uncertain, though S. montanum is believed to be one parent. The flowers are reddish-purple with a dark eye, and rather short petals.

S. globuliferum. The plant grown under this name is apparently a variety or form of S. montanum. It has rosettes measuring up to 3 in.

This plant of Sempervivum globuliferum is producing offsets freely around the central rosette.

across and pale yellow flowers. It is an easily grown and attractive kind.

S. grandiflorum has the largest flowers of any of the hardy Houseleeks. Superficially it resembles S. tectorum, but may be distinguished by its leaves of dull green, clothed with clammy hairs. The flowers are yellow, and its long, leafy offsets and curious strong odor still further distinguish the plant from S. tectorum and S. montanum. The flowers are sometimes as much as 2 in. across.

S. Heuffelii is near S. tectorum, but is distinguished by its yellow flowers. It forms solid compact clumps, not increasing by stalked offsets as does S. tectorum. It is a variable plant and not among the most important horticulturally.

S. Kosaninii is a handsome and distinct Houseleek from Macedonia. It has downy, purple-tipped leaves in rosettes 2 in. across, flat and dense, and red flowers.

S. montanum is one of the most familiar Houseleeks in the Alps, and it is common in gardens. It is a variable plant. The leaf rosettes are usually smallish, dark dull green, and densely covered with fine glandular hairs. There is a large form, Burnatti, in the Maritime Alps, the hairy leaves of which might be mistaken for S. grandiflorum, were it not that the flowers of the latter are yellow whereas those of montanum are bluish-purple. White or yellowish forms of montanum occur, but are rare.

S. Pittonii is a pretty plant, with hairy leaf rosettes and yellow flowers. The rosettes are small and dense and compactly clustered together. It is not common in cultivation.

S. pumilum is one of the smallest of the Houseleeks. It is not unlike a small, sharp-leaved S. montanum; the flowers resemble those of S. arachnoideum, but the plant is quite devoid of cobweb, and the color of the flowers is rosy-purple. It is rare in cultivation, but is a desirable and free-flowering plant.

S. ruthenicum has pubescent leaves and yellow flowers. It is common in southeastern Europe.

S. Schlehanii itself is a rare and comparatively unimportant plant from the Balkans, like a small edition of S. tectorum. There is, however, in cultivation an extremely beautiful variety known as brunneifolium (rubicundum) with leaves of a crimson color margined with green.

S. soboliferum is common in gardens and is popularly known as the Hen and Chicken's Houseleek. It produces numbers of very small offsets which at once become detached from the parent plant and lie about until they take root. It is a shy flowerer. This pretty plant, with green, half-open rosettes was planted by Linnaeus in his garden at Hammarby, in Sweden, where it still grows. Rosettes are carried off as souvenirs by visitors. The plant is a native of northern Eurasia, extending as far north as Archangel.

One of the most popular Sempervivums or Houseleeks for general planting, the handsome S. tectorum.

S. tectorum is represented by a large variety commonly grown on tiled roofs in Europe. It has escaped from cultivation and run wild in some parts of North America. It is an extremely variable plant and it hybridizes with several other species. S. tectorum has been given more synonyms and false names than any other Houseleek.

S. tectorum itself is very clearly defined as a species, first by its purplish flowers, as opposed to yellow or yellowish flowers; secondly, by its leaves, which are smooth, and have purple tips. It is a curious thing that the large form of S. tectorum as grown on roofs and in gardens is unknown in the wild state.

Two of the best of the forms or varieties of S. tectorum are calcareum, very glaucous leaves, definitely purple-tipped; and robustum, which includes some really gigantic forms with rosettes up to 6 in. or more in diameter, and flower stems up to 18 in. tall.

S. Wulfenii is near S. tectorum, but is distinguished by having fewer leaves to each rosette, and the leaves are gray-green, without purple tips, but purplish at the base. The flowers are yellow.

SENECA SNAKEROOT. Polygala Senega, which see.

SENECIO—*Groundsel, Ragwort, Dusty Miller, German Ivy* (Sene'cio). This extensive group comprises a large number of hardy and tender plants of annual, biennial or perennial duration, and of herbaceous, shrubby or climbing growth. Senecio, which belongs to the Daisy family, Compositae, is one of the largest groups of plants, for it contains over a thousand species. In addition to the kinds discussed here, the florists' Cineraria, Senecio cruentus, is popular. In this Encyclopedia it is described and discussed under Cineraria, which see.

Senecios are found wild in nearly every country of the world, being particularly abundant in southern Europe; other cultivated kinds are natives of South Africa, Australia, New Zealand, Japan, China, the United States and Mexico. They vary greatly in size and habit, and especially

Senecio elegans, often known as Jacobaea elegans, is a beautiful annual kind.

in their foliage, but nearly all have yellow or purple daisy-like flowers. The name Senecio is derived from *senex,* an old man, and refers to the white or graying hairlike pappus.

A Free-flowering Hardy Annual. The principal hardy annual is Senecio elegans (Jacobaea), which grows up to 2 ft. in height, has pinnate (feathery) or deeply lobed leaves, and bears terminal compact heads of purple, crimson, mauve, rose or white single or double flowers in summer. It requires a sunny position and thrives in ordinary, well-cultivated soil. The seeds are sown broadcast in irregular patches near the front of the border in spring. The seedlings are thinned out to 6 in. apart. The flowers are freely produced and are excellent for cutting.

Senecio elegans is also a useful plant for growing in pots or in benches of soil in a cool, sunny greenhouse for flowering in spring.

Seeds sown from September to January, according to the size of plants desired, will give satisfactory results. The seedlings are transplanted to small pots and, when well established in these, are transferred directly to benches of soil or are potted into larger containers. They may finish in 5-, 6- or 7-inch pots.

In their young stages they should be pinched once to induce branching. A night temperature of 40-50 degrees suits them, with a rise of 5-10 degrees in the daytime permitted. They grow well in any fairly rich, well-drained soil.

Hardy Herbaceous Kinds. Of the hardy herbaceous plants now or previously included in Senecio, those known in gardens as S. Clivorum, S. Veitchianus and S. Wilsonianus are now included in Ligularia. (See Ligularia.) A hardy herbaceous Senecio which is sometimes cultivated is S. Doria, 4-6 ft., flowers yellow. This handsome plant, a native of Argentine and Uraguay, is hardy in sheltered locations in southern New York and southern New England.

S. aureus, the Golden Ragwort, a native of North America from Newfoundland to Florida and Texas, attains a height of about 2 ft. and has showy heads of bright golden yellow flowers. It is a useful kind for naturalizing in wild gardens.

Other hardy herbaceous kinds are S. adonidifolius, 12-18 in., orange; S. Doria, 4 ft., yellow; and S. Doronicum, 2½ ft., orange or yellow.

Waterside and Border Plants. The herbaceous Senecios are excellent plants for grouping by the waterside, where the roots have free access to abundance of moisture. They also make good border plants on heavy, moisture-holding soil, but are not suitable for dry, sandy or gravelly ground. Planting should be done in fall or early spring. They benefit from an annual mulch of well-decayed manure in spring.

Propagation is by division at planting time. Seeds may also be sown in drills ½ in. deep in early summer. The young plants are planted out, 1 ft. apart, in a reserve bed, and grown until large enough to be planted in their permanent positions.

Silvery-Gray Shrub. Senecio laxifolius, often erroneously called S. Greyii, is a dwarf shrub with oblong or obovate silvery-gray leaves and large clusters of bright golden-yellow flowers in late summer; it is a suitable plant for a sunny rock garden, front of a mixed flower border, or the shrub border.

This plant is recommended for mild climates only. It should be planted in spring in well-drained soil. Propagation is by inserting well-ripened shoots in a bed of peat moss and sand in autumn; they are kept in a cold frame until they are well rooted, then planted outdoors.

The leaves of Senecio tropaeolifolius resemble those of the garden Nasturtium.